# Roger's
## PROFANISAURUS

# Viz

# Roger's
# PROFANISAURUS

BOXTREE

First published 2002 by Boxtree

This edition published for Index Books Ltd by Boxtree 2003
an imprint of Pan Macmillan Ltd
Pan Macmillan, 20 New Wharf Road, London N1 9RR
Basingstoke and Oxford
Associated companies throughout the world
www.panmacmillan.com

ISBN 0 7522 1507 8

15 17 19 18 16 14

A CIP catalogue record for this book
is available from the British Library.

Typeset by seagulls
Printed by Mackays of Chatham plc, Chatham, Kent

A quotation falsely attributed to Bamber Gascoigne on the flap
of earlier copies of the *Profanisaurus* was inserted without
his knowledge and has been removed at his request.

I would like to dedicate this book to my darling girlfriend Candy who, twenty minutes after the tragic death of my wife, showed me it was possible for me to love again. And again, twenty minutes later.

*Roger Mellie, Fulchester, 2002.*

P.S. Oh, and cheers to all the *Viz* readers who sent in entries too. Keep them coming.

*A Foreword by*
# TERRY JONES
*off Monty Python*

T he Profanisaurus is a rich and deeply compelling book which time and again brings the reader face to face with the nature of the human condition. Here, exposed for all to read, are human beings caught in their moments of extremity. This is not a sober, contemplative book, such as we look for when we take down a volume of St Thomas Aquinas. Nor will the volume you are now holding provide an answer to those essential questions about humanity - about life or death - that have preoccupied the human race for so many millennia. Here is no easy blueprint for surviving the cold truths of universal entropy - no quick guide to deliverance from the darkness that surrounds our fragile and momentary existence on this planet. But what you will find here are words and phrases to assist you as you grapple with those inexplicable forces of darkness, as you confront destruction, debilitation, misdirection, inappropriateness and plain fucking bad luck.

*Terry Jones*

# Aa

**a bit** *1. n.* An imperial unit of *the other*, slightly less than an entire *portion*. *2. n.* Unspecified quantity of sex, usually partaken *on the side.*

**aardvark's nose** *n.* An uncircumcised *cock.* See *anteater.*

**abnormal load** *n.* An *arse* so large it necessitates a motorcycle outrider.

**abra-kebabra** *n.* An illusion performed after a night on the *piss*, whereby a kebab is made to disappear down the performer's throat, only to reappear a short time later on the back of a taxi driver's head.

**ACAB** *acronym.* All Coppers Are Bastards. Popular knuckle and forehead tattoo.

**access time** *1. n.* The time taken between requesting and receiving data in computing. *2. n.* The time taken for a woman to produce enough *moip* to allow smooth penetration without feeling like one is scraping one's *giggling stick* on the Great Barrier Reef.

**acorn** *n.* A little *bell end* nestling forlornly in the *pubage* of a fat German naturist.

**activity** *n.* A 'hands on' style of *mammary management.*

**address the speaker of the house** *v.* To *suck* the honor-*able member for Pantchester off.* To engage in *horatio.*

**adult** *adj.* Something to *wank* at, on or over eg. ~channel, ~magazine, ~phoneline, ~text messages.

**ADW** *abbrev.* All Day Wank. A 24 hour trip to the *Billy Mill Roundabout* with no hand signals. Something to do when the Queen Mum dies and the telly is off.

**aeroplane blonde** *n.* A dark-haired female who dyes her hair blonde, ie, is equipped with a *black box.*

**after dinner bint** *n.* A *bird* you have to take out to dinner to *fuck.*

**afterburner** *n.* A pyroflatulatory *anal announcement.* A *blue streak, St. George's ruin.*

**aim Archie at the Armitage** *euph.* To *point Percy at the porcelain.*

**air bags** *n.* Huge breasts. *Oomlaaters.*

**air biscuit** *n. Fart, botty burp.* Floating body of *trouser gas.* 'Could you open a window, Your Highness? I think your mother has launched an air biscuit.'

**air buffet** *n.* A lingering, gaseous meal, more nourishing than an *air biscuit*, to which one may make several visits.

**air lingus** *n*. A sexual position adopted by soft porn *jazz mag* lesbians, where one is just about to lick the other one's *twat.*

**air tulip** *n*. A delightfully fragrant *fart,* as dropped by Lady Di or Grace Kelly. But not Jocky Wilson.

**air your guts** *v*. To *puke.* To *shout soup.*

**alcopoop** *n*. The loud, smelly, life-affirming *shit* you have the next morning after a heavy night on the pop.

**ale stones** *n*. A downpour of marble sized *tods* after a night spent quaffing Youngers Scotch Bitter.

**almond** *1. rhym. slang.* Penis. From almond rock ~*cock. 2. rhym. slang.* Socks. *3. n.* An imperial measure of *spongle,* approximately one stomach full.

**almond flakes** *n*. *Mandruff, dried taddies.* Also *mammary dandruff.*

**ambassador's hedge** *n*. An immaculately trimmed *bush.*

**American tip** *1. n.* A piece of advice given by someone from the USA. *2. n.* A short *rubber*

*Johnny* that just covers the *herman gelmet* and prevents the *wanked-up spunk* going on the hotel sheets.

**American trombone** *n*. A *spit roast.* A horny trio of two men and one woman, who plays the *pink oboe* of one of the men, whilst the other strikes up the *double bass.*

**anal announcement** *n*. *Fart, chuff, beefy-eggo, trouser trumpet.* A *rumpet voluntary.*

**anal delight** *1. n.* A soft, light, fluffy chocolate or butterscotch-coloured pudding served in a large porcelain bowl. *2. n.* Pleasures taken in *tradesman's practices.*

**anchovy's fanny** *n*. The *fishiest* of all possible *suppers.*

**Andrex runway** *n*. The long strip of *arsewipe* stretching from *pubes* to throat on the prone body that provides a landing strip for airborne *jizz.* A *wank runway.*

**angel** *1. n.* Spin-off series from 'Buffy the Vampire Slayer'. *2. n.* A passive *hur-mur.* A buggeree.

**ankle spanker** *1. n.* An extremely long *cock. 2. n.* A normal sized *cock* on a man with extremely short legs.

**Anne Frank** *rhym. slang.* To masturbate. Whilst hiding in a cupboard for five years.

**anteater** *n.* An uncircumcised penis.

**anus** *n. medic.* The *council gritter, brass eye.*

**apache** 1. *n.* Sex without a condom, riding *bare-back.* 2. *n.* Popular instrumental hit by sixties guitar combo 'The Shadows.'

**apeshit** *1. n.* That which is flung at your granny in a zoo. *2. adj.* State of mental perturbation. *Fucking radgy.*

**apple catchers** *n.* Generously proportioned *dung hampers* for the more generously *arsed* lady.

**aquafresh** *n.* A *skidmark* created on the inside of the trousers of someone wearing a G-string ie. three stripes of two different colours.

**aris** *rhym. slang.* Convoluted rhyming slang for anus. From Aristotle ~bottle ~bottle and glass ~*arse.*

**Ark Royal Landing Deck** *n.* Descriptive of the state of the 'U' bend in a student house toilet.

**Armani & Navy** *n.* Poorly-made imitation designer clothes purchased from a scouser in a street market.

**armbreaker** *euph.* A particularly vicious *wank.* 'What with excellent browsing and sluicing and a couple of armbreakers and what-not, my afternoon passed quite happily.' (from 'Wooster Wanks Himself Daft', by PG Wodehouse).

**around the world** *n.* Sexual practice costing about £25. *Anilingus.*

**arse** *1. n.* The *Gary Glitter*, the *chuff*, the *nick*, the *tradesman's, the chamber of horrors. 2. exclam.* A negative reply, expressing denial. 'Did you steal my pencil?' 'Did I arse'. 3. v. ~**about.** To have a bit laugh and carry on.

**arse baby** *n.* A *ring ripper,* a *dreadnought.* A huge *turd.*

**arse bar** *n.* Unappetising *bum-toffee* confection.

**arse cress** *n.* Spindly anal vegetation that doesn't get much light. The hairs that attach the *winnets* to *Dot Cotton's mouth.*

**arse feta** *n.* The barely-edible cheese that forms inside Clive James's trousers.

**arse grapes** *n.* Haemorrhoids, *farmers, Chalfonts, Emmas, ceramics.*

**arse like the top of a sauce bottle** *sim.* A less than clean rectum. One where slight spillages and leaks have dried in situ, and which will have to be picked clean.

**arse man** *n.* One who's boat is floated by *derrieres* in preference to legs or *thruppennies*.

**arse piss** *n.* Diarrhoea, *rusty water, anal fire water, Jap flag juice.*

**arse spider** *n.* A tenacious, well-knotted *winnet* that cannot be removed without bringing eight spindly hairs with it.

**arse tex** *n.* Public lavatory bowl render.

**arse tramp** *n.* A cleft-dwelling vagrant who hangs around in the bushes long after his pals have been moved on by the prudent use of *bumwad*. A tenacious *winnet*.

**arse vinegar** *n.* The acidic contents of the *arseovoir*.

**arse wasps** *n.* A swarm of aggressive imaginary insects that attack and sting your *anus* after a particularly hot curry.

**arse wipe** *1. n.* Bathroom tissue, *bumwad, shit-scrape. 2. n. pej. US.* Contumelious epiphet for a *tosser*.

**arsecons** *n.* Of e-mails and phone texting, resourceful use of punctuation to illustrate the condition of someone's *jacksie*. eg. Normal *arse* (-!-) Lard *arse* ( -!- ) Tight *arse* (!) Sore *arse* (-\*-) Slack *arse* (-0-) etc. *Arse* icons.

**arsed** *adj.* The state of being bothered. *'CEDRIC: Come onto the balcony, Lavinia. The moon is so terribly, terribly enchanting this evening. The stars are twinkling like the lights in your eyes when you laugh. LAVINIA: (off stage) In a bit. I can't be arsed at the minute.'* (from *'Don't Put your Daughter on the Game, Mrs. Worthington'* by Noel Coward).

**arsehole** *1. n.* The *dirtbox, the tea towel holder. 2. sim.* Measure of the roughness of someone or something. *'That bird is as rough as arseholes without her make-up on. When she's got it on she's rough as fuck.' 3. n.* Descriptive of a person with a character comparable to that of Eddie Irvine or Dave Lee Travis.

**arseholed** *adj.* To be completely *wankered. Shit-faced.*

**Arsenal are at home** *euph.* Of a bird, to be *up on blocks,* *chasing the cotton mouse, dropping clots, smoking short cigars* etc. Arsenal can be replaced by any football team who play in red: (Scotland – Aberdeen *are at hame*).

**arseovoir** *n*. The little indent just above a builder's *arse* that holds about half a pint of sweat.

**art pamphlet** *n*. A *jazz magazine, bongo periodical*. Any one-handed reading material.

**artichoke** *n*. *Aus*. Ugly *slapper*.

**ass** *n*. *US*. That part of the body the *whupping* of which indicates a comprehensive victory, and of which the invitation to kiss is often rhetorically made.

**assets** *n*. *journ*. *Charms*.

**asstrash** *n*. *US*. Rectal garbage.

**at it** *adj*. To be engaged in copulation like knives. The use of this term is restricted to disapproving neighbours. *'Tssch. Sounds like those two next door are at it like knives again.'*

**atomic mutton** *n*. A mature woman trying to look younger than she obviously is and ending up looking like a *tart* in the process, eg. Diana Dors.

**audition the finger puppets** *v*. A single act, one man show, not suitable for children. *Shuffling the Kit-Kat*. See *Kit-Kat shuffler*.

**Augustus** *n*. A *hur-mur sexual*. A *botter*. From Charlie and the Chocolate Factory, where Augustus Gloop got stuck up the chocolate pipe.

**aunt Mary** *n*. A lady's hairy *fadge*.

**auntie** *1*. *n*. Affectionate term for the BBC coined by the BBC. *2*. *n*. Elderly *botter*.

**auntie's round** *euph*. A *visit from Aunt Flo*.

**Aussie kiss** *n*. Similar to a *French kiss* but performed down under.

**autograph the gusset** *v*. To allow the newly-born *turtle's head* to sign the inside of one's *bills*.

**awaken the bacon** *v*. Sexually arouse the *puh-seh*. To turn on the *blip tap* prior to a *Dutch breakfast*.

**axle grease** *n*. A budget lubricant used in *grumble flicks*. *Hockle flobbed* onto a *herman gelmet* before it's pushed in.

**Aztec two-step** *n*. Diarrhoea dance along the lines of the *Tijuana cha-cha*. *Turkish two-step*.

# Bb

**babia majora** *exclam. US.* A gaggle of *flange*, a flange of *quim*.

**baby gravy** *n. Spaff, speff, spongle, spungle, spangle.* Also *baby bouillon.*

**baby's arm** *n* . ~holding an apple. Descriptive of a substantial penis, ie. 10 inches long with a bend in the middle. Sometimes covered in jam.

**baby's dinners** *n. Assets, airbags, norks.*

**bacardi geezer** *n.* A gentleman who, inexplicably, chooses to quaff *tart fuel* as his favourite tipple.

**Baccus Marsh** *n.* A *dobber.* From the spongy area halfway between *Melbourne* and *Ballarat.*

**baccy pouch** *n.* Overgrown *mapatasi.* A *pant moustache,* a *St. Bruno.*

**back beauty** *n.* A woman who appears to be attractive from behind, but when seen from the front is a bit of a horse. Back beauties form a staple joke in Benny Hill's oeuvre.

**back door boogie** *1. n. Heterosexual.* The ritual dance which accompanies a game of *hide the salami* when playing *canine rules. 2. n. AC/DC*

The theme tune for *Pot Brown.*

**back on solids** *sim.* Descriptive of a woman who has recently been *drinking from the hairy goblet,* but who is now back eating *beef on the bone.* A cured lesbian.

**back one out** *v.* The act of reverse *parking your breakfast,* usually involving much looking over the shoulder, grunting and sweating.

**back passage** *n.* Rear exit and/or entrance.

**back scuttle** *v.* To *scuttle* from the back.

**back seat driver** *1. n.* Car passenger who offers useful advice and helpful tips to the driver. *2. n.* Gentleman who puts his *sixth gearstick* up someone else's *exhaust pipe.*

**back tits** *n.* The folds of fat which spill over the rear panels and fastenings of a *munter's* bra, giving her the appearence of having *knockers* on her back.

**back wheels** *n. Bollocks, balls. 'What a gob, your Royal Highness. You've even managed to get my back wheels in.'* (Peter Sellers overheard behind a hedge at Kensington Palace).

**backfire** *v.* A *fart* capable of startling a police horse.

**backstage pass** *n.* Privileged admittance to a tightly restricted area. *'I don't know why she's got the hump, the way she was acting, I was sure I had a backstage pass.'*

**backter** *rhym. slang.* A lady's *front bottom.* From back to front ~*cunt.*

**backwards burp** *n. Fart, air dump, tree monkey.*

**bacon bazooka** *n. Pork sword, spam javelin, mutton musket.* Penis.

**bacon strips** *n.* Female external genitalia, presumably with the word 'DANISH' printed on in blue ink. A *ragman's coat.*

**badge . badger** *n. Fanny.*

**badger loose** *euph.* RAF. An air force issue *air biscuit.* *"I say, Ginger', cautioned Biggles. 'I think number 2 engine is on fire.' 'No, that's me', confessed Algie. 'I've just let a badger loose."* (from *'Biggles Follows Through',* by Capt. W.E. Johns).

**badly packed kebab** *n.* An untidy vagina that looks appetising only after 10 pints. A *butcher's window,* a *ripped sofa.*

**badunkadunk** *n. onomat.* A big *arse.*

**bag ladies' period** *sim.* Unpalatable. *'Don't buy Mrs Timpkin's home made jam, vicar. I've tasted nicer bag ladies' period.'*

**bag** *n. Slapper, boot.*

**bag of slugs** *n.* A particularly slimy *mingepiece.* *'Jeeves answered on the first ring. 'What-ho, old chap', I said. 'Fish out those French letters from my dressing table, there's a fellow. I'm out with the Duchess of Worcester and I've just got my fingers off her. By Jove, it was like putting my hand in a bag of slugs."* (from *'I'm Coming, Jeeves!'* by PG Wodehouse).

**baggage boy** *n.* Of *pooves* and *poovery,* the opposite of a *pillow biter.* A *backseat driver.*

**bagging** *v.* Discreet public lavatory *cottaging* involving one participant standing in a shopping bag to mislead any *tit-head* peering under the cubicle door.

**bagpipe** *v.* To ignore *the pink* and *the brown,* and shove the cue straight into the top corner pocket. *Hawaiian muscle-fuck.* Armpit sex.

**bagpuss** *n.* An old, fat, furry *cunt.*

**bagsy** *v. legal.* An assertion of claim upon something, based solely upon the legal precedent that the one who speaks first gets it. *'Right. Bagsy me the Sinai. Yous lot of had it since the Six-Day War in 1967. It's not fair.'* (Anwar Sadat, Israeli-Egyptian Summit, 1978).

**bahookie** *n. Scot. Arse.*

**baibhe** *n. Gaelic.* Rough old *slapper. Bag.*

**bairn brine** *n. Baby gravy.*

**bairn's sock, trying to get a roll of carpet into a** *sim.* Gentleman's excuse for not wearing a *jubber ray.*

**Bakerloo breeze** *1. n.* The pungent wind that precedes the London underground train moments before it exits the tunnel. *2. n.* The pungent *wind* that precedes the *cocoamotive* moments before it exits the *bonus tunnel.*

**baking one** *v.* The act of not going for a *shit* when you really ought to.

**bald man in a boat** *n.* Lady's *clematis.* The *wail switch.* (not to be confused with the *skin boat*).

**bald man** *n. Kojak, Captain Picard, Spurt Reynolds* etc. The penis. Also the *old man* (not to be confused with *bald man in a boat*).

**bald-headed hermit** *n.* See *bald man.*

**Balkans** *n.* In British Carry-On films, a vague euphemism for the testicles, *bollocks.* Also the *Urals,* the *Balearics.*

**ball bag** *n.* Bag in which *balls* are kept. A *nadsack,* scrotum.

**ball glaze** *n. medic.* The clear, colourless solution secreted by the *clockweights* which gives the tadpoles something to swim in. Also *guardsman's gloss.*

**ball** *v.* To *poke, nob, bang.*

**Ballarat** *n. Aus.* A fully erect penis. *'Are you ready yet Bruce?' 'Almost there, Sheila. I'm nearly at Ballarat'.* See also *Lake Wendouree.*

**ballbearings in a condom** *sim.* Descriptive of an older woman's saggy *knee shooters* whilst she's on top.

**ball-buster** *1. n.* Unpleasant neighbour who puts a garden fork through your football when you kick it over the fence. *2. n.* Sexually aggressive female. A *cock chomper.*

**balloon knot** *n. Ringpiece,*

*chocolate starfish, Dot Cotton's mouth.* A puckered *gazoo.*

**ballrooms** *rhym. slang.* Diarrhoea. From the Sweet song 'Ballroom Blitz' ~ *Brads.*

**balls** *1. n.* Testicles, those spherical *spunk* factories on the *Scrots Road Industrial Estate. 2. n.* Courage, guts. *'I like him. He's got balls'. 3. exclam.* Denial. *'Has he balls got balls!' 4. n.* Rubbish, nonsense. *'Balls! Of course he's got balls'. 5. n.* Round things you play football with.

**balls deep** *adj.* A *pork sword* buried to the hilt. The maximum *length* which it is possible to *slip* someone. In a *sausage and doughnut situation,* the maximum extent to which the *sausage* can *fuck* the *doughnut.* In *up to the apricots,* in *up to the maker's nameplate.*

**balls like bats' wings** *sim. medic.* Descriptive of deflated, leathery testicles, often accompanied by insanity, blindness and stunted growth. *Knackers* that have been *wanked* flat.

**bally heck** *exclam.* Wartime form of *bloody hell* when swearing was rationed. Strong expletives and eggs were reserved for soldiers on the front line.

**baloobas** *n.* See *bazoomas.*

**bampot** *n.* Survivor of the mental health system. A *mentalist,* a *headbanger,* a *heed-the-ball.*

**banana hammock** *n.* Skimpy *undercrackers* or swimming trunks. The male equivalent of *genital floss.*

**banana yoghurt** *n.* Not particularly healthy breakfast alternative to *porridge,* to either *swallow* or *spit.*

**bang** *v.* To copulate like a *shithouse* door in the wind.

**banger hangar** *n. Sausage wallet, cock wash.*

**bangers and mash** *n.* The contents of a well used but badly flushed toilet, the bangers being the *turds* and the mash being the *bumwad.* Usually found in the bogs of pubs, campsites and non-stop coaches to Spain. *"Cinders and ashes, Thomas, your coaches are a disgrace', cried the Fat controller. 'There are used tickets on the floor, soot all over the windows and Clarabelle's cludgy is full of bangers and mash."* (from *'Thomas and the Dyno-Rod Man'* by Rev. W. Awdrey).

**bangles** *1. n.* All female pop group consisting of one *fox* and a pack of *hounds.* *2. n.* Most delicate part of the *crown jewels*: the *orbs*, rather than the *sceptre.*

**bangover** *n.* The hangover headache that, temporarily vanquished by the act of love, returns with all its mates at the moment of *stackblow.*

**banjo** *1. n. US.* Musical instrument played by inbreds in the deep south, that makes a twanging sound when plucked. *2. n.* The thin ridge of skin on the penis connecting the *roll-neck* to the *bobby's helmet*, that makes a twanging sound when plucked. The *guy-rope.*

**banjo cleaner** *n.* Of ladies' dentition, that gap between the two upper front incisors which effectively scrapes detritus from a gentleman's *banjo* during *horatio.* Guy Ritchie has one of the cleanest *banjos* in showbusiness.

**banjoed** *adj. Pissed-up, wankered, arseholed, shit-faced, rat arsed.*

**bannocks** *1. n.* Unappetising Scottish bread buns. *2. n.* Unappetising Scottish *knackers.*

**BANT** *acronym.* Big Arse No Tits.

**banty** *n.* One who nods at *stoats.*

**baps** *1. n.* Soft bread rolls. *2. n.* Tits.

**barber's floor** *n.* A particularly hairy *biffer.*

**barber's pole** *n.* Result of *parting the whiskers* while the *painters are in.*

**Barclays** *rhym. slang. J. Arthur.*

**barf bag** *n.* Sick bag, as found on an aeroplane. Also a useful alliterative insult.

**barf** *v.* To *vomit, huey, puke, bowk.*

**bargain bucket** *n.* An over-employed and overstretched *fanny.* A *Mary* like a *welly top.*

**barge-arse** *n.* A lady of rotund posterior aspect.

**bark at the ants** *v.* To *yoff.*

**barker's egg** *n.* Poodle *shit.* A dog *turd* so old it has gone white.

**barking carrots** *v. Parking tigers,* to *vomit, puke, sing a rainbow, barf.*

**barking spider** *n. Ringpiece, freckle, chocolate starfish.*

**Barnes Wallis** *n.* The type of *turd* released from the *bomb* *bay* which sends a splash of water onto your *undercarriage*. A *panbuster*.

**barney rubble** *n.* That which, in a good natured protest, is torn up from pavements, walls etc, and *hoyed* at the *tit-heads*.

**barse mallow** *n.* A light, pink fluffy substance that forms spontaneously in a *salad dodger's taint*.

**barse** *n.* The little bit of skin between the *bannocks* and the *freckle*. Also *biffin bridge, stinkers bridge, chin rest, taint* etc.

**Barthez** *1. n.* Manchester United goalkeeper. *2. n.* A bald *twat*.

**barumph** *v. Garboon, poon, snarf, snurdle,* etc. To sniff a lady's bicycle seat, an act that seems to be named more often than performed.

**bash the bishop** *v.* To *pull the Pope's cap off*, to *box the Jesuit*. To *bank with Barclays*.

**basket making** *v. arch.* Medieval sexual intercourse. Basket meaning *'bastard'*.

**bastard** *n.* A football referee.

**bat in the cave** *n.* A precariously suspended *bogie* that hangs upsettingly in someone's nostril.

**bat wings** *n.* Thin, leathery, nocturnal flaps. *Beef curtains*.

**Batmobile** *n.* Descriptive of the state of one's brass eye after a particularly hot *Ruby Murray*. *'I had a real ring stinger at the Rupali last night. My arse is like the back end of the Batmobile.'*

**bat's wings** *n.* Delicate alternative to beef curtains.

**battered kipper** *n.* A frothsome *gash* on your old *trout*. A *blippy mackerel*.

**batting for both sides** *euph. Bowling from both ends*, as opposed to just the *gasworks end*.

**batting on a wet wicket** *v.* To not be the first man in. To *stir the porridge. Sloppy seconds*.

**batty-boy** *n. W. Indies.* Tailender who habitually bowls from the *pavilion end*.

**baw bag** *n. Scot.* Oor Wullie's scrotum. A tartan *chicken skin sporran*.

**bawd** *n. arch.* Old fashioned term for a *rub-a-tug shop* proprietress.

**bazongers** *n.* Gravity-defying, surgically-enhanced hemispherical breasts that explode in aeroplanes.

**bazoomas** *n*. See *begonias*.

**bead curtains** *n*. *Dangleberries, toffee strings, mud-buttons, tagnuts*. Also *beaded curtain*.

**beadle** *1. n*. A *cunt* with a neatly-cropped bikini line. A *bushell*, a *Californian wax*. *2. v*. To fondle a pair of *Kelly Brooks*.

**Beaker's mouth** *n*. The involuntary movement of the vaginal lips when being taken up the *bonus tunnel* (as seen in many a *grumble flick*). From the lip movement of the Muppet character Beaker 'me-mo-ing'.

**bean flicker** *n*. A lady of lesbicious tendencies. A wearer of *comfortable shoes*.

**bear trapper's hat** *n*. An excessively hairy *front bottom*. A *biffer*, a *Davy Crockett hat*. *'Put my ladder up to the flat / Saw a nun with bear trapper's hat / I get a wank out of things like that / When I'm cleaning windows'*. (from *'The George Formby Song Book'*, 1945).

**beard** *1. n. arch*. Fulsome *twat-thatch, mapatasi*. *2. n*. A woman married to a *batty-boy* in order to conceal his true sexuality. *'Do you reckon*

*that Sophie's a beard then, or what?'* See also *whiff of lavender, frock*.

**bearded clam** *1. n*. An edible mollusc. *2. n. Aus*. An edible *fanny*.

**beast with two backs** *n*. A strange, grunting animal with 2 heads and 4 legs, commonly found in bus shelters after midnight.

**beaten like a ginger step-child** *adj*. A particularly ferocious and merciless thrashing, for example, off a bouncer at a nightclub, a policeman in a cell, or Bjork at Bangkok Airport. *'This is dreadful. I don't think Hawking can take much more of this punishment. Bruno's raining the blows down now, left right left right. I can't look, this is terrible. Hawking's being beaten like a ginger step-child.'* (Harry Carpenter, commentating on charity boxing match, *BBC Children in Need*, 1998).

**beat-the-meat** *v*. To avail oneself of a *ham shank*, perform the *five-knuckle shuffle, pull your pud*.

**beaver** *1. n. US. Gorilla salad*. Female pubic hair. *2. n. Blart*. Collective term for women.

**beaver cleaver** *n*. Primitive male weapon for splaying *beaver*.

**beaver lever** *n*. See *beaver cleaver*.

**Becksfart** *n*. Brand-specific lager hangover *flatulence*. Has an aroma a bit like egg mayonnaise.

**bed flute** *n*. Woodwind instrument closely related to the *pink oboe* that responds well to double tonguing.

**bed glue** *n*. Liquid that adheres people firmly to their mattresses, especially students. Beer.

**bed muscle** *n*. The *old fella*.

**bed** *v*. A tabloid term, to *fuck*. *'I went out with Tracey last night and ended up bedding her in the bus shelter.'*

**bee stings** *n*. Small *tits*. *Chestnuts*.

**beef bayonet** *n*. See *bacon bazooka*.

**beef box** *n*. A container into which *sausages* are put.

**beef curtains** *n. medic.* Of women's genitalias, those folds of skin known as the *labia majorca*, or big lips. Or indeed *piss-flaps*.

**beef dripping** *n*. The spreadable extract found in a *butch-er's window*, traditionally used in the preparation of *fish suppers*.

**beef** *n*. A *fart*. A *beefy eggo*.

**beef wellington** *n*. A *wizard's sleeve,* a *clown's pocket*. A voluminous *Mary*.

**beer armour** *n*. The invisible protective clothing that prevents injury on the way home from the pub by shielding the body from all sensation of damage on contact with the pavement.

**beer callipers** *n*. Miraculous leg splints which enable *wankered* stragglers to make their way home at closing time.

**beer coat** *n*. An invisible, yet warm coat worn when walking back from a club at three in the morning.

**beer compass** *n*. A homing device that ensures your inexplicably safe arrival home after a night on the pop.

**beer cones** *n*. Invisible contraflow system surrounding a drunkard staggering up the road, allowing traffic to move freely around him without injury.

**beer goggles** *n*. Booze-fuelled optical aids which make *hounds* look like *foxes*.

**beer lag** *n*. The disruption to human sleep patterns encountered after intense lunchtime drinking which leaves one unable to stay awake for 'Heartbeat', but wide awake at two in the morning.

**beer monkey** *n*. A mythical simian creature which, during a drunken slumber, sneaks into your bed, ruffles your hair, steals your money and *shits* in your mouth.

**beer muffs** *n*. Invisible ear defenders that attach themselves to a man's head after several pints, rendering him unable to hold a conversation without shouting or to watch TV at anything but full volume.

**beer mugger** *n*. The man you discover has hit you over the head and taken £35 out of your wallet the morning after you 'nip out for a couple of pints'.

**beer scooter** *n*. Miraculous method of transport employed when leaving the pub after drinking large amounts of beer. So called due to the 'lost time' effect when returning home seemingly in no time and at incredible velocity.

**beer shoes** *n*. Gloves

**beer wood** *n*. The thing that feels like an erection, but isn't, whilst attempting sexual congress under the influence of alcohol.

**beeriod** *n*. Twice weekly malady suffered by men after a night *on the pop*. Symptoms include headache, mood swings and a bloated stomach. *'Leave me alone, woman, me beeriod started this morning.'*

**beertent** *n*. Jocky Wilson's shirt.

**beerwolf** *n*. One who wakes up in unfamiliar surroundings with torn clothes, aching limbs, the taste of blood in the mouth and nightmarish flashbacks to terrible events of the previous evening.

**Beethoven's fifth** *n*. A large, stirring movement of the bowel which may leave the performer deaf.

**beetle bonnet** *n*. Female pubic mound as viewed through tight garments. From the design of the VW car. *Camel's foot, camel's lip.*

**begonias** *n*. See *bejonkers*.

**bejonkers** *n*. See *bouncers*.

**Belfast taxi** *n*. Battery powered shopping scooter for old people too fat or idle to walk. A *Disneyworld dragster.*

**Belgian biscuit** *n.* Sexual practice of Flemish origin and costing over £100.

**Belisha beacon** *n.* Flashing orange globe on a black and white pole, named after the British Transport Minister in 1934.

**bell end** *1. n.* An amusingly named tent. *2. n. medic.* The *bobby's helmet,* the *herman.* The glans of the penis.

**bell end Brie** *n. Helmetdale.*

**bell** *n. Clit, the devil's doorbell,* found just above the *snail's doorstep.*

**bell tower** *n. Knob* shaft. *Bean stalk.*

**bell wringing** *v.* A harmless pastime that builds up the arm muscles, popular with monks for the last two thousand years.

**bell-swagged** *adj.* To be endowed with a large *bell end* on a contrastingly small stem or *shaft. Mushroom rigged.*

**belly flopper** *n.* A clumsy *brown trout* whose graceless entry into the water causes splashing of the *arse.*

**belly warmers** *n.* Big, droopy *tits. Overblaaters.*

**belt-fed mortar** *sim. milit.* A measure of the sexual enthusiasm of a lady. *'I bet she bangs like a belt fed mortar.'* See also *shithouse door in the wind, kangaroo shagging a space hopper.*

**bend the elbow** *v.* To go for a *beer goggles* fitting.

**bender** *1. n.* Prolonged drinking spree. A *Leo Sayer. 2. n.* A crustie's tent. *3. n.* A *pinch of snuff.*

**benefactor** *n.* Of *farts* and *farting,* the altruist who supplies it. Also known as the *donor.*

**beneficiaries** *n.* Those who benefit from the smelly largesse of the *benefactor's* fart.

**Benny Hill** *rhym. slang.* A form of contraception. *'It's nothing to do with me, Mrs. Gamp. You told me you was on the Benny Hill'.* (from *'Nicholas Nickelby',* by Charles Dickens).

**bent** *1. adj.* To be not straight. *'He was as bent as a nine bob note.' 2. adj.* To not be an honest policeman.

**Beppe's beard** *n.* A severely but neatly trimmed *muff,* named after the severely but neatly trimmed chin growth of the former EastEnders character. A *clitler*.

**Berkeley Hunt** *rhym. slang.* *Fanny.*

**Bermuda triangle** *n.* A mysterious area where *skin boats* full of seamen seem to disappear.

**berry** *1. n.* A sexual deviant, a kinky person. A goddam prevoit. *2. n.* One who has *carnival knowledge* of animals.

**Bertie** *1. n.* Male homosexual. *2. n.* A proper *Charlie*.

**bespectable** *adj.* Respectable in glasses.

**Betty Swollocks** *n.* Polite term for *knacker* discomfort. *'Forgive me, your Majesty whilst I adjust my doublet and hose. I have sailed the oceans these last six months and have not changed my codpiece since we left the New World. I fear I have the most awful Betties.'* (Sir Walter Raleigh, Audience with Queen Elizabeth I, 1584).

**bevvy** *n. Booze,* drink.

**biffer** *n.* A particularly hairy *minge. 'Gaw, you've got a right old biffer on you there, Your Majesty'.*

**biffie** *n. Bog, shitter, dunny, cludgy.*

**biffin bridge** *n.* See *barse.*

**biffin** *n.* Perspiration which condenses in the *biffin bridge* area during coitus.

**biffing plate** *1. n. Beetle bonnet, monkey's forehead. 2. sim.* That which is flat. *'Christ! This lager's as flat as Kate Moss's biffing plate'.*

**biffon** *n.* That part of the female anatomy between the *council gritter* and the *fadge,* which the man's *clockweights* 'biff' on during intercourse. The *taint.*

**big bamboo** *n.* Penis.

**Big Ben** *1. n.* A large bell in St. Steven's Tower, London. *2. n.* An enormous *erection,* possibly with Robert Powell hanging off it.

**big cock day** *n.* A day, quite possibly in spring, the arrival of which is greeted with the *dawn horn,* and throughout which the sap continues to rise. *'As he wrestled himself into his shreddies, D'Arcy knew it was going to be a big cock day.'* (from *'Pride And Prejudice'* by Jane Austen).

**biggie smalls** *n.* Fat lasses' knickers.

**bike** *n.* A frequently ridden woman, one who has had thousands of gentlemen swing their legs over her. Often prefixed with a location. *'You don't want to go near her, mate. She's the office/factory/London Symphony Orchestra & Festival Chorus bike'.*

**bikini burger** *n*. A *vertical bacon sandwich*. See *hairy pie*.

**bilge tanks** *n*. The 'double gut' effect caused by an overly-tight belt on an overly large belly. eg. Simon Bates.

**Bill Grundies** *rhym. slang. Undies, trollies, dunghampers.*

**Billingsgate box** *n*. *Minge*. Based on a comparison between the smell of a cockney fish market and a cockney *fanny*.

**billposter's bucket** *sim.* Large paste-filled *fanny*. *'I was stationed in Scutari Hospital for six months, the only woman amongst thousands of soldiers. By the end of my first shift I had a twat like a billposter's bucket'.* (from *'My Poor Cunt – The Wartime Memoirs of Florence Nightingale'*).

**bills** *n*. *Shreddies, dung hampers.*

**Billy Connolly's beard** *n*. A *ragweek fanny*.

**billy goat's mouth** *n*. An exceptionally loose vagina. With bits of the Mayor's hat sticking out.

**Billy Mill roundabout** *n*. Climactic point of a bout of masturbation. From the end of AI058 Coast Road near Newcastle. *'My mum walked in just as I was coming up to the Billy Mill roundabout.'* The *vinegar strokes.*

**Billy No-Mates** *n*. A lonely little buoyant *turd* that remains hanging around in the pan after all the others have gone to the beach.

**Billy Wright** *n*. Legendary Wolverhamtpon Wanderers footballer, latterly immortalised as rhyming slang for *shite*.

**bilp** *n*. The watery substance of female love. *Fish cream, nog juice.*

**biltrum** *n*. The *chin rest*. See *wannocks*.

**bimbo** *n*. Jordan or Joanne Guest.

**bimboid** *adj*. Appertaining to Jordan or Joanne Guest.

**Bin Laden's beard** *n*. A particularly luxuriant, yet unruly *stoat*. The antithesis of a *Hitler tash*.

**bingo wings** *n*. Upper arm

adipose underhang found on post-menopausal ladies of a common bent.

**bint** n. Derogatory term for a daft *slapper*, a *bird*. Jordan or Joanne Guest.

**bird** n. An inanimate young woman. *'Phoar! Is this your new bird? She's a bit of alright, ain't she. Fantastic tits'.*

**biscuits** 1. n. UK. Contents of the stomach after a heavy night's drinking. *'Get me a bucket, quick, Your Honour, I'm gonna chuck me biscuits.'* 2. n. US. Tight *buns*. Attractive *arse cheeks*.

**bishop rage** n. To *spank your monkey* with such vigour as to appear to have flown into a rage. Very popular with Popes.

**bishop's dick** n. The condition of muscular and joint rigidity after a 20 mile walk. *'With Striding Edge safely negotiated, I wearily descended the Victorian pony track down Birkhouse Moor with its fine views across to St Sunday Crag. At the foot of the slope I crossed Grisedale Beck and joined the tarred road for the difficult last eight miles, finally entering Patterdale as stiff as a bish-*

*op's dick.'* (from *'Coast to Coast the Miserable Way'* by Alfred Wainwright).

**bit of fluff** n. Singular piece of *totty*.

**bit of rough** n. Sexual partner, usually male, from a lower echelon. One who would wipe his *cock* on your curtains. eg. Mellors, Lady Chatterley's Lover.

**bitch tits** n. Large flabby breasts found on overweight men of any age. Particularly amusing on American children on 'Oprah'. *Triple-hearters, dog udders.*

**bitchwhore** n. A woman who is not only a bitch, but is also a whore.

**BJLs** n. Blow job lips. See *DSLs*

**blaaters** n. *Oomlaaters.*

**Blackbeard's ghost** n. A triangular, white, spooky apparition occasionally glimpsed by the *one-eyed lookout* in one's *crow's nest*. A mature lady's once-raven *mapatasi*. A *fanny badger*.

**bladdered** adj. See *blitzed*.

**blanket drill** n Mil. An early morning *mutton musket* practice that results in the loss of the *officer's mess*.

**blanket ripper** *n*. Back-draught in a *Dutch oven*.

**blart** *1. n.* Vagina. *2. n. coll.* Women, *totty*. *'Golly gosh! This nunnery is heaving with blart'.*

**blart attack** *euph*. A strange feeling, starting in the *pills* and spreading down the right arm, upon finding oneself surrounded by large numbers of quality *totty. Acute vangina.*

**blart gallery** *n*. Pub containing wall to wall *totty*.

**bleed the lizard** *v*. See *siphon the python*.

**bletherskate** *n. Scot. Shit-for-brains, fuckwit, twat.* Literally meaning *bag of shite.*

**blick** *n*. Pubic scurf, *muff-druff.*

**bliff mag** *n. Rhythm journal, art pamphlet.* Pornographic magazine.

**bliff** *n. Minge, front bottom.*

**blimplants** *n. Knockers*, surgically enhanced to comic proportions, as sported by the likes of Jordan and Lolo Ferarri.

**blind cobbler's thumbs** *n*. Large, well-hammered *nipples. Pygmies' cocks.*

**blind dirt snakes** *n*. A mal-odorous, legless lizard inhabiting *cak canyon,* which migrates south every morning. A *Richard the Third.*

**blip fountain** *n. medic*. The Bartholin's gland that secretes vaginal lubrications. The *batter tap.*

**blit** *n*. See *blivvet.*

**blitzed** *v*. See *blotto.*

**blivvet** *n*. See *blart.*

**blob** *1. n.* Condom, *French safe, French letter, rubber Johnny.* *2. v.* ~**it.** To over sleep. *'Jesus, Phil, look at the time. Get up, quick! I'm being coronated in half an hour and we've blobbed it.'* (HRH Princess Elizabeth, Coronation Day, 1952). *3. v.* To inadvertently make pregnant. *"You look a little green around the lemon, old chap. Bad news is it?' I asked as Jeeves continued to study the letter. 'I'm afraid so sir', he replied. 'I attended a party of the downstairs staff of Brokenbury Manor, and afraid things got a little out of hand. To cut a long story short, sir, it appears that I have blobbed the cook"* (from *'Use the Back Door, Jeeves'* by PGWodehouse).

**blobsleigh** *n*. Unexpected

barefoot skid on last night's discarded *johnny*.

**blobstopper** *n*. A *fanny mouse*, a *slim fanatella*. A tampon.

**Blofeld brunette** *n*. A natural blonde who dyes her hair dark to feign intelligence. However, inspection of her lap reveals a white *pussy*. And draft plans for world domination. Opposite of an *aeroplane blonde*.

**blonde herring** *n*. A blonde woman who looks like she ought to be a nice bit of *mackerel* from the back, but who turns out to be an *old trout*.

**blongle** *n. medic*. Seminal fluid containing traces of blood. *Blunk, blism, blimphet*.

**blood orange** *n*. The *arsehole* after being savaged by a particularly vicious *chocolate shark*. *Japanese flag*.

**bloody** *adj*. Swearword.

**bloomers** *1. n*. A voluminous item of women's underwear. *2. n*. A large loaf of bread. *3. n*. Any unfunny and self-indulgent 'mistake' made on camera by a BBC employee which can later be transmitted as part of a tiresome 'comedy' compilation.

**blooper** *1. n*. An actor's mistake which provides Dennis Norden with something to do while he waits to die. *2. n*. A sub-aquatic *fart*. A *tottle*, an *edwardwoodward*.

**blootered** *adj*. See *banjoed*.

**blotto** *adj*. See *blootered*.

**blow job** *n*. Dangerous sex act whereby the female inflates the male's testicles like balloons by blowing air into his penis.

**blow mud** *v*. To noisily expel a loose stool, *crop spray, pebbledash*, release a *flock of pigeons*.

**blow off** *v*. To trumpet through the trousers, *parp* in the pants.

**blow sisters** *n*. Lesbian nuns, often seen in candle shops.

**blow your biscuits** *v*. To *puke, yawn in technicolour*.

**blue balls** *n. Bollocks* which are fit to burst through lack of use. *DSBs, Sir Cliff's nuts*. Nuts like two tins of Fussels milk.

**blue dart** *n*. That brief but exciting pyrotechnic display achieved by igniting one's *air biscuits*. An *afterburner, blue streak*.

**blue-veined piccolo** *n*. A tiny, high-pitched *cock*.

**blumpkin** *n. US.* An American rock groupie speciality. To administer a *gobbie* to an artiste whilst the latter is *dropping his kids off at the pool.*

**blunderguff** *v.* To expel an horrendous-smelling *fart* only to realise that the tastiest *bird* in the office is fast approaching.

**blunkett** *n.* Facial expression adopted when two oncoming attractive ladies are forced to pass one to either side.

**blurter** *1. n. Aus. Chocolate starfish, ring.* 2. *n.* A little fishy that thou shalt have on a little dishy, when the booert comes in.

**boak** *v.* See *bowk.*

**bob** *n.* A *neck massager,* a *dildo.* A *Battery Operated Boyfriend.*

**bobbery** *n.* Female-on-male *strap-on*-assisted *arse-banging.*

**Bobby Charltons** *n.* Rogue pubic hairs trapped under the foreskin that stick themselves across the dome of your *bell end,* in the manner of the erstwhile centre-forward.

**Bobby Splithead** *n. prop.* Affectionate term for a *herman gelmet.*

**bobby's anorak** *n. Kojak's roll-neck, fiveskin, cock collar.*

**bobby's helmet** *n. Bell end.* From the distinctive shape of the British police constable's hat which manages to look like a *tit* and a *cock-end* simultaneously.

**bobfoc** *acronym.* Body Off Baywatch, Face Off Crimewatch. Having a *welder's bench* inexplicably mounted on a finely carved *rack and pegs,* eg. Sarah Jessica Parker.

**boff** *v.* See *bonk.*

**bog library** *n.* Reading material that builds up around the toilet of a bachelor. *Shiterature.*

**bog** *n. Shit house.* Lavatory.

**bog snorkelling** *n. Dirtbox diving. Anilingus.*

**bog-mess monster** *n.* A legendary brown beast that curls its body out of the water in at least two places. May be a *brown trout* or a *dead otter.*

**boh!** *exclam.* The noise made by a man after a particularly heavy woman has bounced up too far and sat down hard on his *gut stick,* breaking it in two. Reportedly Prince Albert's last word.

**boiled eggs for four** *n.* Visual impairment enjoyed by two reciprocating *homo horatiolists* in the *69* position. *Double Dutch blindfold.*

**boiler** *n.* An ugly woman who is lucky to get *serviced* once a year.

**boilerdom** *n.* The state of being a *boiler* into which many fat lasses pass directly upon reaching puberty.

**boilersuit** *n.* The charge that you did wilfully, and with phallus aforethought score with a pig ugly lass on Friday night. Usually brought by a kangaroo court convened in a pub on Saturday.

**bolitics** *n.* The practice of talking utter *bollocks* about politics. Often performed by drunks in pubs, students in halls of residence and Estelle Morris.

**bollock jockeys** *n.* See *willipedes.*

**bollock rats** *n.* Scrotal vermins. Crabs.

**bollock service** *n. Wank.* '*My balls are blue. It's about time I had them in for a bollock service.*'

**bollocks** 1. *adj.* Nonsense. '*That's utter bollocks, that is*'. 2. *n. Knackers, balls.* '*Them's massive bollocks, thems is*'.

**bomb bay bedbath** *n.* To *shit* the bed after a pleasant night of curry and lager. Also *Mrs Chegwin's facepack.*

**bomb bay duck** *n.* A *dog's egg* that quacks to let one know it wants to come out.

**bomb bay mix** *n.* A single lavatorial sitting that produces a pot-pourri of stool consistencies, from *copper bolts* to a *rusty water* geyser, and all points in between. *Shitterish Allsorts, variety cack.*

**bomb bay** *n. medic.* The last lock on the alimentary *shit* canal. The rectum.

**bomb China** *v.* To release your *payload* over the *Yellow River.* To have a *Billy Wright.*

**Bombay roll** *n.* Like a sausage roll, but with *tits* instead of pastry and a *cock* instead of a sausage. And it costs £25 instead of 30p.

**bone of contention** *n.* A *stonk on* that causes an argument, eg. one that arises whilst watching beach volleyball with one's wife.

**bone on** *n.* A *panhandle.*

**bone** *v. US.* To *fuck.*

**bone xylophone** *n. medic.* Gynaecological term for the interior of a woman's rib

cage. Her *slats*. *'Let's go play
the bone xylophone.'*

**boner** *n*. *US*. That which is
used to *bone*.

**boneshaker** *1*. *n*. An
unsprung Victorian bicycle,
named for its teeth-loosening
progress along cobbled
streets. *2*. *n*. An act of sexual
intercourse that has to be finished by hand.

**bongo mag** *n*. *Rhythm literature, spangle book.*

**bonk** *v*. Tabloid term for *fuck*.

**bonk-on** *n*. Splendidly tumescent member. *'A copy of
'Splosh' and a box of tissues
please, Mr Newsagent. I've
got an almighty bonk-on.'*

**boobies** *n*. See *boobs*.

**boobs** *n*. See *boobies*.

**boot** *n*. *Can*. A woman who is
too easy to *shag*.

**booze flu** *n*. A non-viral ail-
ment that strikes suddenly
after an evening at the pub
and causes the sufferer to
take the next day off work.
Symptoms include staying in
bed and feeling like shite.

**booze tardis** *n*. A four dimen-
sional *beer scooter*.

**boregasm** *n*. An act of *self-
pollution* for want of anything else to do.

**Boris** *n*. Term used by females
for their *farmyard area*,
apparently.

**born again fistian** *n*. One
who has recently become single and is once again spend-
ing a lot of time *praying for
milk*.

**Bosch** *v*. Of bishops and farmers – to drill a hole between
cubicles in a public lavatory
for the purpose of spying on,
or making your penis available to the farmer or bishop
in the adjacent *trap*.

**bosphorus** *n*. The bit that
connects the fishy pleasures
of the Mediterranean with
the exotic mysteries of the
Black Sea. The *taint, tinter,
notcher, biffin bridge*.

**bott** *v*. A sex act performed by
*botters*.

**bottee** *n*. One who is *botted* up
the *bottom* by a *botter*.

**botter** *n*. One who *botts* a *bottee* up the bottom.

**bottled Bass** *n*. Descriptive of
the lubricity of a *stoat*. *'You
may be knocking on a bit,
love, but your granny's oysters
are frothing like bottled Bass.'*

**bottom log** *n*. A scuttled
*dreadnought* that hits the sea
bed whilst still exiting the
*windward passage*.

**bottom** *n.* That part of the *bottee* which is *botted* by a *botter.*

**botty burp** *n.* A burp from the *bottom, trouser trumpet, fart.*

**bouncers** *1. n.* Unsportsmanlike, short-pitched deliveries in cricket aimed at intimidating the batsman. *2. n.* Muscle men, *ripped to the tits* on steroids, who keep the riff raff out of pubs and clubs. *3. n.* Big, wobbly *tits.*

**bourbon** *n.* Someone who is good at *horatio.* A fancy 'licker.'

**Bourneville boulevard** *n. Arse, fudge tunnel.* Used to denote homosexuality. *'I believe he strolls down the Bourneville boulevard'.*

**Bovril bullets** *n.* Stools, excrement. Faeces.

**bowel bugle** *n.* A *trouser trumpet.*

**bowel howl** *n.* Fearsome wailing of the anus, the *sound of your supper.*

**bowel trowel** *n.* One of a selection of tools at the disposal of the *uphill gardener.* See also *cheesy wheelbarrow, trouser rake. One-eyed purple-headed blue-veined hairy pink hedgeclipper.*

**bowk** *v.* To *barf, vomit, spew, yak, hoy up, bake a pavement pizza.*

**bowl from the Pavilion end** *v.* To *bott,* travel on *the other bus.*

**box** *1. n.* The vagina. *'I wouldn't mind getting into her box.' 2. n.* In cricket, a gentleman's protective device worn around the *undercarriage. 'Ooyah me pods! I wish I'd worn a box.'*

**box doc** *n. medic.* A gynaecologist. A *fanny mechanic.*

**box of assorted creams** *n. Aus.* She who has recently been over-accommodating to a number of gentlemen. A promiscuous female with a *fanny like billposter's bucket.*

**box the Jesuit** *v. 17thC.* How Friar Tuck may have referred to *strangling the parson* behind a bush in Sherwood Forest.

**brace** *rhym. slang.* To defecate. From brace and bit ~ *tom tit.*

**Brad** *1. n. rhym. slang.* A *dump. 'Give me the paper, I'm off for a Brad.' 2. n. rhym. slang. ~s The Earthas. 'Can you pass me some moist wipes in? I've got a bad case of the Brads.'*

**Brahms and Liszt** *adj. rhym. slang. Wankered.*

**brain donor** *n.* Thick *cunt.*

**brap** n. The volume rating of a *fart (Bp)* governed by three variables – rectal pressure *(r)*, buttock friction *(f)* and sprouts consumed *(SpC)* such that $Bp = fx\ SpC/r$. Buttock friction *(f)* can be reduced to zero by pulling the *ringpiece* open wide during emission.

**brass eye** n. *Hog's eye, brown eye, red eye, chocolate starfish.*

**Brazilian wax** n. A bald *monkey's forehead. A shaven haven, a Barthez.*

**breach the hull** v. To push one's digit through inferior quality *bumwad* when wiping one's *arse. Push through. 'Day 82, and the men are getting restless. Squabbles are beginning and tempers are short. John Norton handed out the ship's biscuits, but Mr Christian refused to eat, accusing him of breaching the hull and not washing his hands.'* (from *'The Log of HMS Bounty',* 1764).

**break company** v. To disrupt a gathering of *beneficiaries* by the release of a *McArthur Park.*

**breaking the seal** v. The first *piss* at the pub, usually after three or four pints. After breaking the seal of your bladder, return visits to the toilet are required every fifteen minutes throughout the evening.

**breast fest** n. Those summer months during which women sunbathe topless.

**breasticles** n. Particularly small, wrinkly bosoms of the type you'd expect Dot Cotton to have.

**breather ring** n. An anular indentation on a long *turd,* indicating where the *cable layer* has had to pause for breath, allowing the *nipsy* to partially contract. A faecal aneurism. *'Fuck me! That was a bastard to part with. I left it with three breather rings on it.'*

**brew one up** v. To be *burbulent,* to bake an *air biscuit. 'For your own safety step back please ladies, I'm brewing one up over here.'*

**brewer's droop** n. Marshmallowing of the penis due to excessive *turps nudging.*

**brewer's fart** n. A particularly sulphurous *bowel howl. 'Jesus, he's just dropped a brewer's fart, grains and all.'*

**brice** v. *Vict.* To engage in a sexual act in which one party is tied to a large stake known as the *bricing post*

**bricing post** *n.* Stake to which someone is tied, who is to be *briced.*

**brick shithouse** *sim.* Built like a Bradford Bulls prop forward. Heavy set, stocky. *'Is that your missus. Fucking hell, she's built like a brick shithouse.'*

**bridge the gap** *v.* See *TUB-FUF.*

**bridger** *n. Bottom log.*

**Brillo pad** *sim.* Coarse vaginal foliage. A red headed Scots lassie might be described as having *'A mott like a rusty Brillo pad.'*

**brim** *n.* Wainscotting around the base of the *helmet. The wankstop,* the *sulcus.*

**bring off** *v.* To cause to have an orgasm.

**Bristol Channel** *n.* The cleavage.

**Bristols** *ryhm. slang. Tits.* From Bristol Cities – *titties.*

**broat** *n.* See *vurp.*

**Bronx cheer** *n. arch.* Obsolete whoopee cushion term for a *fart.*

**brother** *n. Bean flicker, tuppence licker, carpet muncher.* A lesbian.

**brown admiral** *n. zoo.* The common and far from beautiful butterfly that can be found in the pants of someone who has failed to *draw an ace.* A *gusset moth.*

**brown bear's nose** *n.* A cute little round *turd* that hibernates at the bottom of the *pan.*

**brown bullet-hole** *n. Bumhole, barking spider.*

**brown daisy** *n.* An unpleasantly-scented flower which attracts flies instead of bees. A *bronze eye.*

**brown eye** *n.* The *ring* through which the *brown trout* jump on their daily migration to the sea.

**brown hatter** *n.* A *bottsman* with a *shit* on his helmet.

**brown jewels** *n.* The Queen's *winnits.* The *dangleberries* of state.

**brown lilo** *n.* A buoyant *Tom Tit* that, left alone, will eventually float out to sea.

**brown pipe engineer** *n.* An *arse mechanic* who always calls at the *tradesman's entrance.*

**brown tie** *n.* The dirty mark left between a lady's *jugs* by a man who has a *sausage sandwich* after taking her up the *council gritter.*

**brown trout** *n.* A *turd, big job, shite.*

**brown wings** *n.* Hell's Angel term – the honour bestowed on one after performing *bumilingus* on a lady Hell's Angel.

**Bruce Lees** *n.* Hard *nips.*

**BS** *abbrev. US.* Booooool-shee-it.

**BSH** *abbrev.* British Standard Handful. The unit by which breasts are often measured.

**bubbies** *n.* Coy term for *breasts,* much beloved of writers of cod-Victorian pornography. *"Ooh, zur! What does you think of moi bubbies, then?' asked Molly the Milkmaid, as she unzipped the Squire's heaving breeches.'* (from *'A Roll in the Hay',* by Jeffrey Archer).

**bubbing** *v.* To rub one's *knob* on one's partner's *freckle* whenever possible (usually accompanied by an Ainsley Harriot-esque chinny grin and head wobble), in the hope that one day she'll say 'Oh, go on then.'

**bubble poo** *n. Fizzy gravy.*

**bucket fanny** *n.* Spacious or roomy vagina. *Tardis twat, cathedral, welly top.*

**budgie smugglers** *n.* Extremely tight gentlemen's bathing trunks.

**budgie's tongue** *n.* Descriptive of the female erectile bit, particularly when her *fanny* has climbed a little plastic ladder to ring a bell.

**buffage** *n. US.* Highly offensive and sexist term used by women to describe men. *'Hey girls, check out the buffage in here.'*

**buffet slayer** *n.* A female *lard of the manor.* A lady with a penchant for eating more than her fair share of free food.

**buffing** *v. Gusset typing.* The act of female masturbation.

**buffty** *n. Scot.* Gay fellow.

**bugger** *1. n.* He who pokes animals, arseholes or animals' arseholes. A *berry. 2. v.* To break or damage. To *fuck. 3. exclam.* A cry of dismay. *'I'm afraid you have lung cancer, and it's spread into your lymph nodes' 'Bugger!'*

**bugger's grips** *n.* Sideburns. Any tufts of facial hair on the cheeks. *Bugger's handles, face fannies.*

**Bugner's eye** *n.* Flapless female genitalia, resembling boxer Joe Bugner's closed-up eye in any fight he ever had.

**build a log cabin** *v.* To pass a

series of sturdy stools. *'I wouldn't go in there, mate. Someone's just built a log cabin.'*

**builder's bum** *n* . The protrusion of sweaty *arse* cheeks above the sagging waist of the jeans. Common among builders, council workmen and top fashion designer Alexander McQueen. *Bricky's crack, Dagenham smile.*

**bull** *abbrev. US. BS*

**bulldog chewing a wasp** *sim.* Descriptive of a lady's face that does not conform to conventional ideals of beauty. Also *bulldog licking piss off a nettle, welder's bench, stripper's clit.*

**bulldog eating porridge** *sim.* Poetic term describing the vagina in the aftermath of sex. *'When I'd finished with her, she had a fanny like a bulldog eating porridge, I can tell you.'*

**bulldyke** *n.* Butch, masculine or aggressive lezza. *Diesel dyke.*

**bullshit** *1. n. Feeshus* of male cattle. *2. n.* Rubbish, nonsense, *bollocks. 2. v.* To lie, deliberately mislead, talk rubbish to. *'Don't you bullshit me now, you hear, bitch, or I'll cut yo' jive-ass face wide open.'* (Sir Neville Chamberlain to his wife, after she informed him that Hitler had invaded Poland).

**bum** *1. n. Arse, bottom, poopchute. 2. n. US. Harold Ramp, pan handler.* A homeless person. *3. v.* Of cigarettes, to scrounge, scavenge. *4. v.* To *bott. 5. adj. US. legal.* Of *raps*, to be unjust, unfair. *6. n.* Trebor mint preservation apparatus.

**bum bandit** *n.* A robber, outlaw or highwayman, who steals people's *bottoms*.

**bum brake** *n.* The *nipsy.*

**bum chain** *n.* A rather intimate version of the Conga, danced around the streets at the end of a gay party.

**bum chums** *n.* Primary school term for any two boys who always sit next to each other.

**bum cigar** *n.* In after dinner conversation, a stool. *'Well, if you'll excuse me ladies, I think I shall retire to the bathroom and light a bum cigar.'*

**bum conkers** *n.* Shiny, brown spherical agglomerations which hang off the *arse*, and can be baked in the oven or soaked in vinegar.

**bum crumbs** *n.* *Kling-ons* which have ceased to kling on. Usually found in the bed or in the gusset of the *trolleys*.

**bum fluff** *n.* Risible pubescent attempt to grow a moustache.

**bum goblin** *n.* A gnarled, malevolent *turd* that jumps out from behind you, casting a painful spell on your *ring-piece*.

**bum grapes** *n.* Painful, juice-filled, seedless fruit which grow well in the moist, shady regions of the *Khyber Pass*.

**bum gravy** *n.* Diarrhoea, *rusty water*.

**bum tongue** *n.* A large piece of *shit* hanging from *Dot Cotton's mouth* just before it licks the bowl.

**bummange** *n.* A light, fluffy *arse* dessert. *Angel deshight*.

**bummer** *1. n.* One who *bums*. *2. n. US.* A disappointing situation.

**bumpies** *rhym. slang. Fun bags.* From bumpy bits ~*tits*.

**bumscare** *n.* Severe pressure in the lower abdominal region prior to a controlled explosion.

**bumshee** *n.* A blood-curdling howl of anguish coming from a toilet cubicle.

**bumtags** *n. Dangleberries.*

**bumwad** *n.* Toilet tissue.

**bun in the oven, to have a** *v.* To be pregnant, *up the stick, in the club, in trouble*. *'Guess what love. I've got a bun in the oven.' 'Oh! Is my tea ready, yet?'*

**bung hole** *n.* Vagina. See *fizzing at the~*.

**Bungle's finger** *n.* A short, stocky *turd*, named after the ursine simpleton from the 70s children's show 'Rainbow.'

**bunion ring** *n.* An old lady's *jacksie*.

**bunk up** *1. n.* A utility poke. *'Darling, you look beautiful tonight. Any chance of a bunk up?' 2. n.* Assistance in climbing. *'Shit. I'm so pissed I can't get onto the bed. Any chance of a bunk up?'*

**bunko booth** *n.* Paul Daniels's *shithouse*. A lavatory cubicle.

**bunk-up badge** *n.* A love bite, usually found on really ugly people's necks to prove they have a love life. A *hickie*, a *bub,* a *shag-tag*.

**bunny rub** *n.* A *tit wank, Bombay roll*.

**bunny-boiler** *n.* A determined

woman who misinterprets a one-off drunken *scuttle* as the overture to a deep and lasting relationship, then tries to win your affections when you go back to the missus by boiling your kids' pets.

**buns** *1. n.* Regional variation of *baps*. *2. n. US. Ass* cheeks.

**burbulence** *n.* The uncomfortable alimentary rumbling which precedes the breakage of wind. *'Over Nova Scotia I finished the last of my egg sandwiches. Half an hour later I hit a pocket of burbulence, and had to fasten my seat belt and extinguish all lights.'* (from *'Across the Atlantic- the autobiography of Amelia Earhart'* 1938).

**burial at sea** *n.* The dignified delivery of a stool, without *splashback*. The opposite of a *depth charge* or *belly flopper*.

**burly** *n. Bum wipe*, toilet paper, *chocolate shark bait*, *turd tokens*.

**BURMA** *acronym.* Secret code used on military correspondence – Be Upstairs Ready My Angel. See also *Norwich, Polo.*

**burn bad powder** *v. arch. milit.* Of *trouser trumpetry*, to *light a tyre*, emit a *fyst*.

**burp the worm** *v. Bash the bishop.*

**bury a quaker** *v.* To dispense with the contents of one's rectum. *Crimp one off*, release a payload from the *bomb bay.*

**bury the hobbit** *v.* To lose *Bilbo Bellend* in the *wizard's sleeve.*

**bush meat** *n.* Meat found under *bushes.*

**bush** *n. Gorilla salad, ladygarden, mapatasi.* Female pubic hair.

**bush pig** *n.* A slightly more polite term for a *swamp hog.*

**bush tents** *n.* Ladies' *knickers.*

**bushcraft** *1. n.* Survival techniques employed in the Australian Outback. *2. n.* Recreational techniques employed in the *Tasmanian Outfront.*

**bushman's hankie** *n. Aus.* Term given to the process whereby mucus is expelled from the nose by placing a finger over a nostril and blowing. Popular amongst professional footballers. A *single barrelled snot gun.*

**bushtucker** *n.* Anything on the menu when *eating out* in Tasmania.

**butcher's dishcloth** *sim.*

Descriptive of the *drip tray* of a lady's knickers when *the fleet is in*.

**butcher's dustbin** *n.* A sight grimmer than a *butcher's window*.

**butcher's turd** *sim.* Descriptive of the richness of something. *"Do have some more gateau, Mr. D'arcy'. 'Well perhaps just a little slice, Mrs. Bennet. It's as rich as a butcher's turd".* (from 'Pride and Prejudice', by Jane Austen).

**butcher's window** *n.* An appetizing display of female genitalia.

**butler in the pantry** *n.* A polite *turd* which knows its place, remaining below stairs, occasionally coughing discreetly until summoned.

**butler's cuff** *n.* A tightly-buttoned vagina, the opposite of a *wizard's sleeve*. A *fanny like a mouse's ear.*

**butler's revenge** *n.* A silent but deadly *fart*.

**butler's ringpiece** *adj.* Descriptive of something that is nipping clean. *"What can you see, Holmes?' I expostulated, as the great detective peered into his microscope. (I need not remind you of how in the past, he had solved the mystery of the Pope's cap when he found gibbon's tooth marks on the cardinal's walking stick.) 'I'm examining the handle of this dagger of unusual oriental design in the hope of finding a speck of tobacco, only available from one shop in London, or a hair from a rare species of Patagonian chinchilla. However, I fear our murderer has wiped it as clean as a butler's ringpiece."* (from 'The Brown Hatted League' by Sir Arthur Conan-Doyle).

**butt cutlet** *n.* A wholesome organic *loaf* baked in the *chamber of horrors*. A vegetarian's *turd*.

**butt nuggets** *n.* Piles.

**butt plug** *n.* A medical appliance used to prevent water from the bath going up your *arse*.

**butt slammers** *n. US.* Members of the gay community. *Turd burglars.*

**butt sneeze** *n. US. Fart.*

**butt's fizz** *n.* Celebratory *bubble poo.*

**buttered bun** *n.* A well-used *snatch.* A *box of assorted creams.*

**butterface** *n.* A woman with a great figure, but the face of a darts player's wife. From the phrase *'A good body, but her face...'* A *bobfoc.*

**buttflood** *n.* The *squirts,* the *Earthas.*

**buttock broker** *n.* Controller of prostitutes, pimp. A *titty farmer, pussy farmer, gash baron.*

**buttock hall** *n. Meat market.* Pub or club frequented by slappers.

**buttock jig** *n.* A close horizontal dance that takes place after chucking out time.

**button groove** *n. Hairy axe wound,* the *snapper.* The vulva.

**button** *n. Clitty.* The *Devil's doorbell.*

**BVH** *abbrev.* Blue Veined Hooligan. A hard, six-inch tall, one-eyed, skinhead.

**Byker tea cake** *n.* A *Glasgow kiss.* A head butt.

# Cc

**cab man's rests** *rhym. slang.* *Bristols, thrupenny bits.*

**cabbage fart** *n.* An *old dog's alarm clock.* A *fart* that smells of rotting vegetation.

**cabbage gas** *n.* Naturally occurring renewable fuel used to power *Dutch ovens.*

**cabbage** *n.* Girls, *totty, blart.* *'What-ho, Jeeves. I've just been down to the Pink Flamingo club. Never seen so much cabbage in all my born pecker.'* (from *'Achtung, Jeeves',* by PG Wodehouse).

**cable laying** *v.* To excrete solid stools.

**caboose** *n.* The *anchor man* in a *bum train. Lucky Pierre's* rear attendant.

**cack . cacka . cak** *1. n. Shit,* excrement, *feeshus. 2. v.* To *papper,* usually one's *trolleys.*

**Cadbury alley** *n. Bourneville Boulevard.*

**cajooblies** *n. Oomlaaters.*

**call down for more mayo** *v. Jack the beanstalk.*

**call Huey** *v.* Vomit, *puke.* Also *call Ralph, call Ruth.*

**camel's foot** *n. Twix lips.* See *beetle bonnet.*

**camp** *adj.* To be as butch as Kenneth Williams.

**Campbell's condensed** *n.* A small-volume double-strength *fart* which, when diluted with air, can feed a whole room.

**can** *1. n. US.* Bottom. *2. n. US.* A quantity of *Bob Hope, marijuana. 3. n. US.* Prison. *4. n. US.* Toilet, *shithouse. 'They put me in the can after I was caught in the can sticking a can up my can.'*

**captain** *1. n.* Penis. *'Don't be shy, love. Go below deck and say hello to the captain.' 2. v.* to do a~. To display one's *buttocks* through the back window of a coach, usually to a couple of nuns in a Morris Minor. To do a *moonie.*

**Captain Caveman** *n.* A yodelling *biffer.*

**Captain Hogseye** *n.* Curly bearded seafarer with a shiny, bald, purple head who trawls in *cod cove.* And spits a lot.

**Captain Oates, to do a** *v.* To altruistically leave the pub early when struggling with the pace, so as not to hold your fellow drinkers back.

**Captain's pie** *1. n.* Tasty *slice* caught fresh by Captain *Hogseye. Haddock pastie. 2. n. milit.* Of naval catering, that pie which belongs to the captain.

**capuccino fanny** *n.* When the *furry cup* has reached its maximum froth.

**card table** *n.* A position whereby a lady engages in simultaneous oral/vaginal pleasures with two gentlemen who, should they wish, could play a game of cards on her back. A frankly unlikely scenario. A *spit roast.*

**cardinal's cap** *n. medic.* A swelling and reddening of the *herman* brought on by chronic *bishop rage. Fireman's helmet.*

**carnival knowledge** *n.* Biblical phrase meaning to have sex. *'And it came to pass that Mary was up the spout, yea though Joseph had not lain with her, and certainly had not carnival knowledge of her.'* (from *St. Paul's letters to the Gas Board, Chapter 6, vv. 3-5*).

**carnival** *n.* A sexual game where a woman sits on a man's face and he has to guess her weight.

**Carolgees' cuff** *n.* To have one's *wanking spanner* wrist deep in a *biffer.*

**carpenter's dream** *n.* sexually promiscuous woman – 'flat as a board and easy to *screw.'* A *boot.*

**carpet duster** *n.* A dense, heavier-than-air *fart* which forms a thin layer over the whole floor surface.

**carpet muncher** *n.* A lady who enjoys *gorilla salad*, but turns her nose up at *meat and two veg.*

**carse** *n.* The female equivalent of the *barse.*

**carwash** *n.* View of the vagina whilst performing *cumulonimbus.* The hair of the *muff* looking like them big whirly brush things.

**Casanova's rubber sock** *n.* Condom, *blob, French letter, Coney Island whitefish.*

**cashpoint cripple** *n.* See *video cripple.*

**casting Churchill's reflection** *sim.* A political impression involving a porcelain bowl with water in the bottom, your *arse* and a *bum cigar.*

**cat flaps** *1. n.* Means by which a cute little pussy can enter the house. *2. n.* Means by which a *cock* can enter a cute little *pussy.* Labia minora, *beef curtains.*

**cat's face** *n.* Mrs. Slocombe's *cunt.*

**catcher's mitt** *n.* A contraceptive diaphragm, a *fuck-plug.*

**cathedral** *sim.* Describing an oversized vagina which is too echo-y for a satisfactory *organ recital.* A *bucket fanny.*

**cattle** *rhym. slang.* To engage in coitus. From cattle truck *~fuck.* Also *trolley* (and truck), *Friar* (Tuck) or *Russian* (duck).

**cauliflower** *1. n.* Sex. *'Hey! Your missus gave me a bit of cauliflower while you were at work last night.'* 2. *n. 18thC. Lettuce.*

**cauliflower cheese** *n. Smegma.*

**cavalier** *n.* Uncircumcised penis. With a big feather stuck in the top.

**cedar burp** *n.* Small outbreak of *chocolate thunder.* A *fart.*

**CGI** *1. abbrev.* The City and Guilds Institute. *2. abbrev.* Cunt Gap Index. A measurement on a scale of finger widths of the size of a woman's *Toblerone tunnel.*

**Chalfonts** *rhym. slang.* Piles, *bum grapes.* From the town of Chalfont St. Gemerroids, Buckinghamshire.

**Champagne corks** *n.* Bullet-hard *nipples* that pop out of the *tit pants* with enough force to take your eye out.

**change at Baker Street** *v.* During intercourse, to decide to *play the B-side.* From the only station on the London Underground where it is possible to change from the Pink line *(Hammersmith & City)* to the Brown line *(Bakerloo).*

**change holes and ball** *exclam. Meat movie* director's instruction to his actors, informing them of his wish that they swap ends to ensure variety in his production.

**chap** *v.* To gently slap your penis in the face of your sleeping wife, girlfriend or party guest, take a Polaroid photograph and leave it in a place where they are bound to come across it, eg. fridge door, car windscreen, internet.

**chapel hat pegs** *sim.* To describe large, erect *nips. Pygmy's cocks, Scammell wheel nuts, JCB starter buttons.*

**Charlie** *1. rhym. slang.* Cunt. From 'Charlie Hunt'. *'You look a right Charlie'.* 2. *n. Showbiz sherbert.* 3. *n. Hampton Wick,* the penis. 4. *n.* A *tit.*

**Charlie Carolli's hat** *n.* A lady's *minge,* brimful of *spoff.* From the erstwhile clown's blancmange-filled bowler.

**Charlie Dimmock's nipples** *n*. Term used by vicars to describe the hat-pegs in their chapels.

**Charlie in the chocolate factory** *n*. *Bolivian marching powder* snorted in a public *shithouse* eg. the *crappers* at the Groucho Club.

**Charlies** *n*. 1970s *tits*.

**charms** *n*. Of British tabloid journalism, the breasts. Usually prefixed 'ample'.

**charver . charva** *1. v. US*. To have sex, *shag*. *2. n*. Boy, lad, adolescent. *3. n*. Aerosol snorting, be-tracksuited *twocker*, *borstal boy, car radio removal mechanic. 4. n*. A ten-year-old mother of several *pastie babies*.

**chasing the cotton mouse** *adj*. To have the *painters in, flags out, surf the crimson wave*, be *up on blocks*.

**chauffeur's glove** *n*. A tight-fitting *flunkey*. Possibly with three buttons on the back.

**cheapies** *n*. Schoolboy sexual thrills. *'Miss Pollard bent down to pick up the chalk and gave William his cheapies.'* (from *'William Stirs Below'* by Richmal Crompton).

**chebs** *n*. *Tits, norks, headlamps*. Breasts.

**check the roast** *v*. To see if what you've been baking is ready to come out. To go for a *shit*.

**cheddar apple** *n*. A very large, cheesy *bell end*.

**cheek flapper** *n*. A *fart* which registers highly on the *brap scale*. A *clapper rattler, a drive on the cat's eyes*.

**cheese ridge** *n*. The fertile area of the *cheesepipe* where *knob cheese* is matured for weeks and months. The *brim* of the *lid*.

**cheese-cutter** *n. medic*. A rogue *pube* caught in the *five-skin*, whilst still attached to the body. Results in two-fold agony; it simultaneously cuts into *Captain Picard's head* whilst trying to tear itself out at the root.

**cheesepipe clingfilm** *n*. Condom, *rubber Johnny*.

**cheesepipe** *n*. The tubular organ that secretes *chucky cheese*.

**cheesey wheelbarrow** *n*. A self-explanatory sexual position utilised by two *uphill gardeners*.

**cheezer** *n*. That which is a cross between a *chick* and a *geezer*, eg. Julian Clary or Richard Branson.

**chef's arse** *n.* An uncomfortable, perspiring, smelly *bum* cleft, so called because of its prevalence amongst catering professionals, eg. Gordon Ramsay and Delia Smith.

**cheps** *n. Chebs.*

**Cherie Blair** *n.* A mouth conducive to group fellatio. A *Carly Simon*, a *three-dick gob.*

**cherry boy** *n.* A crimson, hormone-filled adolescent male with an intact *virgin string.*

**cherry** *n.* An intact *virgin string.* One that has not been *popped.*

**chest pillows** *n. Chebs.*

**chestnuts** *n. Stits, juglets.*

**chew your own arm off** *v.* To have difficulty getting away from a *coyote* with whom you wake up no longer wearing your *beer goggles.* If she was asleep on it, you would 'chew your own arm off' in order to escape.

**Chewbacca after a fight** *sim.* Descriptive of a particularly untidy *biffer.*

**chewie** *n.* An act of *horatio*, a *sucking off*, a *gobbie.*

**chewing a toffee** *v.* During perambulation, descriptive of the unpleasant sensation of anal chafing and squelching following insufficient wiping of the *freckle.*

**chewing on a brick** *v.* Of *logs* and *logging*, that desperate point when the *turtle's head*, and indeed *shoulders* protrude, and the *arse* is left *'chewing on a brick.'*

**chichis** *n. Mex. Tits,* breasts.

**chicken** *n.* Young gay male. A *botter's apprentice.*

**chicken skin handbag** *n. Scrot, nadbag.*

**chickenhawk** *n.* The time-served *botter*, to whom several *botter's apprentices* are apprenticed.

**chimney sweep** 1. *n.* A soot-covered man who cleans your chimney. 2. *n.* A soot-covered man who *bangs* you up the *dirtbox.*

**chimney sweep's brush** *n.* Dick Van Dyke's penis.

**chimping** *v. Spanking the monkey* whilst grinning from ear to ear. And having a cup of PG Tips.

**chin rest** *n. Duffy's bridge.*

**chin splash** *n.* Condition caused by trying on a *pearl necklace* that is too big.

**Chinese gravy** *n.* Something that tastes foul. *'I was dining at the Y the other night and* *my fish supper tasted worse than Chinese gravy.'*

**Chinese helicopter pilot** *sim.* Descriptive of someone sitting up and controlling their *chopper.*

**Chinese singing lesson** *n.* A *gypsy's kiss.* A *piss.*

**Chinese tool** *n.* A feeble penis, ie. barely up to the job in hand.

**chinstrap** n. The small piece of skin which holds the *German helmet* safely in place. The *banjo.*

**Chipperfield** *n.* A proper leathering you get off a bouncer for no good reason.

**chips 'n' hame** (home) *phr. Scot.* The observed state of someone's failure to *score* and their resulting departure from the pub or club. *'Wee Angus has had nae luck the neet.' 'Aye, Hamish. He's chips 'n' hame.'*

**choad** *n. Cock, knob.*

**chocolate cha-cha** *n.* Rooftop dance in the style of Dick Van Dyke, but performed by *chimney sweeps* of the *chocolate* variety.

**chocolate chimney sweep** *n.* A soot-covered man who is not interested in cleaning ladies' chimneys.

**chocolate eclair** *n.* A *Cleveland steamer.*

**chocolate eye** *n. Bumhole.*

**chocolate fountain** *n.* A spectacular, anal, upside-down firework ignited in the lavatory to celebrate having a belly full of beer and a dodgy curry the night before.

**chocolate iceberg** *n.* Giant *turd* sitting in the pan, nine tenths of which remains below the surface. A *growler.*

**chocolate sandwich** *n.* A sexual act performed in the presence of Arthur Lowe in the film 'Oh Lucky Man!' involving a black man and two white lady strippers.

**chocolate speedway** *1. n. Bumhole, poop chute. 2. n. ~rider.* Purple-helmeted star of the *dirt track.*

**chocolate starfish** *n. Rusty sheriff's badge, Bovril bullet hole.* The *arse.*

**chocolate thunder** *n. Tail winds,* a *trouser typhoon.* Also *under thunder.*

**choke a brown dog** *v.* To apply the *bum brake* too early. To nip a *shite* halfway through.

**choke the chicken / goose** *v.* To masturbate.

**chooza** *n. NZ.* A *choad.*

**choozies** *n. Aus.* Breasts.

**chopper** *1. n.* Penis. *'That (insert name of striker currently having a run of bad form) couldn't score in a brothel with a £50 note wrapped round his chopper.'* *2. n.* Fancy orange bike that fat kids owned in the 1970s. *3. n.* Helicopter. *4. n.* Axe.

**chorus from Mama Jo's bongos** *n.* An early morning *fart* that sounds like someone from 'Scooby Doo' running on the spot before scarpering from the ghost. *Morning thunder.*

**chrome-dome** *n. Slap head, baldy.*

**chubblies** *n.* Fat bird's *choozies.*

**chuck up** *v.* Vomit, *honk up, barf.*

**chuck your muck** *v.* To *lose your mess, spend your wad.* To ejaculate.

**chuckies** *n.* Balls.

**chucky cheese** *n.* Vomit-inducing tangy cheddar matured in unwashed *brims.*

**chudleighs** *n. Chuds, chebs, charlies, charms, chichis, choozies.* Ladies' *tits.*

**chuff** *1. v.* To *pass wind, shoot* a bunny rabbit. *'Oops! Best open a window vicar. I've just chuffed'.* *2. n.* Vagina, lady's front bottom. *3. n. zoo.* Anus of a gnat.

**chuff chowder** *n.* A pungent soup served as a first course when *dining at the Y.* Hopefully without croutons.

**chuff mountain** *n.* Surplus of *cabbage* at a party.

**chuff muncher** *n.* A *woman in comfortable shoes.*

**chuffdruff** *n. Muffdruff.* Residual flakes of desiccated *mess* and *fanny batter* found on the *mapatasi.* Pubic equivalent of *mammary dandruff.*

**chuff-nuts** *n. Dangleberries.*

**chuftie plug** *n. Cotton pony.* Tampon.

**chug** *v. Choke the chicken, spank the monkey, burp the worm.*

**chugnuts** *n.* Extremely big piles. *'A cushion, Mrs. Bennet, a cushion! I fear the frivolities at Lady Marchmain's ball has brought down my chugnuts no end.'* (from *'Pride and Predudice',* by Jane Austen).

**chumbawumbas** *onomat.* A rather predictable use of a pop group's name as slang for breasts. Also *Bananaramas* (penises), *Wurzels* (testicles) and *BeeGees* (hairy twats).

**chumblies** *n medic. Nuts, knackers.*

**chunder** *v. Aus.* To *chunk.*

**chunk** *v.* To vomit. Also *blow chunks.*

**churns** *1. n.* Breasts. *2. n.* Testicles. *3. n.* Seemingly any vessel containing white fluid.

**chutney ferret** *n. Chocolate speedway rider.*

**chutney locker** *n. medic.* The *bomb bay,* rectum. Also *date locker.*

**cider visor** *n. Beer goggles* for the younger street drinker.

**cigarbutts** *n. JCB starter buttons, Bruce Lees.*

**circle jerk** *n.* A communal *hand shandy* session. A *milk race.*

**cistern chapel** *n.* The porcelain font where *Meatloaf's daughter* is baptised.

**clabby** *adj.* Exceptionally pink. Used to describe *bacon strips.*

**clacker** *1. n.* One half of a dangerous, finger-breaking 1970s toy. *2. n. Aus.* The *anus.*

**clackerbag** *n.* A leathery receptacle for *clockweights.*

**Clacton chinwag** *n.* The oral intercourse that takes place between a man and a kneeling woman who has had a couple of bottles of *tart fuel.* A *blow job.*

**clagnuts** *n. Dangleberries, tagnuts.*

**clam jousting** *n.* A fanular encounter between two ladies afflicted with lesbism. Also *velcro fastening.*

**clam ram** *n.* A *gut stick, cock.*

**clam shandy** *n.* A lady's version of a *hand shandy.* A few scales on the *invisible banjo.*

**clam smacker** *n. Bean flicker.*

**clamoflage** *n.* Thick, impenetrable *bush* which makes the target impossibly hard to spot at first glance. The *pubes* on a *biffer.*

**clankers** *n. onomat.* The same as *clinkers,* only bigger.

**clap** *n. medic.* Any sexually transmitted disease, but usually gonorrhoea. *Cockrot.*

**clapometer** *n.* Imaginary medical instrument used by doctors to diagnose the clap. *'Don't touch her. I hear she scores ten on the clapometer.'*

**clappers** 1. n. In *farting,* the buttocks. *'Christ! That one didn't half rattle the clap-*

*pers.'* 2. *n*. That part of a bell like which a lady *goes*.

**clapping fish** *n*. Female genitalia.

**clarts** *n*. Tacky excrement, such as would cling to the lavatory bowl above the water line rather than slip below the surface.

**claypit** *n*. A source of the raw material for making *coil pots*. The *arse*.

**clear the custard** *v*. To have a long overdue *wank*. *'I've got ten minutes before I have to take mass. I'll just nip upstairs and clear the custard.'*

**Cleveland steamer** 1. *n*. A merchant cargo vessel operating on Lake Erie. 2. *n*. A sexual act much favoured by the Hun that doesn't bear thinking about. A *chocolate éclair*.

**climb on** *v*. The culmination of a romantic evening. *'Lavinia was powerless to resist. His eyes burned into hers like sapphires. His strong arms enfolded her tender body as she felt herself being swept away in a whirlwind of passion. Then he dropped his trolleys and climbed on.'* (from *'The Lady and the Gentleman'* by Barbara Cartland).

**clinkers** *n*. *Aus*. Difficult to remove *poo* particles, *toffee strings, winnets, kling-ons, dangleberries, bum conkers*.

**clit and run** *n*. A light-hearted indecent assault whereby one makes a playful grab for *Captain Caveman's nose* followed by a swift getaway into a crowd.

**cliterati** *n*. A dazzling array of *grumble vid* starlets.

**cliterature** *n*. One-handed reading matter.

**clitler** *n*. A fashionable clitoral moustache, as seen on the women of porn who leave a daft little tuft. A *toothbrush muff*.

**clitty litter** *n*. Vaginal detritus in the *drip tray* of a lady's *dung hampers*.

**clock springs** *n*. Very strong, curly pubic hairs usually found around the *clock-weights* or coiled tightly around the top of the *belltower*. Often found stuck onto bars of soap.

**clockweights** *n*. Large, metal, adjustable testicles that have to be cranked at least once every eight days.

**clodge** *n*. Vagina.

**close-up pink** *n.* Anatomically explicit *cliterature.*

**clot mops** *n.* Feminine napkins.

**clout** *1. n.* Clunge. *2. n.* South African lesbian rock band.

**cloven hoof** *n. Camel's foot, camel's mouth, camel's lips.* In fact, any part of a camel.

**clown's hat** *n.* A *bald man in a boat.* A *clematis.*

**clown's pie** *n.* A very, very wet *clodge. 'Finding ourselves alone in the shooting lodge at Balmoral, Her Majesty bade me descend to her ladygarden. After fifty years of widowhood, I found her to be considerably aroused. It was like being hit in the face with a clown's pie.'* (from *'The Memoirs of Queen Victoria's Ghillie'* by John Brown).

**clown's smile** *n.* Facial make-up donned when performing at the *red ring circus. Mexican lipstick.*

**clown's pocket** *sim.* To describe the bigger, baggier and perhaps yellow and red checkered vagina. *'May I introduce my wife, your worship. She has a fanny like a clown's pocket.'*

**cludgy** *n. Shitehouse,* lavatory, *thunderbox.*

**clumper** *n.* The *nipsy.*

**clumsy beekeeper, face like a** *sim.* Descriptive of a lady with a lovely personality. She with a face like a *stripper's clit.*

**clunge** *n.* A *clout,* a *furry hoop.*

**clusterfuck** *1. n.* A group of people unable to make a simple decision, e.g, friends standing on a pavement outside a pub wondering where to eat, or a group of PC World salesmen on a team-building course trying to construct a raft. *2. n.* A gang bang.

**coal hole** *n.* Any grubby little hole around the back of something. A popular entry point for burglars and tradesmen.

**coat hangers** *n.* Large erect *nipples* that can double up as an emergency car aerial.

**cobblers** *ryhm. slang. Bollocks.* From cobbler's awls ~ *balls.*

**cobs** *n. Nads, pills, pods.* Testicles.

**cock** *1. n.* Penis, *willy, knob. 2. n.* A person to whom a chirpy cockney wishes to speak, often prefixed by 'Wotcha...' *3. n.* A gentleman chicken.

**cock block** *n.* Bed. *'I wouldn't mind lying that on me cock block.' Shag slab.*

**cock book** *n.* Literature which encourages one to whip up a quick *cheese-based white sauce.*

**cock clamp** *n.* A *'v' clamp,* a *mouse's ear.* A tight *muff.*

**cock collar** *n.* The *fiveskin.*

**cock holster** *n.* A romantic term for a lady's mouth. *'Felicity was powerless to resist. His eyes burned into hers like sapphires. His strong arms enfolded her tender body as she felt herself being swept away in a whirlwind of passion. Then, she knelt before him and he stuck his eight-inch Charlie into her cock holster.'* (from *'The Officer and the Gypsy Duchess'* by Barbara Cartland).

**cock knocker** *n.* A gentleman who bangs at the back door.

**cock lodger** *n.* A bloke who lives in his bird's house without paying rent.

**cock mess monster** *1. n.* A *grumble flick* actress, transformed by a small fortune in *money shots.* A *plasterer's radio.* *2. n.* A cryptozoological beast occasionally sighted floating round the bath after playing *up periscope.*

**cock porridge** *n.* Messy load fired from the porridge gun.

**cock rot** *n. medic.* V.D, a *dose.*

**cock smoker** *n.* A lady who doesn't mind a puff on one's *Whitehouse cigar.* A *fellatrix.*

**cock snot** *n.* Semen.

**cock sucker** *n.* A motorist who cuts you up.

**cock tease** *n.* A woman who wears *fuck me shoes* and then changes into *fuck off slippers* when you get back to her place.

**cock-a-doodle-poo** *n.* The *shit* that, needing to come out, wakes you up in the morning.

**cock-a-fanny** *n.* The act of hiding one's *wedding tackle* between one's legs to give the appearence of having female genitals. Popularised by Captain Sensible and East German female shot-putters of the 70's.

**cockfest** *n.* A pornographic film featuring quantities of *skinclad tube.*

**cockless pair** *n.* A particularly athletic looking lesbian couple.

**cocknuckle** *n.* The sixth knuckle, that always comes at the top of the deck in a *five knuckle shuffle.*

**cockoholic** *n.* One addicted to cockohol.

**cockwash** *n.* Vagina. *'My charlie's absolutely filthy. I think I'll stick it through the cockwash on Sunday morning.'* See also *token for the cockwash, municipal cockwash.*

**cockwasher** *n.* A *fellatrix* who takes it to the *biffin bridge.* A *deep throater,* a *pork sword* swallower.

**cocoa sombrero** *n.* Mexican *brown hatter.*

**coconut minge-mat** *n.* Pubic hair you could wipe your feet on.

**coco-pops** *n. Winnets,* known briefly as Choco Krispies.

**cod cove** *n. Fish mitten.*

**cods** *n. Balls.* Often prefixed *'A kick in the'.*

**coffin-dodger** *n.* Affectionate term for an incontinent, elderly relative. An *oxygen thief.*

**coilus interruptus** *n. Lat.* Method employed by God to prevent the birth of *Meatloaf's daughter* whereby the Jehovah's Witnesses ring the doorbell just as you are laying the foundations of a *log cabin.*

**Colchester condom** *euph milit.* Anal sex, one up the *bonus tunnel,* as used by squaddies in the garrison town. *'Please be careful, Field Marshal'. 'Don't worry, sweet tits, I'll be using a Colchester condom when I meet you behind the skip.'*

**collar and cuffs** *euph.* Matching hair colour, up top and down below. *'See that blonde? Do you reckon her collar matches her cuffs?'.*

**Columbo's mac** *n.* A rumpled *fiveskin* that is much too long for the *one-eyed bobby* it covers. *Delaney's overcoat.*

**Colwyn Bay** *1. n.* Welsh seaside resort famous for its multi-storey Safeway's and its elephant-less zoo. *2. rhym. slang.* Homosexual. *'This is your cellmate, Lord Archer. Try not to drop anything on the floor, only he's a bit Colwyn.'*

**combustoflatulation** *n.* Anal flame-throwing. *Pyroflatulation.*

**come** *1. v.* Cum. *2. n.* Cum.

**come in Tokyo** *n.* To manipulate both a lady's breasts at the same time in the manner of a WWII radio operator. *Finding Radio Luxembourg.*

**command module** *n. Bell end,* glans.

**committee shitty** *n.* A motion that is seconded after the paperwork is complete. A *council dump*.

**con artiste** *n. Fr.* A *cunning linguist, muff diver*, a *Jacky Danny Cousteau*, a *puba diver*.

**con** *n. Fr. Cunt, fanoir.*

**concrete donkey** *n.* A *horse's handbrake*, a *diamond cutter.*

**cones are out** *euph.* ie, only one lane in use. *Rag week.*

**cones** *n.* Pointy, orange, dayglo breasts found alongside the M25.

**conker water** *n. Spangle, spooge, spadge, gunk.*

**conkers deep** *adj.* To be in a state of total intromission.

**conkers** *n.* See *hairy conkers.*

**convoy cock** *n. milit.* A squaddie's *travel fat.*

**cooch** *n. US.* A Yankee *fanny.*

**cooking lager** *n.* Utility pub booze. *Wallop.*

**cooter** *1. n. prop. US.* A character from 'The Dukes of Hazzard'. *2. n.* The visible contents of Daisy Duke's shorts in the 'Dukes of Hazzard'.

**cooter cutters** *n. US.* The type of shorts worn by Daisy Duke in 'The Dukes of Hazzard'.

**cop a feel** *v.* To get one's *tops*

or *fingers*. Or *tops and fingers*.

**copper bolt** *v.* Very heavy or dense *sweaty morph*. With a clockwise thread.

**copper wire** *n.* A stray pube appearing in a handful of loose change.

**corks** *1. n.* Nipples. *2. exclam.* 1950s schoolboy cry of surprise. *"Corks', cried Darbishire. 'I've just seen Matron's corks. Anyone for a daisychain?"* (from *'Jennings and the Sticky Sheets'* by Anthony Buckeridge).

**corn beef cudgel** *n.* Short, thick *trouser stick* the 'taking up' of which relieves *gentlemanly tensions*, and so aids restful sleep.

**corn beef lighthouse** *n.* Big thing that flashes to attract sailors.

**corn on the cob** *n.* A *spitroast*, where two gentleman revolve the lady in a shallow dish of *melted butter.*

**cornbeef sandwich** *n.* The contents of Daisy Duke's *cooter cutters.*

**cornhole** *1. n. US. Brass eye, ring, balloon knot. 2. v.* To shove one's *cock* up the same.

**corybungo** *n. Arse,* backside.

**costume drama** *n*. The frantic behaviour of a woman who cannot decide what to wear for a party.

**cottage cheese pastie** *n*. A well-*shagged fanny*.

**cottage** *v*. To visit a thatched public lavatory with climbing roses round the door looking for a bit of *Colwyn Bay* action.

**cotton mouse** *n*. *Jam rag, chuftie plug*.

**cotton pony** *n*. A *fanny mouse*.

**cough cabbage water** *v*. *Tread on the gloy bottle*, ejaculate.

**cough your filthy yoghurt** *euph*. A romantic expression for ejaculation. A *money shot*. '*Ursula was powerless to resist. His eyes burned into hers like sapphires. His strong arms enfolded her tender body as she felt herself being swept away in a whirlwind of passion. Then he dropped his trolleys and coughed his filthy yoghurt in her hair.*' (from '*The Gentleman and the Lady*' by Barbara Cartland).

**council gritter** *rhym. sIang. Gary Glitter, apple fritter, pint of bitter. Shitter*.

**council twat** *n*. A scraggy utility *fanny*. Not very good quality, but it does the job.

**court Madam Knuckle** *v*. To woo your right hand. See *Madam Palm and her five daughters*.

**Covent Garden nun** *n*. A *fuckstress*. A *Fulham virgin*. A *ho'*.

**covered wagon** *n*. To drive your old cow under canvas after you've had a bellyful of beans. A *Dutch oven*.

**cowboy walk** *n*. Broad, rolling gait required when walking to the *bog* with the *turtle's head*.

**cowgirl** *n*. A sexual position much favoured by the choreographers of American *grumbleflicks* involving a lazy man and a bow-legged woman. A *fucking bronco*.

**coyote** *v*. See *chew your own arm off*.

**crab ladder** *n*. *Gut stick*, penis.

**crabe** *n*. A measure of *shite*, thought to equal about two crates.

**crabs** *n*. *Bollock jockeys*, pubic lice.

**crack** *1*. *n*. *Minge, fanny*. '*Close your legs honey, folks* *will see your crack.'* (Ronald Reagan at his presidential inauguration, 1980). *2. n.* Pointless *bollocks* spoken after four pints of Guiness in Irish theme pubs. *3. n.* The cleft of the *arse* cheeks.

**crack a fat** *v.* To achieve a *bone on.*

**crack a stiffy** *v. Crack a fat.*

**crack maggot** *n.* See *man overboard.*

**crackerjacks** *n.* Testicles. *'It's Friday, it's five to five, and I'm off upstairs to whack me crackerjacks.'*

**crackling** *n. Totty, talent.*

**craddock** *n.* A *cock-a-fanny.*

**crafty butcher** *n.* A male homosexual, ie. a man who likes to take his meat around the back.

**cranberry dip** *n.* A special sauce for sausages available only during *rag week.*

**crane operator** *n.* A *stick vid* actress with a *gut stick* in each hand, the motion of which gives the appearance that she is positioning a crane or wrecking ball. Also *Madam two-swords, downhill skier.*

**crank** *1. n.* Penis. *2. rhym. slang.* To have a *wank* in the

style of someone attempting to start a vintage car. A *ham shank.*

**crap** *1. n. Shit. 2. v.* To *shit. 3. n. US.* ~s. A shit game with dice.

**crapper** *n.* Lavatory. Named after the inventor of the self-cleaning water closet, Thomas Shitehouse.

**crappuccino** *n.* A particularly frothy form of diarrhoea which one gets abroad. See *kexpresso.*

**craptain Webb** *n.* A long *turd* that 'dips its toe' in the water before diving in.

**crash mat** *n.* A *pap baffle*, a *turd raft.*

**crash the yoghurt truck** *v.* To *shed one's load* at the *Billy Mill roundabout. Empty the wank tanks.*

**cream rinse** *n.* A bubbly hair-care product that is often provided gratis with every facial. A *sperminant wave.*

**cream** *v.* To *crash the yoghurt truck*, esp. in your pants. To *milm.*

**crepitate** *v.* To discharge a noxious fluid accompanied by a slight explosive sound. How Bamber Gascoigne would describe a *fart.*

**crescent wank** *n.* To arrange one's favourite *jazz periodicals* in a half-moon display, before kneeling down to perform a five finger exercise on the *spunk trumpet*.

**cricket week** *n.* A five day test, when a gentleman must *bowl from the pavilion end* while his wife is *padded up*.

**crimp off a length** *v. milit.* Naval slang for *curling one off*.

**crimson wave** *n.* Also *crimson tide*. See *surfing the crimson wave*.

**crinkle cuts** *n. medic.* The large, crenellated *scallop lips* that protrude from a salty bag. *Real McCoy's, Nicki Lauda's lugs, turkey's wattles*.

**crop spraying** *v.* See *pebble dashing*.

**crotch crickets** *n. Crabs.*

**crouching tiger, hidden dragon** *n.* Ancient Chinese sexual position. *Doggy style* sex with a woman so *fugly*, one can't bring oneself to look her in the face.

**crouton** *n.* An erection that floats in one's soup.

**crow** *1. n. US.* That *muck* which has been *chucked*, esp. onto the *mapatasi*. Post *porking* residue on the *hairy*

clam. *Muffdruff*. *2. n.* Nostril carrion. *Bogie, greb, greenie*.

**crowd pleaser** *n.* Unusual or noteworthy stool which one feels an urge to show to someone before flushing.

**crumpet** *1. n.* A traditional Scottish cake made of soft light dough, eaten toasted and buttered, and much craved by the late Sid James. *2. n.* 1970s *blart*.

**crunchie** *1. n.* A tasty confectionary snack. *2. n.* A brittle sock worn the day after one has *wanked* into it.

**crunk** *n.* The *taint, blarse, tintis, tinter*.

**crusties** *1. n.* Dog-on-a-string owning soapophobes. *2. n.* Over-worn *bills* somewhat lacking in 'April freshness'. *Dung hampers* with a dirty *drip tray*.

**Cuban wank** *n.* A *diddy-ride*, a *Bombay roll*. A *tit-wank*.

**cuckold** *n.* A man whose wife allows another *cock* into her *nest*.

**cuffing the dummy** *v. US mill. Wanking, scrubbing the cook*.

**cum** *1. v.* A sexiness-enhancing mis-spelling of *come* used by the authors of bongular literature to describe male ejaculation. *2. n.* A sexiness-enhancing mis-spelling of *come* used by the authors of bongular literature to describe male ejaculate.

**cumbeard** *n.* A white coagulated sperminiferous goatee beard worn by a lady who has helped herself to a double portion of *spangle*.

**cumbrella** n. A *jubber ray*.

**cumchugger** *n.* A bird who enjoys guzzling *spadge*.

**cumster** *n.* A small hamster-like female who fills her cheeks with your *nuts*.

**cumulo nimbus** *n. Lat.* Oral sex. Tongular stimulation of the lady's *clematis*.

**cunnifungus** *n. Lat.* Female equivalent of *knob cheese*.

**cunny** *n. Lat. Fadge*, vagina. From cunnus ~ *shagpipe*.

**cunt** *1. n. 14thC. medic.* Polite term for lady's genitals. *2. n. 21stC.* Impolite term for lady's genitals. *3. n.* A traffic warden.

**cunt book** *n.* The *dog house*. *'16th August 1945. Went down the Feathers with Joe and Dwight to celebrate winning the War. Back to Downing Street 4am. Lost keys. Climbed up drainpipe and fell into bins. Woke kids up.*

*Clementine came down to let me in. I reckon I'm in the cunt book for at least a fortnight.'* (from *'The Diary of Sir Winston Churchill'*).

**cunt bubble** *1. n.* An air lock up the *fanny*, often leading to a *Lawley kazoo. 2. n.* A traffic warden.

**cunt buster** *1. n.* An enormous erection. A *diamond cutter. 'Olivia was powerless to resist. His eyes burned into hers like sapphires. His strong arms enfolded her softly yielding body as she felt herself being swept away in a whirlwind of passion. Then he dropped his trolleys revealing a right cunt buster.'* (from *'The Lady and the Gypsy'* by Barbara Cartland). *2. n.* A large baby.

**cunt guff** *n.* The dropping forwards of a lady's hat.

**cunt rug** *n.* A *muff*, a *merkin*.

**cunt scratchers** *n.* Humorous term for hands. *Wanking spanners*.

**cuntitude** *n.* A *cuntish* attitude.

**cuntstruck** *adj.* Besotted, hopelessly in love.

**cunty booby** *adj.* To be in a state of confusion. *'I don't pretend to understand the universe – when I start thinking* *about it I go all cunty booby, me.'* (from *'Latterday Pamphlets Number 6',* by Thomas Carlyle).

**cupcake** *n.* Small quantity of *fart* gas caught between the palms of the hands and released in a person's face.

**Cupid's toothpaste** *n.* Oral *gunk.*

**curd** *n. Jizz.*

**curl one off** *v.* To carefully deliver a mudchild. See also *three coiler.*

**curler** *1. n.* A lump of excrement. *2. n.* Something in your wife's hair. *3. n.* A lump of excrement in your wife's hair.

**curryoakie** *n.* An enthusiastic but tuneless *fart* performed after a gallon of bitter and an Indian meal. A *blanket ripper.*

**curtain call** *n.* A return to the lavatory for an *encore dump.* A *second sitting.*

**curtain drop** *n.* Labia length, size of a woman's *beef curtains.*

**curtain rings** *n.* Labial ironmongery.

**cushion creeper** *n.* An upholstery-muffled *fart.*

**custard cannon** *n. Lamb cannon, mutton musket, pork sword,* etc, etc, et fucking cetera.

**cut the cheese** *v.* To *fart.* Also *cut the Brie, open the ham.*

**cybertranny** *n.* Man or woman who pretends to be of the opposite sex in internet chat rooms. eg. 16 year-old Brenda turns out to be 35 stone tattooed American man called Jim-Bob. With his dead mother in a fridge.

**Cyclops** *n.* A legendary purple-headed monster with the eye of a hog. And two big hairy *bollocks* underneath.

**Cyprus manoeuvre** *n.* To remove the penis during *doggy sex* and re-enter 'accidentally' up the *bonus tunnel.* The *Limasol slip.* Invented in 1972 by scientists in Cyprus.

# Dd

**D' Oyley** *rhym. slang.* D' Oyley Carte ~ *fart.*

**Daddy's sauce** *n. Baby gravy, pineapple chunk.*

**Dagenham handshake** *n.* Sexual practice whereby the gentleman inserts a finger in the *pink,* a finger in the *brown,* then uses a third to ring the *devil's doorbell.*

**Dagenham smile** *n. Builder's bum.*

**dags** *n.* Shepherd-speak for sheep's *dangleberries.*

**daisy chain** *n.* Series circuit of *AC* or *DC* sex. The sort which only occurs in *bongo films* and Stephen Fry's public school dormitory.

**daisy cutter** *n.* A heavyweight *fart,* in breach of the Geneva Convention, that leaves nothing standing within a wide radius.

**dalek** *n.* An erection reminiscent of a forehead-mounted sink-plunger.

**dance the blanket hornpipe** *v.* A sailor's jig, performed below decks.

**dancer's lance** *n.* An unwelcome dalek that appears when dancing closely with a lady. A *Saturday night lever, St. Vitus pants.*

**dancing bear** *n.* A grizzly brown monster that stands on its end in the pan and refuses to be flushed away unless hit with a stick.

**dancing with the captain** *v.* To masturbate. Wearing a bowler hat. See *grandma's party.*

**dang** 1. *n.* Penis. 2. *exclam. US.* Expression of annoyance. *'Dang them pesky Al Qaeda varmints.'* (George W. Bush, State of the Nation Address, 2002) 3. *n.* A word which, together with ding and dong, features prominently in the lyrics of Eurovision Song Contest entries.

**danger wank** *n. Self-abuse* whereby you shout your parents from downstairs, and then try to *blow your tanks* before they get to your bedroom. A *dangerous spurt* for an adrenaline *jizz-junky.*

**dangermouse** *n.* A tampon.

**dangleberries** *n. Winnets,* excrement adhering to the *arse cress* around an inefficiently-wiped *ringpiece. Fartleberries, toffee strings, bead curtains, kling-ons, clinkers.*

**dangler** n. A dangling *donger.*

**danglers** n. *Hairy conkers.*

**dangly ham** *n. Beef curtains, bacon strips.*

**darb** *v.* To *shag, bonk, bang.*

**dark star** *n.* Black, or rather brown hole from which the *pink Darth Vader* might emerge wearing a *shitty* helmet.

**Darth Vader's hat stand** *n.* A sinister, six foot tall, wheezing *cock.*

**Darth vulva** *n.* The act of eating a *fish supper* with such gusto that it makes a sound not unlike Darth Vader trying to eat a squid without taking his helmet off.

**dash for gash** *n.* The desperate last half hour before chucking out at a night club.

**date locker** *n.* Rectum, *bomb bay.*

**dawn horn** *n.* Early morning *tent pole, bed flute.* See also *big cock day.*

**dead heat in a zeppelin race** *sim.* Large *tits, knockers, bazookas, oomlaaters, Gert Stonkers.*

**dead otter** *n.* A single stool of immense proportions.

**death by chocolate starfish** *1. n.* An incredibly disgusting *fart. 2. n.* A chronic attack of the *Earthas.*

**Deirdre's neck** *n.* The strings supporting the *nadbag* that are under immense tension.

**Delhi belly** *n.* Delicate stomach condition leading to the *Eartha Kitts, red ring, liquid Thoras, Mexican screamers.*

**dell** *1. n. 16thC.* Prostitute, *tom.* 2. n. Original Hampshire venue of Southampton F.C.'s annual relegation battle.

**depth charge** *n.* Large or heavy stool, *copper bolt.* Also *belly flopper, Admiral Browning.*

**designer vagina** *n.* Any *muff* which has been trimmed into an unusual shape eg. a heart, a *Hitler tash* or Craig David's beard. *Armani fanny, Versnatche.*

**desk lifter** *n.* An attractive lady teacher who, on bending over to pick up some chalk can cause 30 desks to be raised simultaneously.

**devil's kiss** *n.* A *fart* released during sex in the *69* position. *Hell's mouth.*

**devil's handshake** *n.* Roman Catholic *wank.* To *tug* oneself into the eternal lake of fire.

**dew on the lily** *1. euph.* A lubricated *flange.* 2. n. Knob glaze, pre-cum. Perseverance soup.

**DFKDFC** *abbrev. medic.* Used in patients' notes during diagnosis – Don't Fucking Know, Don't Fucking Care. *'Patient: Female. Age: 72. Presented: Hot flushes, swollen tongue, racing heart, low blood pressure, tingling down right side, loose finger nails. Diagnosis: DFKDFC. Treatment: Amoxyl 3 times a day.'*

**diamond cutter** *n.* The hardest erection known to man. *Pink steel.*

**diamond in the muff** *n.* A genuinely attractive woman in a *grumbleflick.*

**dibble** *1. v. 14thC.* To *shag. 2. n.* Cartoon police officer in 'Top Cat'. *3. n.* To playfully prod around at the *hangar doors.*

**Dibnah dick** *n.* A sudden loss of erectile strength causing the *skin chimney* to collapse. Can be brought on by catching a whiff of badly-wiped *arse* when *changing at Baker Street.*

**dick** *1. n. US.* Penis, *pud, plonker. 2. n.* Idiot, *plonker. 'Rodney, you fucking dick.'* (Only Fools and Horses, Christmas Special, 1955) *3. v.* To *fuck.*

**dick docker** *n.* A rabbi.

**dick head** *n.* Fool, *idiot, joskin, brain donor.*

**dick skinners** *n. medic. US. Wanking spanners, cunt scratchers.* Hands.

**dick splash** *n.* Urine on trousers or suede shoes caused by shakage or *splashback.* See also *forget-me-nots.*

**dick van dyke** *n.* A strap-on cockney. A lesbotic twat rattler, a dildo. A *Mary Pop-in.*

**dick weed** *n. US.* Goldang *melon farming Fuckwit.*

**dick wheat** *n.* Male pubic hair.

**dickwit** *1. n.* Probably a character from a Charles Dickens novel. *2. n.* A fellow who thinks with his *charlie. 3. n.* A foolish fellow.

**diddies** *n. Scot.* Ladies' *tits.*

**diddy ride** *n. Scot.* A deep fried *sausage sandwich.*

**diesel dyke** *n. US.* Butch or masculine lesbian, *fanny nosher.* Also *bulldyke.*

**difficult brown** *n.* Tricky option in *bum games. 'I'd rather take the easy pink than the difficult brown.'* See also *Irish, snookered behind the red.*

**difficult child** *n.* One who, once *dropped off at the pool,* refuses to go into the water and clings onto the side.

**dig in the whiskers** n. Aus. To *split the beard*. '*Fuck me, look at that Sheila. She's worth a dig in the whiskers, wouldn't you say, Rolf?*'

**dildo** n. Practice version of the *pork sword*. A *bob*, a *neck massager*.

**dill** 1. n. An unpleasant thing put in burgers by the staff at McDonalds. 2. n. A type of pickle.

**dillberries** n. *Dangleberries, wufflenuts*.

**dilm** n. Unpleasant tasting spermicidal lubricant on a *dunkie*.

**ding! dong!** exclam. arch. Caddish expression of delight when Terry-Thomas spotted a woman with *dunce's hats*.

**ding-a-ling** n. Chuck Berry's *cock*. With two silver bells hanging off it.

**dingleberry roast** n. A lighted *fart*, an *afterburner*, a *blue streak*.

**dinner lady's arm** 1. n. medic. *Bingo wings*. 2. sim. A large, but nonetheless unhealthy looking *cock*.

**dinner masher** n. *Botter*.

**dip your wick** v. To put one's

*dill* in the *hamburger*.

**director's cut** n. The point in an 18th generation *jazz video* where a previous *Chinese helicopter pilot* has inadvertently pressed 'record' instead of 'pause', leaving the viewer with a four second clip of Panorama circa 1994.

**dirtbox** n. *Date locker, chamber of horrors*. Rectum.

**dirty Beppe** n. A *dirty Sanchez,* but with coverage extended to the chin.

**dirty fart** n. A *fart* with delusions of grandeur. A *follow through*.

**dirty Sanchez** n. To stick one's finger up a lady's *back bottom* during *doggy style* sex. Then one draws a moustache on her top lip, apparently.

**dirty spine, snip a length** of v. To *lay a cable, drop a copper bolt*.

**dirty water** n. medic. A medical term for seminal fluid. *Bollock bile*.

**disco fanny** adj. The full strength flavour achieved by a vigorous evening of giving it six nowt on the dance floor.

**dishonourable discharge** n. milit. The shameful result of knocking the *little general's* helmet off.

**ditch pig** *n*. An affectionate lighthearted epithet for an ugly fat girl.

**divot** *n*. A particularly hairy *fanny*.

**DIY** *euph*. A single handed job done around the house at the weekend using one *tool* and a bag of *nuts*.

**Dizzy Gilespie** *n*. A formidable blast on the *spunk trumpet* where the lady's cheeks puff out like a bullfrog's.

**dizzyade** *n*. Beer. Also *dizzy pop*.

**do a Southampton** *sim*. To score and stay up when you haven't really got it in you.

**do** *v*. To give someone *one*. *'No kissing, just cold, hard sex. And absolutely no simulation – these birds are really being done.'* (from advertisement for erotic videos, Daily Express).

**dobber** *n*. Semi-erect *dill*. A lazy *lob on*.

**dock** *1. n*. Arse. The polite term by which horsey types refer to their steed's *fudge tunnel*. *2. v*. To *shag*. Up the horse's *arse*.

**docker's omlette** *n*. A glistening gobbet of rubbery phlegm with remarkable anti-traction properties. A *gold watch*, a *rolex prairie oyster*.

**docker's tea break** *sim*. Descriptive of something very long. *"Oh, what a tiny little man', laughed Verruca Salt as she saw the Oompa Lumpa. 'He may be small', cautioned Mr. Wonka as he turned briskly on his heel, 'but he'll have a cock as long as a docker's tea break."* (from 'Charlie and the Chocolate Sandwich' by Roald Dahl).

**docker's thumbs** *sim*. Large, erect nipples. Also *chapel hat pegs, Scammell wheel nuts, pygmies' cocks*.

**docking** *v*. The rolling of one's *fiveskin* over another chap's hat. A *clash of heads*.

**dockyard rivets** *n*. Cigarbutts, *pygmies' cocks*.

**dog** *1. n*. A woman who fails to reach an acceptable standard of attractiveness. A *steg*. *2. n*. A male prostitute. *3. v*. To hang around in car parks at night, in the pretence of walking a dog, in order to spy on courting couples and watch it go in.

**dog catcher** *n*. A man who goes looking for unwanted *hounds* in a nightclub after all the pedigree *blart* has been collared. A *munter hunter*.

**dog eating hot chips** *sim.* A crude and voracious, yet effective *horatio* technique. *'Lusitania was powerless to resist. His eyes burned into hers like garnets. His muscular arms enfolded her body as she felt herself being swept away in a force 10 gale of passion. Slowly, she fell to her knees and unzipped Giuseppe's breeches and went at his cock like a dog eating hot chips.'* (from *'The Countess and the Lion Tamer'* by Barbara Cartland).

**dog eggs** *n.* Dog *turds*, often laid on the pavement.

**dog in a bath** *n.* A bedroom game like *rodeo sex. 'The missus was setting the video last night and I was on me vinegar strokes when I called her by her sister's name. It was like trying to keep a dog in a bath'.*

**dog lime** *n. Dog eggs*, canine faeces.

**dog slug** *n.* The act of licking around, and indeed inside, another person's *rusty sherrif's badge.* A *trip round the world,* a *rim job.*

**dog toffee** *n.* Tacky pavement deposit that readily adheres to the sole of a shoe or supports an upright lollipop stick.

**dog toss** *n.* To grind against a woman's leg in an over-eager fashion whilst dancing at a night club, school disco, or wedding reception.

**dog track** *n.* A song (usually 'Lady in Red') played at 10 to 2 in a nightclub, that precipitates a last attempt mad dash onto the dancefloor by all remaining *hounds.* A *Desperate Dance.*

**dog with two dicks** *sim.* To be incredibly pleased with oneself. *'That's one small step for man, one giant leap for mankind. I'm on the moon and I'm as happy as a dog with two dicks, me.'* (Neil Armstrong, July 1969). Also *tomcat with three balls.*

**dog's arse** *adj.* To be troubled with wind. *'Excuse my wife. I'm afraid she's got a dog's arse today, your Holiness.'*

**dog's bollocks** *n.* Bee's knees, *donkey's knob, monkey's nuts, cat's knackers* etc.

**dog's lipstick** *n.* A shimmery pink retractable cosmetic favoured by magicians' assistants.

**dog's marriage** *n.* A *back scuttle.*

**dog's match** *n.* A sexual encounter in public place. In

bushes, doorways, taxi queues or casualty.

**doggies** *n.* Intercourse in the position adopted by dogs, usually near some dustbins.

**dogging** *v.* To *dog.*

**dog-locked** *n.* To be stuck in a compromising position due to muscular spasm, usually in the back of a car in a 'Confessions of...' film. Also, *dog's lock-in.*

**doley's blackout** *n.* A midafternoon session of *self-abuse* snatched during a lull in daytime television. Achieved by shutting the curtains after 'Quincy' for a quick *tug.*

**dollymop** *n.* An amateur or inexperienced prostitute.

**dolphin skin** *n. medic.* The epidermis of the *herman gelmet.*

**Don King in a headlock** *sim.* Descriptive of a foreign lady's armpits.

**Donald** *rhym. slang. Fuck.* From Donald Duck.

**donger** *n. Whanger, pork sword, dill.*

**donkey kisser** *n.* An inexperienced osculatrix. A lady who *snogs* like a donkey chewing an apple.

**donkey punch** *n.* Of *bum games,* to knock your partner out cold with a blow to the back of the head whilst in the *vinegar strokes.* Said to have the same aphrodisiacal effect as slamming a goose's neck in a drawer whilst committing bestiality. Don't try either.

**donkey rigged** *adj.* Blessed with a sizeable penis.

**donkey's earhole** *n.* A particularly large, flappy, twitching vagina. A *hippo's mouth,* a *clown's pocket.*

**donkified** *adj.* To have a *horse's handbrake,* to be in a state of *tumescence.* To be *on the bonk.*

**donner** *n.* An unattractive woman, a *ten pinter.* ie, someone one wouldn't fancy too much when sober.

**donor** *n.* See *benefactor.*

**doonicans** *n.* Assorted *claps,* NSUs and *doses.* From the initials of the bejumpered Irish rocking chair croonster Val.

**doorbell** *n.* A small button above the *snail's doorstep* that is so difficult to find, it is often easier to use the *knockers.* The *clematis.* Also *devil's doorbell.*

**doormat basher** *1. n.* One

who whacks their partner's *fanny* on the back yard wall to get the dust off. *2. n.* A *lesbo.*

**doos** *n. Tits.*

**dopper** n. A *dork.*

**doppleganger dick** *n.* A *hard-on* of such intensity, that one's own face is seen reflected in the shiny head, affording it the appearance of a miniature double.

**dork** *n.* A *dopper.*

**double adapter** *euph.* *AC/DC* man equipped with a *one pin plug* at the front but also having the benefit of a fully functioning *single pin socket* at the back. A *switch hitter.*

**double bassing** *v.* To have sex from behind, fiddling with the lady's left nipple with your left hand and her *clematis* with your right – a position similar to the one adopted when playing the double bass, although the sound is completely different.

**double bouncers** *n.* Value for money *tits* that resonate at twice the frequency of the woman's gait. ie. two bounces per step taken.

**double cuffs** *n.* The excessively large *chinstraps* on a *bear trapper's hat.*

**double doors** *n. Beef curtains, cat flaps.*

**double dragback** *1. n.* An impressive football trick as perfected by the likes of David Ginola. *2. n.* A painful *wanking* accident whereby an inexperienced masturbatrix loses rhythm, resulting in one downward stroke being immediately followed by another, thus causing severe *banjo* trauma. Causes an effect similar to being *tossed off* by Ringo Starr.

**double fare** *n.* One who's fat *arse* takes up two seats on a train or bus. A *salad dodger, barge-arse.*

**double the melt** *v.* To give a lady not one, but two portions of hot cheese in her *hambuger.* To supply a second portion of filling to a *vertical bacon sandwich.*

**doughnut puncher** *n.* A *dinner masher.*

**downhill skier** *n.* See *skiing position.* A *crane operator.*

**dowsing rod** *n.* A *gut stick* that involuntarily twitches when approaching an area of great wetness.

**doxy** *n. arch.* Whore, *slag.*

**Dracula's tea bags** *n.* Used tampons.

**dragon food** *n*. Chocolates bought for her indoors when one is in the *cunt book*. *'Shit, I've been out on the piss for three days. I'd better stop by the garage and pick up some dragon food before I get home.'*

**dragon's nostril** *n*. The state of the ringpiece after a hot *Ruby Murray*. *'If you fancy giving yourself a dragon's nostril, then korma along to the Rupali Restaurant, Bigg Market, Newcastle upon Tyne.'* (Press release from Abdul Latif, Lord of Harpole).

**drain your spuds** *v*. To micturate. To have a *gypsy's kiss*.

**draw an ace** *v*. On wiping one's *arse* thoroughly, to eventually have an unsoiled piece of paper which indicates the wiping is over.

**draw mud from the well** *v*. To *follow through*.

**drayhorse's bottom lip** *sim*. A big, floppy *snatch*. Full of carrots.

**dreadnought** *n*. Even bigger than a *dead otter*.

**dress-messer** *n*. A gentleman with a *hair trigger*.

**drink from both taps** *v*. To be bisexual, *bend both ways*. See *double adapter*.

**drink on a stick** *n*. A *suck-off*.

**drip tray** *n*. The often crusty sump in a pair of lady's *dung hampers*.

**dripping like a fucked fridge** *sim*. Of a lady, to be sexually aroused. *'I'm in the mood for love/ Simply because you're near me/ and whenever you're near me/ I drip like a fucked fridge.'* (Song lyric, 'The Mood for Love', by Cole Porter).

**drive stick** *v*. *US*. To be a lady in uncomfortable shoes, to not like tennis. To be a non-*lezza*.

**drive the porcelain bus** *v*. A kneel-down visit to the lavatory during which one holds the rim (like a steering wheel) and does some *psychedelic yodelling*.

**driving on the cat's eyes** *v*. To emit a long, low rumbling *fart* that sounds like it's going to damage one's suspension.

**driving range** *n*. The perineum. Where one hit one's *balls* when practising with one's *wood*.

**drop a clot** *v. medic*. To menstruate. *'It was D'Arcy who spoke first. 'Your disdain takes me somewhat aback, Miss Bennet. I fear I might* have acted in some way inappropriately to cause you such offence.' 'No, Mr. D'Arcy, your behaviour has been impeccable, and the fault lies with me. I am dropping clots at the moment and find myself in the foulest of humours', she replied'. (from 'Pride and Prejudice' by Jane Austen).

**drop a gut** v. To *shoot a bunny*.

**drop a pebble** v. To erroneously emit a *rabbit tod* whilst attempting to *break wind*. See also *follow through*.

**drop anchor in bum bay** v. To arrive at the *rear admiral's* favourite port of call.

**drop fudge** v. To *pinch a loaf, crimp one off*.

**drop one** v. *Let off, chuff.*

**drop the kids off at the pool** *euph.* To defecate in the toilet.

**drop your guts** v. To break wind. *"Fossilised fish hooks',* croaked Venables. 'Which one of you beanfeasters has dropped his guts?"* (from 'Jennings Makes a Daisy Chain' by Anthony Buckeridge).

**drop your hat forwards** v. To *fanny fart, muff chuff.* 'Just as I was donning the beard, she dropped her hat

forwards'. A *Lawley kazoo, a Harry Ramsden's raspberry.*

**drop your hat** v. To *fart.* Also *drop a bomb, drop your handbag, drop a gut.*

**dropout** n. Underpant condition whereby a *knacker* protrudes from the bottom of the *shreddies*, or famously in Peter Beardsley's case, football shorts.

**dropped pie, face like a** *sim.* To resemble one who has been bobbing for chips in a deep fat fryer.

**dropping the shopping** *euph.* See *drop the kids off at the pool.*

**drown a copper** v. To sink a *dreadnought*, give birth to a *dead otter.*

**drown some kittens** n. To pass a litter of small stools which nobody wants to give a home to.

**drown the chocolate slugs** v. Alternative to *light a bum cigar* for those anticipating a looser stool.

**drugs bust** n. Simultaneous entry of two *bobbies' truncheons* through the front and back doors. Also *police raid, SVSA.*

**dry bob** 1. n. A public schoolboy who doesn't row. 2. v.

Fully clothed sex, leading to *milmed kex*. 3. *n.* A bankrupt money shot, a *spaffless stack blow*.

**dry docked** *adj.* Lack of lubrication situation where a low tide of *blip* prevents the *skin boat* sailing into *tuna town*.

**DSB** *abbrev.* Dangerous Sperm Build-up. To have two tins of *Fussels milk*. *'I'm sorry, Sir Cliff, but you are suffering from DSB. As your doctor, the only course of treatment I can prescribe is an ADW.'*

**DSL** *abbrev.* Dick Sucking Lips.

**duck smuggler** *n.* A *Glen Miller,* one who produces a string of pearls, as if trying to smuggle a duck past customs by hiding it up his *arse*. One who *farts* whilst walking.

**duck's breakfast** *n. Welsh.* Early morning sausage and *split kippers*. Accompanied by gentle quacking and a flurry of feathers.

**duel fuel** *n. Fighting water.*

**duel with the pink Darth Vader** *n.* A *Hand Solo*.

**duff** *n. Bum, arse.*

**duffy's bridge** *n.* The *biffin bridge, tinter, taint, barse*. The perineum.

**dugs** *n. Baps, paps*. Olde worlde version of *jugs*.

**Duke of giblets** *n.* A *salad dodger.*

**dump** *1. n.* A forty minute reading session in the *dunny*. *2. v.* To *curl one off*.

**dump station** *n.* The *chod bin.*

**dumplings** *1. n.* baby *dumps*. *2. n.* Particularly filling breasts that go well with *meat and two veg*.

**dunce's hats** *n.* Them conical pointed *tits* found underneath woollen sweaters in 1950's America. *Twin peaks.*

**dung dreadlocks** *n.* Haile Selassie's *beaded curtains*. Laid-back *tagnuts*.

**dung funnel** *n. medic. Fudge tunnel.*

**dung hampers** *n. Undercrackers, trolleys, bills.*

**dung puncher** *n.* A gentleman homosexualist. A *doughnut puncher*.

**dunk** *1. n.* To dip a biscuit in a cup of tea. *2. n.* to dip one's *wick* into a *fanny*.

**dunky** *n.* Protective sheath to prevent the penis going soggy and falling off into the *hairy goblet* during dunking.

**dunny budgie** *n. Aus.* A fly

buzzing round an Australian *bog*.

**dunny** *n. Aus.* Toilet, *bog, netty, cludgie, shite house.*

**dust the duvet** *v.* To *hitch-hike under the big top*, to *starch the sheets.*

**Dutch Alps** *n.* Small breasts, *fried eggs, stits, patsies.* Also *Lincolnshire Cairngorms.* As scaled by a *Dutch mountaineer.*

**Dutch blindfold** *n.* When in the *69* position, with the woman on the bottom and the gentleman's *clockweights* fitting nicely in the eye sockets.

**Dutch boy** *n.* A lady in *comfortable shoes*, a *tennis fan*, a lesbian. ie, one who always has their finger in a *dyke.*

**Dutch brylcreem** *n.* A glutinous product that you don't particularly want in your hair. *Gunk.*

**Dutch door** *n.* A *bird* who *swings both ways.*

**Dutch floor polish** *n. Spunk.*

**Dutch miracle** *n.* The magical appearance of *bongo mags* under a mattress or on top of a wardrobe in a hotel bedroom.

**Dutch** *n. Sausage sandwich, tit wank.* Also *Dutch fuck.*

**Dutch oven** *n.* The act of cooking one's partner's head beneath the bedclothes using cabbage gas.

**Dutch satay** *n.* The epilogue of a *stick vid* where the starlet sucks on the leading man's rapidly softening phallus after she's been front and back *fucked* with it, and had it smear *spunk* all over her *tits.*

**Dutch souvenir** *n.* A little something brought back in the urethra to surprise the wife and help you remember Amsterdam.

**Dutch wink** *n.* The flashing of the *bacon rasher* when crossing and uncrossing the legs. *'The film has action, drama, suspense and a superb Dutch wink from Sharon Stone.'* (Barry Norman, reviewing *'Basic Instinct'*).

**DVDA** *abbrev.* Double Vaginal, Double Anal. The Holy Grail of bongo video acts, presumably involving four India-rubber men and one uncomfortable woman.

**dyke** *n.* Lesbian, *tuppence licker, carpet muncher, three wheeler,* a *woman on the other bus.* See also *diesel dyke, bulldyke.*

# Ee

**Eartha Kitts** *rhym. slang.* *Shits*, diarrhoea. Also *Brads*.

**Easter Island statue with an arse full of razor blades** *sim. Aus.* A permanently grave, sour expression. First used by Paul Keating to describe Malcolm Fraser when in opposition, but actually describes Jimmy Nail to a T.

**eat breakfast backwards** *v.* To *drive the porcelain bus.*

**eat cockroaches** *v. 18thC.* To engage in the filthy, disgusting act of *self pollution.*

**eat out** *v.* To *lap fanny*, to *dive muff*, to *cumulonimbulate*. To *lick out.*

**eating sushi off a barbershop floor** *sim. Cumulonimbus.*

**eau de colon** *n. Rusty water, fizzy gravy.*

**EC flag** *n.* Nipple.

**Eccles snake** *n.* A penis with warts.

**Edinburgh** *rhym. slang.* A *fur burger.* From Edinburgh fringe ~ *minge.*

**Edward Woodward** *onomat.* A bathtime *fart.*

**e-gasm** *n. Web-grumble* assisted *stack blow.*

**egg Mcwhiff** *n.* A particularly sulphurous mid-morning *air buffet* produced after breakfasting at a fast food restaurant.

**egg white canon** *n.* A four inch *blue-veined blunderbuss* loaded with two *balls.*

**egg-bound** *adj.* Blocked of *dung-funnel*, constipated.

**Egyptian PT** *1. n. milit.* Sleep. *2. n.* Masturbation.

**eighteen spoker** *n.* A particularly hairy woman's *arsehole* resembling a tiny bicycle wheel.

**elbow bender** *n.* A *bar fly*, a *boozer.*

**elepants** *n.* Jumbo sized ladies' trunks.

**elephants** *adj. rhym. slang.* Drunk. From elephant's trunk.

**Elvis's leg** *n.* The onset of the *vinegar strokes* whilst *fucking* upright in a doorway, bus shelter or taxi queue. Often accompanied by an 'Uh-huh-huh' vocalisation and involuntary curling of the lip.

**Emmas** *rhym. slang.* Haemorrhoids. From Emma Freud, Clement's chimp-eared daughter. Also *Nobbies.*

**empty one's back** *v.* To *crimp off a tail*, to *lay Al Jolson to rest.*

**empty threat** *n.* A terrifyingly loud *fart* that mysteriously fails to assault one's nasal passages. The opposite of an *SBD.*

**Ena Sharples' mouth** *n.* A disapproving, puckered *rusty bullet hole.* Commonly seen on *grumblemag* models bending over a snooker table. Also *Dot Cotton's mouth.*

**enamel bucket** *n.* A big, dry, cold, rattly *fanny.*

**Engelberts** *rhym. slang. Eartha Kitts.*

**English disease, the** *n.* Homosexuality, as defined by the French.

**English overcoat** *n.* The French equivalent of the English *French letter.* A *Coney Island whitefish.*

**erection section** *n.* The top shelf of a newsagents.

**Eric** *n.* Schoolboy alternative to a *Jake.*

**escape sub** *n.* A technologically advanced brown, sea-going vessel in which an evil hangover makes its getaway. An *alcopoop.*

**ESD** *abbrev.* Eat Shitty Dick. To *smoke a pink cigar* fresh from *kak canyon.*

**etch-a-sketch** *v.* To attempt to draw a smile on a woman's face by simultaneously twiddling both of her nipples. *Finding radio Luxembourg, come in Tokyo.*

**Ethelbrown the Ready** *n.* A pretender to the *porcelain throne.* A *King Richard* in waiting.

**eticlit** *n.* The observance of rules of correct decorum when *dining at the Captain's table.*

**Excalibur** *n.* A magic *turd* of legendary proportions that rises eerily out of the water in a mist-shrouded toilet.

**Exchange and Mart** *rhym. slang.* To *drop a gut.*

**exhaust pipe engineer** *n.* One who tinkers with *exhaust pipes.*

**exhaust pipe** *n. Bumhole, fudge tunnel.* Also *tailpipe.*

**exhibition position** *n.* Variation on *doggy-style* sex. The man takes the kneeling position from behind, places one hand on the lady's back and the other jauntily on his hip. Then turns and smiles at an imaginary audience, pretending to be a moustachioed German porn star.

**exit wound** *n.* The state of the *freckle* after a particularly fierce *Ruby Murray*.

**exorcist** *n*. One who is gifted with the power to rid a place of spirits, ie. the top shelf behind the bar.

**extras** *n*. Something one tentatively asks for whilst winking at a masseuse or osteopath. The *tugging* as opposed to the *rubbing* in a *rub-a-tug shop*.

**eye magnets** *n*. Lovely *tits*.

**eyes like sheep's cunts** *n*. *medic*. Symptom of an extremely bad hangover.

# Ff

**face fannies** *n. Bugger's grips*, sideburns. As sported by the singer out of 'Supergrass' and Anne Robinson.

**face grating** *n.* Performing the act of *cumulonimbus* upon a woman with advanced *five o'clock fanny*.

**face painting** *v.* To adorn one's spouse with *jelly jewellery*.

**fadge** *n.* A cross between a *fanny* and a vagina.

**faecal touch** *n.* Opposite of the Midas touch, ie. everything this person touches turns to *shit*, eg. Clive Sinclair.

**fag** 1. *n.* An eight year old boy who has to fetch tea, fetch toast and *fetch off* a prefect. 2. *n. Tab, ciggie,* a *cancer stick.* 3. *n. US.* A *bummer.*

**fag hag** *n.* A wizened old woman who prefers the company of homosexuals.

**fagnet** *n.* A man who, when out clubbing, only manages to attract *botters.*

**faint on** *n. medic.* A devastating condition affecting certain males who are *hung like rogue elephants.* When a *fat is cracked*, the shaft drains the body of its blood, causing the patient to become light headed.

**fairy hammock** *n.* A tart's *dung hampers.*

**fairy wings** *n.* The gossamer tracery of *arse* sweat left on the seat when a lardy chap gets up off the *bog* on a warm day.

**fallen off her bike** *euph.* A monthly cycle accident leaving a woman bleeding from the saddle area.

**fallen to the communists** *euph.* Of a woman, to be *flying the red flag. 'Any luck last night?' 'No. She's fallen to the communists.'*

**falling down juice** *n.* Beer. Also *fighting water, dizzyade.*

**family jewels** *n.* Priceless heirloom *knackers.*

**fan your arse** *v.* Male courtship display, masculine showing off. *'Well you can tell by the way I fan my arse/ I'm a woman's man, with a sweaty barse.'* (Song lyric, 'Stayin' Alive' by The Bee Gees).

**fancy wank** *v.* To use an ugly bird's *fanny* to save wear and tear on your hand.

**fannicure** *n.* A pampering of the *bush.* A *quim-trim,* a *Hitler tash.*

**fanny** 1. *n. UK.* Snatch, snapper, quim, cunt, puh-seh.

Female genitals, ladies' *pudenders*. 2. *n. US. Arse, backside.* 3. *n.* Fictitious Great Aunt.

**fanny badger** *n.* See *Blackbeard's ghost.*

**fanny batter** *n.* The substance which leaves one's chin greasy after a *fish supper.*

**fanny battering ram** *n.* A stout length of *wood* used to burst *Mary hinges.*

**fanny bomb** *n.* The female organism. *'How was it for you, pet. Did the old fanny bomb go off?'*

**fanny flange** *n.* The vaginal escutcheon.

**fanny fright** *n. medic.* Nervous condition affecting some macho men who suddenly find themselves unable to have *a bit* when presented with an opportunity.

**fanny hopper** 1. *n.* A two foot diameter inflatable orange vagina with handles at the top. 2. *n.* A gentleman who hops from one *fanny* to another. A *stickman*, a *skippy.*

**fanny magnet** *n.* Something or someone to which top drawer *blart* is inexplicably drawn, eg. Ferrari, Rolex watch, Mick Hucknall.

**fanny mechanic** *n. medic.* One who performs *MOTT* tests, a *box doc*, a *snatch quack*, a *scrape doctor.* A gynaecologist.

**fanny nanny** *n.* A feminine napkin.

**fanny nosher** *n.* A *woman in comfortable shoes* who takes the *other bus* to *dine at the Y.* A *tennis fan*, a *lady golfer.*

**fanny rat** n. Sexually promiscuous male. A *skippy*, a *bed hopper.*

**fanny tax** *n.* Surcharge paid on drinks in a bar staffed by top class *blart.*

**fannytastic** *adj.* Anything wonderful to do with the female genitals.

**fanoir** *n. Fr.* French insult. *'Vous etes une fucking grand fanoir, M. D'Artagnan.'* (from *'The Three Musketeers'* by Alexander Dumas).

**FANTA** *acronym.* A one night stand. Fuck And Never Touch Again.

**farmers** *rhym. slang. Emmas.* From Farmer Giles.

**FARO** *acronym.* A gentleman's post-coital afterplay. Fart And Roll Over.

**fart** 1. *n.* A *bottom burp*, the expulsion of foul air from the *chamber of horrors* causing the *clappers* to vibrate musically like a tuning fork. A *beefy eggo*, a *poot*, an *air biscuit*. 2. *v*. To *drop one* of the above, *step on a duck*.

**fart catcher** 1. *n*. Male homosexualist. 2. *n*. Derogatory term for one who waits on another person, eg. a valet or footman.

**fart higher than your arse** *euph*. To have an inflated opinion of oneself. To *think one all that when one ain't*, eg. talentless fat fuck Chris Moyles.

**fart knocker** 1. *n*. *Bum bandit, fudge nudger*. 2. *n*. One who criticises another's *farts*.

**fart sack** *n*. Bed. *'Malaria was powerless to resist. His eyes burned into hers like Swarovski crystals. His strong arms enfolded her body as she felt herself being swept away on a monsoon of passion. Roughly, Pablo took her by her heaving shoulders, pushed her down and did her on his king-sized fart sack.'* (from *'The Countess and the Matador'* by Barbara Cartland).

**fart sauce** *n*. A *raspberry coulis* that is served with *arse cress*. The rancid juice accompanying a wet *poot*.

**fart sucker** *n*. A sycophantic *arse licker*, eg. BBC Royal 'Correspondent' Jenny Bond.

**farting clappers** *n. medic*. Small, fragile castanet-like bones up one's *nick* that resonate at particular frequencies, producing an unexpectedly loud 'braaap!' sound in polite company.

**farting crackers** *n*. Trousers. *'When invited to a black tie function, the correct mode of attire for gentlemen would be ~white dress shirt and collar, cummerbund, black shoes, black dinner jacket and corresponding farting crackers.'* (from *'Debrett's Guide to Etiquette'* by Buckridge Pottinger).

**farting sideways** *v*. To have a bad case of piles. *"Do please sit down, Mr. Willoughby,'* Lady Marchmaine invited. *'Thank you, Madam,'* he replied, *'but if it is all the same with you, I shall remain standing. I rode a fox to earth over three counties yesterday and I fear I am farting sideways."* (from *'Sense and Sensibility'* by Jane Austen).

**farting strings** *n. medic*. Tendons or ligaments in the *lisks* which are prone to snapping during periods of excessive mirth. *'In a landmark court case, a Birmingham pensioner with an IQ of 6 is suing the BBC after snapping her farting strings laughing at the sitcom 'My Family.'* (*BBC News report*, Michael Buerke).

**fartleberries** *n. Dangleberries, winnets, toffee apples, chocolate raisins.*

**fasturbation** *n.* Emergency, hurried *self-abuse.*

**fat rascals** *n.* Playful *titties.*

**fatty** *n.* Something that causes much hilarity in the school showers. An erection.

**faux-pwa** *n.* A slip of lapdancing club etiquette. To *milm* one's *kex* when fishing for a tenner to stuff in a bored dancer's *dung hampers.*

**fawn** *v.* To *come*, to *reach the Billy Mill roundabout. 'Felicity was powerless to resist. His eyes burned into hers like sapphires. His muscular arms enfolded her body as she felt herself being swept away in a whirlwind of passion. Then he whipped out his Charlie and fawned all down her dress.'* (from *'The Lady and the Cossack'* by Barbara Cartland).

**feather spitter** *n.* An over-enthusiastic *pillow biter.*

**feck** *exclam. Ir. Fuck.* Popularised by Fathers Ted and Jack.

**feed it a bun** *phr.* Term used to emphasise the enormity of a male member. *'I didn't know whether to suck it or feed it a bun.'*

**feed the ducks** *v.* To *wank.* From an apparent similarity in hand movements when on a park bench *wanking.*

**feed the fish** *v. nav.* To vomit over the side of a ship, *bury one's biscuits* at sea. A nautical *honk.*

**feed the pony** *v.* To *frig* a lady's *front bottom.*

**feel like Andy Warhol looks, to** *v.* To have a particularly severe hangover.

**feeshus** *n.* Excrement.

**felch** *v.* The tender act whereby a gentleman orally retrieves his *spoff* from his partner's *arsehole. 'Birds do it/ Bees do it/ Even educated fleas do it/ Let's do it/ Let's felch some spunk.'* (Song lyric *'Let's Do It'* by Cole Porter).

**felchmeister** *n. Ger.* A man in lederhosen with a shaving brush in his hat who is particularly adept at *felching.*

**fem . femme** *n.* A highly pho-
togenic species of lesbian.
Commonly found in pairs on
TV porn channels.

**femtex** *n.* Hormone-based
explosive which becomes dan-
gerously unstable once a
month.

**fertle** *v.* To *feed a lady's pony*
through her *bills.*

**festival hot dog** *n.* A hand-
held *pap baffle.*

**fetching off** *v.* The gentle art
of *tipping your concrete* into a
lady's knicker drawer whilst
she's out the room.

**fight a turkey** *v. Choke a
chicken.*

**fighter pilot's thumbs** *n.
Chapel hat pegs, pigmies'
cocks.*

**fighting water** *n. Falling
down juice, wreck the hoose
juice,* Spesh.

**fill your boots** *v.* (pref, go on
son~) To make the most of a
sexual opportunity.

**fillet-o-fish** *n.* A *fanny* that is
on the menu, but for which
one has to wait four minutes
whilst it is prepared.

**filthy Ned** *n. Dirty Sanchez's*
brother.

**finger blessing** *v. Ferky-
foodling* sans *dunghampers.*

**finger pie** *n.* A *handful of
sprats,* a *pony feeding session.*

**fingers** *n.* Sucessfully gaining
digital access to one's bird's
snatch. *"Smell them!', cried
Jennings 'Pwoar!' sniffed
Darbishire. 'What an ozard
ronk. What have you been up
to?' Jennings grinned conspir-
atorily. 'I just got my fingers
off Venables' sister in the prep
room and I'm never going to
wash my hand again."* (from
'Jennings and the Strange
Urges' by Anthony Buck-
eridge).

**Finsbury bridge** *n. Barse.*

**fire down below** *exclam.* An
announcement used by a gentleman signifying the discov-
ery of a genuine redhead.

**fire one across the bows** *v.
naval.* A navel engagement
whereby the *pirate of men's
pants* withdraws from the
battlezone just before the *egg
white cannon* shoots its payload.

**firey surprise** *n.* To receive a
brand spanking new electric
fire that one never knew
about.

**firing blanks** *v.* Post-*snip
spoffing. 'You can put the ticklers away love, I'm firing
blanks.'*

**firkin** *1. n. arch.* A measure of ale capacity, equal to nine gallons or half a kilderkin. *2. n.* The fuckwitted epithet for half the pubs in Britain.

**firkyfoodling** *n. arch.* Tudor foreplay. *'Dearest Maid Miriam. Until lately did my husband Henry be a most wonderful and caring lover. But forsooth I am most sad to relate that of recent times he wanteth naught but most hasty coupling with me. He spendeth no time on the firkyfoodling. Yea I fear that my tastes for the courses of love hath declined as a consequence. And now he hath vouchsafed to cut my head from my shoulders. Five wives hath he taken already before me, and of two hath he separated their heads from their shoulders. What am I to do? Pray, pray, pray help me. C. Parr, London.'* (Letter to Daily Mirror, 1545)

**firtle** *v.* To cut a hole in a poster of one's favourite pop star or film actress, and *fuck* it.

**fish box** *n.* A lady's *twat*. *Billingsgate box, fish mitten.*

**fish drowner** *n.* A *clown's pie.*

**fish fryer's cuff** *sim.* Descriptive of a pair of well-worn knickers with a heavily *battered* gusset.

**fish mitten** *n.* A *muff* that keeps the fingers and thumb of one hand warm.

**fish supper** *euph. 1. n.* A Friday night feast with the tang of the sea and plenty of batter. *2. n.* Fish and chips.

**fisherman's sock, pull on like a** *sim.* No-nonsense method of sexual intercourse. *'Concertina was powerless to resist. His eyes burned into hers like zirconium. His muscular arms enfolded her body as she felt herself being swept away on a tsunami of passion. They stood before each other naked, until he could wait no longer. Roughly, he grasped her by the waist and pulled her on like a fisherman's sock.'* (from *'The Lady and the Cheesemonger'*, by Barbara Cartland).

**fist** *1. v.* Of boxers, to punch someone in the ring. *2. n.* Of homosexuals, to punch someone in the *ring. 3. n.* Of heterosexuals, to punch someone in the *quim.*

**fist magnet** *n.* Someone who attracts punches to his face.

**fist rape** *n.* Taking advantage of your fist after inviting it back to your place for a coffee and a flick through a *meat mag. Knuckle glazing.*

**fit** *adj.* Attractive, worthy of *one.*

**fitbin** *interj.* The rudest word in the English language, so rude that its meaning has been encased in 500 tons of concrete and dumped in the Irish Sea.

**five against one** *n.* A very one-sided but none-the-less enjoyable game of wrestling in which *Madame Palm and her five sisters* attempt to *strangle Kojak.* The game ends when one *makes the bald man cry.*

**five finger spread** *n.* Counter-productive attempt to suppress *upchuck* with the hand. A *chuckspreader.*

**five knuckle shuffle** *n. One-handed workout* to a Gerri Halliwell yoga video.

**five o'clock fanny** *n.* A stubbly *ladygarden.* A *Flintstone fanny,* a *face grater.*

**five-pinter** *n.* A very ugly woman who one would only happily chat up after five pints of *dizzyade.* A *St. Ivel lass.*

**fives** *n.* A traditional Etonian game played with four fingers, a thumb and a *cock.*

**fiveskin** *n. Fourskin.*

**five-to-two-er** *n.* Five minutes uglier than a *ten-to-two-er.*

**fizzing at the bung hole** *adj.* Descriptive of effervescent sexual arousal in a woman.

**fizzle** *n.* A gentle or quiet *fart.*

**fizzy gravy** *n.* Diarhorrea, *rusty water.*

**fizzyjizz** *n.* Aerated semen caused by overenthusiastic *cat stabbing. Bubblecum.*

**flackets** *n. medic. Beef curtains.*

**fladge and padge** *abbrev.* Of *rub-a-tug shop* services, *Mr Whippy* off a whore in a nurse's outfit. From flagentry and pageantry.

**flags are out** *adj. Wet paint* warning, fixture list shows *Arsenal are playing at home.*

**FLAME** *abbrev.* Fanny Like A Mouse's Ear.

**Flanders poppy** *sim.* A *ringpiece* that has been through the wars, ie. bright red and shot to pieces.

**flange** *1. n.* A *fish mitten. Muff, beaver, minge. 2. n. coll.* A group of baboons. *3. n. coll. Fanny, blart, tush.*

**flannelled** *adj.* The state of one's face after *going down* on a *fish drowner.*

**flap snack** *n.* A quick *fish burger* or *bacon sandwich.* Elevenses at *the Y.* Token *cumulonimbus.*

**flap snot** *n. medic.* A *fannular discharge. Lizzie dripping, clam jam. Gleet.*

**flap-flops** *1. n.* The shoes commonly worn by old ladies in naturist resorts. *2. n.* The *tits* commonly worn by old ladies in naturist resorts.

**flapjack** *1. n.* A dense, syrupy cake that has pretentions to healthiness. *2. n. medic.* A *quim quack's* tool for jacking *flaps* apart. A speculum.

**flapmonger** *n.* One who mongs *flaps.* A *tart farmer,* a *pimp.*

**flash in the pan** *n.* A *spooge-*free male orgasm. A cashless *money shot.*

**flash the ash** *exclam.* A gentle reminder of a person's social responsibility to share his cigarettes with others in his peer group. *'Oi, fuck face! Flash the ash, you tight fisted cunt.'*

**flash the upright grin** *v.* To expose the female genitals, *flash the gash.*

**flash** *v.* To treat a lucky lady to a surprise private viewing of one's *fruitbowl.*

**flasher** *n.* A gentleman who frequents parks wearing a mac, beret, little round glasses and trouser bottoms tied round the knees with string.

**flat as a kipper's dick** *adj.* Descriptive of unleavened *baps.*

**flative** *adj.* Of food, that which induces *flatulence,* eg. cabbage, *musical vegetables.*

**flatulence** *n.* The whole kit and kaboodle of *farting.* Fr. Lat. *flatus* ~to start & *lentus* ~a cold tractor.

**flembrandt** *n.* A distinctive piece of pavement art seen adorning much of London's walkways. *Lung paint.*

**flesh wallet** *n. Hairy cheque book, pubic purse.* Somewhere to put one's *money shots.*

**fleshbombs** *n.* Two large wads of *jubbly gelignite* packed in a woman's *titpants.*

**fleshy flugelhorn** *n.* Tuneful variation on the *bed flute, pink oboe.*

**flick finger** *n. medic.* The finger with which a woman *flicks herself off.*

**flingel** *rhym. slang. Cunt.* From The Shadows' instrumental hit 'The Rise and Fall of Flingel Bunt.'

**float an air biscuit** *v*. To release a *tree monkey* from captivity.

**floater** *1. n*. A *turd* in the pan which will not flush away. *2. n*. A member of the crap 70s soul band, eg. Larry (Cancer), who likes a woman that loves everything and everybody.

**flock of pigeons** *n*. The sound of a loose bowel movement.

**flog the log** *v*. To whup one's *wood, spank the plank*.

**flogging on** *v*. Accessing the internet in search of *left-handed websites*.

**flop out** *n*. Condition whereby the flaccid penis protrudes through the bottom of the underpants, this often occurring during the transfer from a sitting to a standing position.

**flop to pop** *n*. A standard interval used to measure the quality of *horatio* techniques. The time taken to ejaculate from a flaccid start. *'Egbert was powerless to resist. Her eyes burned into his like sapphires. Her ladylike arms enfolded his masculine body as he felt himself being swept away in a whirlwind of passion. Then she knelt down in front of him and took him from flop to pop in three minutes flat.'* (from *'The Officer and the Gypsy'* by Barbara Cartland).

**floppy red cup** *n*. Hairy goblet.

**Florida fartbox** *n*. *US*. An *abnormal load. Orlando dirtbox*.

**florins** *ryhm. slang*. The *shits*. From pre-decimal 'florin' coins known as *two bob bits*.

**flub** *1. onomat*. The sound of a *fanny fart*. *2. v. Fuck* in flowerpot man language.

**fluff** *n. nav*. A maritime *fart*.

**fluffer** *n*. In a *bongo vid* studio, a *fellatrix* employed between takes to ensure tumescence of the male actors.

**flum** *n. Ladygarden, cunt rug, pubes*.

**flunkey** *1. n*. A Royal slave, one who fawns on a *nob*. *2. n*. A *dunky*.

**flush puppies** *n*. Dalmatian-spotted suede shoes that have been standing too close to a urinal.

**fly sheet** *n*. A *fiveskin*.

**fly's eyes** *n*. A gentleman's party trick whereby the shorts or bathers are pulled tight between the legs so that the testicles bulge out on either side of the *gusset*. *'August 6th. We all go down to Cliveden for the weekend. Gerty (Laurence) and Fanny (Brice) were there as usual. Ivor (Novello) entertained us all by singing King's Rhapsody by the pool, and followed it by doing fly's eyes. How we all shrieked. Benjamin (Britten) laughed so much he shat himself, poor dear.'* (from *'The Diaries of Noel Coward'*, 1938).

**flying pastie** *n.* Excrement wrapped in newspaper and thrown into a neighbour's yard for whatever reason. See *pyropastie*.

**flying scotsman** *n.* A highly complicated sex act that doesn't sound like it's worth the bother.

**fnarr! fnarr!** *exclam.* Suppressed childish exclamation of amusement uttered after a double entendre.

**foaming at the bunghole** *adj.* *Frothing at the gash. Glistening.*

**fog up** *adj.* Of *train pulling*, to be the driver, as opposed to the *porridge stirrer* in the *guard's van*. *'Bagsy me fog up. I don't want any of you lot's sloppy seconds again.'*

**follow through** *v.* To accidentally soil ones *undercrackers* whilst attempting to *fart*. Create *russet gusset, drop a pebble*.

**fomp** *v. US.* To engage in sexual foreplay, to *firkyfoodle*.

**fondleberries** *n.* Testicles.

**food's ghost** *n.* An invisible, eerie presence accompanied by a low humming sound and the stench of death. A *McArthur Park*.

**footwell flavour** *n.* The soul-destroying aroma of *dog's egg* that appears three minutes after turning on the car heater.

**force field** *n.* A thick *fart* that clings to the warp and weft of one's duds, preventing anyone from coming within six feet for a good ten minutes. A *Velcro guff*.

**foreporn** *n.* The token, exaggerated, wooden acting preceding the *spaff candy* of a *grumble vid.* Usually viewed on fast forward.

**foreskinzola** *n.* A pungent, unappetising mature *knob-cheese*.

**forget-me-nots** *n.* The final notes in a *Chinese singing lesson,* droplets which form a tiny but embarrassing wet patch on your trousers. *Dicksplash*.

**form** *1. n.* Means of judging horses by statistics. *2. n.* Means of judging *birds* by statistics. *Fitness, fuckability*.

**Forth bridger** *n.* An irritable and cantankerous woman who seems to *have the painters in* all year round, eg. Germaine Greer.

**foul Paulo** *n.* An Italian *Dirty Sanchez*. A faecal moustache.

**four-man bob** *n.* A large, speedily-ejected *turd*. Possibly rocking backwards and forwards 2 or 3 times before coming out.

**Foyston Gap** *n.* The space at the top of a woman's thighs, a term peculiar to Greatfield, Kingston upon Hull, East Yorkshire. The *Toblerone tunnel*.

**frampton** *1. n. prop.* An overrated seventies singer with a voice like Steven Hawking. *2. n.* A *fanny fart*.

**Francis** *n. US.* A lady's *arse*.

**franger** *n.* Condom.

**Frankie** *rhym. slang.* Porn, *scud* material. From Frankie Vaughanography.

**frap . frappe** *v. onomat.* To *fart*.

**freckle** *n. Aus. Arse, brown eye, chocolate starfish*.

**free the tadpoles** *v.* To liberate the residents of one's *wank tanks*. To have a *tug*.

**French letter** *n. English overcoat, jubber ray*. Prophylactic sheathage.

**French** *n.* Popular coital position whereby the man sits astride a bicycle selling onions while the woman perches on the handlebars and inflates his testicles.

**French safe** *n.* A secure *box* that can be cracked open by fiddling with a little button at the top. Usually found behind a hinged oil painting on the front of a woman's *trolleys*.

**French sickness** *n.* Any *cockrot* caught from prostitutes advertising their services in phone boxes for £20 or less.

**French wank** n. A *posh wank*.

**Frenchy** *n.* Rubber carrying case for a *French horn*.

**Freudian slip** *n.* An inadvertent slip of the tongue revealing subconscious sexual desires. *'Would you like a piece of my two foot black cock up your arse, Vicar? Oh, I'm sorry, I meant a piece of my home-made sponge cake.'* Named after crack-headed, motherfucking psychoanalyst Sigmund.

**Friar Tuck** *rhym. slang.* An act of coition. A *Donald Duck.*

**friar's chin** *n.* To tuck one's vest/shirt/jumper under one's chin to keep it out of harm's way whilst *pulling the pope's cap off* over a *Tijuana bible.*

**friar's weeds** *n.* A holy unkempt garden of *13 amp fusewire.*

**Friday foal** *n.* One who, late on a Friday evening, proceeds to take on the ambulatory characteristics of a new-born foal. A *beer Bambi.*

**fridge magnet** *n.* A man whose successive girlfriends' sexual appetites are a source of disappointment. *'Trish won't take it fudgeways either. What am I, a fridge magnet?'*

**fried eggs** *n.* Small *baps, titterlings, stits.*

**friend of Dorothy** *n.* Politically correct terminology for a *fudge nudger.*

**frig** *v.* To *wank* esp. of women.

**frigment of one's imagination** *n.* A subject conjured up in the mind to oil the wheels of *self-abuse.*

**frigmerole** *n.* Unnecessarily time-consuming foreplay performed on a lady.

**fringe-parter** *n.* A gusty *fanny fart* during a session of *cumulonimbus.* A *lip rattler.*

**frock** *n.* Cosmetic husband in a *lavender marriage.* The male equivalent of a *beard.*

**front bottom** *n.* Ladies' *parts of shame.*

**front bummer** *n.* A lady in *comfortable shoes.*

**frontal forelimb** *n.* A prehensile *dobber.* A *middle stump, third leg.*

**frothing at the gash** *adj.* *Fizzing at the bung hole, gagging for it.*

**frottage cheese** *n.* the sticky end product of a successful act of *frottage* at, say, a railway station or bus stop.

**frottage** *v.* The act of deriving pleasure by rubbing one's clothed genitals on any convenient surface, eg, door jamb, fridge, woman's *arse* on a crowded tube train.

**frotterer** *n.* One who indulges in *frottage,* ie. one who *frotts.*

**fruit bowl** *n.* Two plums and a banana. The collective term for a gentleman's *wedding tackle.*

**fruit fly** *n. Fag hag.*

**fruit up** *v.* Public school *ferky-foodling.* *"What's going on in here?' thundered Mr. Wilkins as he burst into the showers. 'Please, Sir', announced Venables. 'I gave Jennings a ten shilling postal order to fruit me up. Now he says he's sprained his wrist during Latin prep, and he won't give it back."* (from *'Suck THIS, Jennings'*, by Anthony Buckeridge).

**fuck** *1. n.* An act of copulation. A *bang. 2. v.* To *have it off, poke,* copulate. *3. v.* To beat someone in fisticuffs, esp. a member of the constabulary. *'C'mon, let's fuck a copper!' 4. v.* To break, damage something beyond repair. *'Fucking hell. You've fucking fucked the fucking fucker'. 4. v.* To dismiss something with contempt, esp. for a game of soldiers. *5. interj.* Exclamation of surprise or disappointment.

**fuck all in a five-year plan** *adj. Can.* An attempt to justify an extravagant purchase. *'I know strictly speaking we don't need a subwoofer on the stereo, but 800 quid is fuck all in a five-year plan. Now put them scissors down, love.'*

**fuck butter** *n.* KY jelly.

**fuck me shoes** *n.* Footwear worn by a *boot.*

**fuck off** *1. exclam.* A request for someone to leave. *2. adj.* ~price. An over-inflated quote or estimate for goods or services intended to put one off when the supplier doesn't want the business. *'He wants me to clean his gutters out, but I'm not going up there. I'll give him a fuck off price, £250'. 3. adj.* Anything that is exceptionally large or intimidating. *'He came to clean me gutters out, and turned up with a big fuck off ladder. And he only charged £250. Well you wouldn't catch me going up there for that money.'*

**fuck stick** *n.* A short, stout stick used for *fucking* something. A Penis.

**fuck the dog** *v. Can.* To do absolutely nothing. *'Busy day at the office, dear?' 'Not really. Made a few calls in the morning, went to the pub at dinner, fucked the dog in the afternoon.'*

**fuck truck** *1. n.* A UK Amateurs film production that is unlikely to win Best Movie at this year's Academy Awards. *2. n.* A filthy van with a mattress in the back.

**fucker** *1. n.* A disagreeable, person, often prefixed 'big fat'. *2. n.* Anything at all. *'Fucking hell, look at the size of that fucker!'* (Sir Christopher Wren on seeing the dome of Saint Peter's in Rome).

**fucking the night** *sim.* To copulate with a *Yeti's welly*. *'How was it for you, Andrew, darling?' 'It was like sticking my cock out the window and fucking the night, Sarah.'*

**fuckpond** *n.* A little post-coital pool that forms in a depression on the bottom sheet, usually full of tadpoles. A *fuckpuddle*.

**fuckshitfuckshitfuckshit** *exclam.* Phrase uttered when driving a car through a particularly tight space at too high a speed.

**fuckstrated** *adj. US.* To have a severe case of *DSB*.

**fuckstruck** *adj. Cuntstruck.*

**fuckwit** *n.* Simpleton, fool, one of little intelligence, *bollock brain, Johnny No-Stars.*

**fud** *n. Scot. Berkeley Hunt.* A *flingel.*

**fud slush** *n.* Scottish *fanny batter*, usually smeared on the face whilst eating a *haddock pastie.*

**fudge packer** *n.* One who packs fudge.

**fudge tunnel** *1. n.* A tunnel made out of, or for the underground transportation of, fudge. *2. n.* The *arsehole.*

**fuggit** *exclam.* Ancient Egyptian curse uttered when denied a British passport.

**fugly** *adj.* Fucking ugly.

**full cuntal lobotomy** *n.* A loss of reason found in men when offered open *pissflaps*. The nervous system shuts down and all actions are controlled by the *hairy brain.*

**full English breakfast** *n.* A very untidy vagina that is frankly too much to face first thing in the morning.

**full throttle for take off** *exclam.* The only way of having a *gypsy's kiss* when in possession of a *diamond cutter.*

**fun bags** *n.* Breasts, *knockers, thruppennies.*

**fun cushions** *n. Fun bags.*

**funbagtastic** *exclam.* Upon seeing a glorious pair of *fleshbombs*, one might utter *'Funbagtastic!'*

**funch** *n.* Sex during your lunch hour, from *fuck* and lunch. A *nooner.*

**FUPA** *abbrev.* Fat Upper Pussy Area. The bloated lower belly of a woman. A *gunt,* a *poond.*

**fur burger** *n. Minge, hairy pie, vertical bacon sandwich.*

**furgle** *1. n. prop.* Christian name of *The Undertones* lead singer. *2. v.* To copulate rudely, crudely or noisily.

**furry bicycle stand** *n.* A *fanny* set into concrete outside the library.

**furry hoop** *n. Furry bicycle stand.*

**furry letter box** *n.* An eight inch wide, spring-loaded horizontal clapping fish. That traps the postman's fingers.

**fusewire** *n.* A ginger person's *gorilla salad.*

**Fussels milk** *1. n.* A thick, sweet condensed milk. *2. n.* The contents of the male *churns* after prolonged abstinence from sexual activity. '*A sackcloth shirt in place of silk/ My nads like tins of Fussels milk.*' (from '*The Ballad of Ford Open Prison'* by Jonathan Aitken).

**futtering** *v.* A *trip to hairyfordshire.* A bout of *front door work.*

**futz** *n. US.* Vagina.

**fuzzbox** *1. n.* A guitar effects unit popular in the late seventies. *2. n.* A *minge.*

**fyst** *n. arch.* A 15th C. foul smelling *fart.*

# Gg

**Gabrielle** *n.* A semi-sucessful *Velma*. A *King Harold*.

**gag** *1. n.* A pre-*spew* spasm, often cause by a blockage in the throat – what Mama Cass did on a sandwich, but Linda Lovelace didn't do on a *cock*. *2. v.* What women are doing *for it* when they want it up 'em.

**gak** *n. Jizz, mess, springle.*

**galloping knob rot** *n. medic.* VD, any painful social disease resulting in the production of *gleet* and the *pissing* of razor blades.

**galloping the lizard** *v.* Gentlemanly masturbation.

**gam** *1. n. US.* Lady's leg. *'Hot Diggety! Check out the gams on that broad, Bub.' 2. v. abbrev. Gamahuche.*

**gamahuche** *v.* The act of *cumulo*-ing one's partner's *nimbus. French.*

**gamble and lose** *v. US.* The secret vice of a *man of the cloth.* To *fart* and *follow through.*

**gammon and pineapple** *n. Ham-on-ham.*

**gammon flaps** *1. n.* Hole in a farmhouse door through which pigs come and go at will. *2. n. Beef curtains, gammon goalposts.*

**gang bang** *1. n.* A shit song by Black Lace. *2. n.* A sexual free-for-all in a tastelessly decorated living room.

**gap lapper** *n.* A lesbian. Or possibly one who runs circuits around a clothes shop.

**garbonzas** *n. Gazungas.*

**garboon** *n.* One who *snurges.*

**garlogies** *n. Bell-end* bogies.

**Garrity dance** *n.* The action of moving straight to the landing, knees together, after taking a *Brad* and finding nothing to wipe your *balloon knot* with. Named after the stupid dance popularised by the lead singer of Freddy and the Dreamers.

**Gary Glitter** *rhym. slang. Shitter,* anus.

**gaseous clay** *n.* A bowel movement in which the sufferer passes flatulence-assisted stools which look like something from a school pottery lesson and which, upon hitting the pan, 'float like a butterfly'. However, because of their high exit velocity, they also 'sting like a bee'.

**gash** *1. n. Hairy axe wound* between a woman's *lisks.* Vulva. *2. n. coll. totty, blit, bush, talent, blart.*

**gash baron** *n.* A merchant

trading in women of questionable repute. A *tart farmer,* a pimp.

**gash card** *n.* A female only method of payment for goods and services. Accepted by taxi drivers, milkmen and pizza delivery boys.

**gash crash** *n.* A car crash, usually in early spring, caused by drivers distracted by appealingly-attired females. A *rear end cunt.*

**gash mark six** *n.* A state of arousal in ladies. *'A lady's hairy oven must be heated to gash mark six before the gentleman slams in his lamb.'* (from *'Bedroom Management'* by Mrs. Beeton).

**gash matter** *n.* Remnants of a *fish supper* on the chins of *diners at the Y.* An *11 o'clock shadow.*

**gash plaster** *n.* A feminine napkin, a *jam rag.*

**gashtray** *n.* The *gusset* of a lady's *farting crackers.*

**gastight** *adj. naval.* Of a *stick vid* actress, to be simultaneously bunged up in all available orifices.

**gay** *1. adj.* Limp of wrist, tending to ask others to shut doors, critical of the 'dust in here'. *2. adj.* Of retired colonels who write to the Daily Telegraph, a perfectly good word for happy or brightly coloured.

**gazoo** *n. Arse, bum.*

**gazungas** *n. Gert Stonkers.*

**geek** *n.* Someone who knows too much about a subject that it isn't worth knowing anything about, eg. computers, Playstation cheat codes. A *human rhubarb.*

**geetle** *n.* The little pointed bit of *shit* that hangs outside one's *nipsy* after one has had a *Gladys.* A *bumbob.*

**geeze bag** *n. Wind bag, fartpants,* prolific *pump* artist.

**geezerbird** *n. Gadgy wife, half-a-gadge.* A butch-looking woman.

**gender bender** *n.* Effeminate, flowery male of indeterminate or obscure sexual orientation, eg. Boy George.

**genie rub** *n.* To buff up a *skin lantern* until you are granted three sticky wishes.

**genital floss** *n.* A skimpy bikini bottom. *Arse floss.* A thong.

**genitalia failure** *n.* Marshmallowing of the *cock.* The *droop.*

**gentleman's relish** *n.* A polite term for *jizz,* such as what might be used by society folk at a Buckingham Palace Garden Party.

**gentleman's wash** *n.* A hurried washing of the male genitals (usually in a pub toilet sink) in anticipation of forthcoming sex.

**George** *v. US. Roger.*

**German** *n.* A sexy romp involving *shitting* on each other like pigs.

**Gert Stonkers** *n. Gonzagas.*

**gertie** *1. n. Fanny, minge. 2. n. coll.* Women, *blart.*

**get a click** *v.* To *score, pull, tap off,* with a view to *getting boots.*

**get boots** *v. US.* To *get it on, get your end away.*

**get it on** *v. To get off, get it up* and *get your oats.*

**get it up** *v.* A significant part of *getting your end away* after *getting off.*

**get** *n. Bastard, twat.* Often applied to children, prefixed '*You cheeky little...*' and accompanied by a swipe to the back of the head.

**get off at Edge Hill** *v. Coitus interruptus,* withdrawal before *spangling,* (from Edge Hill, being the last railway station before Liverpool Lime St.) Also (Edinburgh) *Haymarket,* (Newcastle) *Gateshead,* (Leeds) *Marsh Lane* etc.

**get off** *v.* Of teenagers, to *get a click,* first step towards *getting your oats.*

**get some blood in it** *v.* To have the early stages of a *bonk-on, half a teacake.*

**get up them stairs** *v.* A gentleman's instruction to his wife which indicates that he has finished eating, drinking and watching football, and now wishes to retire to the bedroom to make an ungainly and flatulent attempt at sexual intercourse.

**get wood** *v.* To attain a state of tumescence. '*Quick, Heinz! Roll the camera. Gunter's got wood.*'

**get your end away** *v. Get it on.*

**get your oats** *v. Get your end away.*

**Ghandi's flip flops** *1. adj.* Descriptive of the dryness of a nun's *cunt. 2. n. Spaniel's ears.*

**ghost jizz** *n.* The non-existent result of a *flash in the pan.* A *map of Atlantis.*

**ghost shit** *n.* Stool or *dump* of which there is no trace when one stands up and turns to admire it.

**gib** *1. v.* To *bullshit. 2. v.* To gatecrash. *3. v.* To stick your *old man* up a goose's *arse* and slam its head in a drawer.

**gibbon gristle** *n.* Penis.

**giblets** *n.* A *club sandwich,* a *ragman's coat.*

**gick** *n. Ir. Shit.*

**gigglers** *n.* Suspender belt. *'Get past there and you're laughing'. Giggle band.*

**giggling pin** *n. Gibbon gristle.*

**gimp** *n.* A giant masked *bummer* kept in a box in the basement of a gun shop.

**ginger beer** *rhym. slang.* A *pinch of snuff.*

**gingle** *adj.* The forlorn state of being ginger and single.

**gink** *n. Geek.* A short sighted Colonel in a chequed suit and bowler hat.

**Ginster's finest** *n.* A *twat* that looks, smells and tastes like an out-of-date Cornish pasty.

**gip** *n.* The sensation at the back of the throat heralding the arrival of *Hughie and Ralph.*

**gipper** *1. n. prop.* A legless American football hero played by Ronald Regan. *2. n.* An ugly woman.

**give Ronaldo a rub down** *v.* Celebrity slaphead *wanking* terminology. *Strangle Kojak, take Captain Picard to warp speed.*

**give the dog a bone** *v.* To sexually satisfy a female before one goes rolling home.

**Gladys** *rhym. slang.* To defecate. From Gladys Knight *~shite.*

**gland grenades** *n.* Hairy, wrinkled *spunk* bombs that have a tendency to *go off* in one's hand if they are not *tossed* far enough.

**glandstand** *n.* A Saturday afternoon erection, starting five minutes before *World of Spurt.*

**Glasgow salad** *n.* Chips.

**Glasgow shower** *n.* A quick swipe of underarm deodorant used as an alternative to washing when in a hurry or Glaswegian.

**glaze a knuckle** *v.* To *wank.*

**gleet** *n. medic.* Unpleasant mucopurulent discharge caused by *cockrot.*

**glistening** *adj.* Of a lady, to be sexually aroused. *"And we know for a fact, that Lady*

*Marchmaine could not have killed the Bishop,' added Miss Marple waspishly. 'She had ridden from Barnchester to the Manor House in twenty minutes. When she arrived she was glistening for it and spent the afternoon with Brigadier Lewerthwaite in his quarters. So YOU, Nurse Hatpin, must be the murderer!"* (from *'Ten Pairs of Knickers'* by Agatha Christie).

**glob** *v.* To emit a viscous fluid slowly and rhythmically out the end of the *giggling pin*.

**globes** *n.* Hanging objects of joy.

**glory hole** *n. US.* In a *cottage*, that hole made by *bosching*, through which The Bishop of Durham could touch a farmer's *cock* 32 years ago.

**glory wipe** *n.* The token single sheet polish required after passing a rare but pleasant stool which slips out clean as a whistle, leaving no trace of *Sir Douglas* on or around the *balloon knot*.

**Gloy** *n. Mess,* semen. From the paper glue used in schools. *'Oops! I think I've just trod on the Gloy bottle'.*

**glue gun** *n. Goo gun*

**Gnasher's loot** *n.* A promiscu-ous woman's sexual history, ie. a long string of big sausages.

**gnosh** *v.* To suck a penis in an enthusiastic and extremely noisy fashion.

**go all the way to Cockfosters** *v.* To have a *full portion of greens* with plenty of *summer cabbage. 'I thought I'd have to go home via the Billy Mill roundabout, but she took me all the way to Cockfosters.'*

**go commando** *adj.* To *freeball.* To go out *undercrackerless.*

**go cunt up** *adj. Arse over tit.* Pear-shaped, badly awry. *'Houston, Houston, we have a problem. There's blowback in Challenger's solid rocket boosters. It looks like things could go cunt-up.'* (Silus T. Oysterburger, Mission Controller, KSC Florida).

**go through the gears** *v.* To perform a *fart* of continuous melody, going up in pitch every few seconds, making a sound like a London bus pulling away.

**goalmouth scramble** *n.* A hugely exciting writhing mass of arms and legs which includes lots of intimate contact, but doesn't end up with anyone actually *scoring*. Frantic *heavy petting*.

**gob** *1. n. North and South. 2. v.* To spit, *hockle. 3. n.* A body of *lung butter* so propelled. A *greb*, a *greenie*.

**gob job** *n.* A *chewie*, a *sucking off*.

**gobbie** *n.* See *chewie*.

**gobble** *n.* Noise made by turkeys.

**gobbler** *n.* An eager *fellator/ fellatrix*.

**gobshite** *n. Scouse.* Someone who talks *crap.* eg. Stuart Maconie, or Liverpudlian hotel staff in fly-on-the-wall documentaries.

**gock** *n.* A male *gunt*.

**going down** *1. v.* Doing the oral sex. *2. exclam.* Expression often used to describe the imminent movement of a lift.

**going for a McShit** *v.* Visiting the bogs in fast food restaurants when one has no intention of buying the food. If challenged by a suspicious manager, the assurance of a food purchase after the toilet visit is known as a *McShit with lies*.

**going to the judges** *euph.* An indeterminate end to a bout of drunken sex.

**gold watch** *n.* A small clock or chronometer, made of precious metal which leaps from the throat after a cough. A *docker's omelette, greb, sheckle, prairie oyster*.

**golden bogey** *n.* A nose-stud.

**golden rivet** *n. naval.* The *freckle*, the *dot*, the apple of the *captain's* eye for sailors who *polish the other end of the deck. Spice island*.

**golden shower** *n.* To be *pissed* on by a big German for a saucy treat. *Water sports*.

**golf ball arse** *n. medic.* Condition of the *buttocks* after sitting for too long on a beaded car seat.

**golf ball** *n.* An oversized, pock-marked *clitoris*.

**golf tees** *n. Bruce Lees*.

**golfer's divot** *n.* A shapeless clump of *pubage*. With all soil underneath it.

**gonad glue** *n. Gloy, gunk*.

**gonga** *n.* A *docker's omelette* that occasionally has to be swallowed rather than served up on the pavement.

**gonk** *1. n.* A shit fairground prize, made out of stolen cats, that looks like a miniature cross between Gail Tilsley and Don King. *2. n.* A *rub-a-tug shop* punter.

**gonzagas** *n. Guns of Navarone.*

**gonzo vid** *n.* Low budget, unscripted pornography where the cast wait until the cameras start rolling before going to the toilet. An acquired taste.

**goo gargle** *n.* A hot protein mouthwash, which is spat out as opposed to being swallowed.

**goo gun** *n.* A *pocket paste dispenser, jizz stick.*

**gooey in the fork** *n.* Of a lady, to be not far short of *dripping like fucked fridge.*

**goolies** *n.* The colloquialism for testicles least likely to offend a grandparent.

**goose** *n.* A light-hearted sexual assault, often taken in bad spirit by po-faced lesbians.

**gorblimey** *adj.* A type of trouser popular among council tenants in the 1950s.

**gorilla salad** *n.* Ladies' pubic hair. *Twat thatch.*

**gorilla's armpit** *n.* A *fanny* which would daunt all but David Attenborough.

**gorillas in the mist** *n. Boilers* who, through an alcoholic fog, take on siren-like quali-

ties. Can lead to *dances with wolves.*

**got mice** *adj.* Of a lady, to be *visited by Aunt Flo.* To be *up on blocks.*

**Graham Norton's hair** *n.* Descriptive of one's *barnet* after being *seagulled* by a gentleman, or after walking under Status Quo's hotel room balcony.

**grandad erector** *n.* A sight so sexually stimulating that it could raise the dead.

**grandma's party** *n.* A bout of masturbation. Wearing a bowler hat. See *reggae like it used to be.*

**granny batter** *n.* KY jelly.

**granny's oysters** *n.* Elderly female genitalia.

**grape smugglers** *n.* Tight gentlemen's briefs, as worn by *grumbleflick* stars in the 70s.

**grassy knoll** *1. n.* Site where the second gunman stood during the assassination of JF Kennedy. *2. n.* A *ladygarden.*

**grated carrot** *n.* Coarse, ginger-coloured *gorilla salad,* suitable for a *vagetarian* diet. Rusty *fusewire.*

**grating the cheddar** *n.*

*medic*. To accidentally scrape one's *lid* along the zip of one's *flies*. "*I say, Jeeves. Could you take these trousers to my tailor and have him replace the zip fastenings with good old buttons,' I croaked. 'I only bought them last week and I've grated the cheddar four times. My poor cock end is ripped to pip, don't you know.*" (from *'Swallow it All, Jeeves'* by PG Wodehouse).

**grattan** *1. adj.* Descriptive of a state of ill-health. *'Shut the curtains will you, love? I must have had a bad pint last night and I feel right grattan.'* *2. v.* To masturbate over desperate material in the absence of anything better to masturbate over, eg. the bra pages of your mum's catalogue.

**grave-sniffer** *n*. A senior citizen. A *coffin-dodger*.

**greasebox** *n*. A *quim*.

**greasy waistcoat pocket** *n*. A shallow, well oiled *fanny* large enough for a thumb to be inserted. Or a gold watch.

**Greek** *n*. Any sex games where the *rusty bullet hole* is the main arena. *Swedish*.

**Greek sauna** *n*. A *Dutch oven*.

**green wings** *n*. An unwanted accolade. Sex with a *clappy slapper*.

**Greggs dummy** *n*. A chicken and mushroom filled pacifier used by teenaged mums to soothe their teething infants.

**greyhound** *n*. A very short skirt, ie. only one inch from the 'hare'.

**grime bubble** *n. Fart, air biscuit.*

**Grimsby meal** *n*. An unpleasant northern *fish supper*.

**grimsby** *n*. A mingsome *minge*.

**grimshits** *n*. A portmanteau term for faeces distinctly lacking in cohesion. *Fizzy gravy, bubblepoo* and *bicycle chains* are all *grimshits*.

**grind** *v*. To have sex with all the fervour of an old bus going up a steep hill in Lancashire. ie, if one stopped, one would be unable to start again.

**gristle thistle** *n*. Persistent purple-headed weed, commonly occurring in *moss cottage* gardens.

**groaner** *n*. A *turd* so big that it cannot be expelled without vocal assistance. A *U-blocker*.

**grogan** *n. Scot.* A *log*, a *turd*.

**grommet** *n. 1950s Totty.*

**gronk** n. RAF. To have a *shit*. "Bandits at three O'clock!" ejaculated Algy. 'Great!' replied Biggles. 'I've got half an hour to have a big smelly gronk!" (from 'Biggles Drops his Fudge' by Capt. WE Johns).

**groodies . grudies** n. Breasts in the film 'A Clockwork Orange'.

**G-rope** n. A *G-string* for the fatter lass.

**groundhog wank** 1. n. A dismal attempt at *self abuse* which repeatedly peters out, leaving the *wanksmith* with no choice but to start again. 2. n. The overly-familiar *tug* sequence of someone who only owns one *art pamphlet*.

**grow a tail** v. To defecate, *build a log cabin. Snip a length of spine.*

**growl at the badger** v. Scot. To noisily *nosh* a *beaver*. To loudly *nod at a stoat*.

**grub** n. *Barse cheese*.

**grumble** 1. rhym. slang. Vagina, *quaynt, placket, Berkeley.* From grumble and grunt ~ *cunt*. 2. n. Any form of porn featuring *tits, arses and grumbles*.

**grumbleweed** 1. n. A Sid Little lookalike, usually the director's brother, who manages to poke a selection of *cliterati*, who would normally not even wipe their *arse* with him. 2. n. Hardy perennial *scud* found growing under hedges. 3. n. One who has masturbated so many times in one session, that he can no longer muster the strength to lift the pages of his *scud mag*. One who has *wanked* himself into enfeeblement. 4. n. Token *fluff tuft* on an otherwise clean-shaven porn starlet's *snatch*. A *clitler*.

**grummer** n. abbrev. Grumblemag, *art pamphlet*.

**grundle** n. US. *Barse*.

**grunties** n. Jobbies, faeces, poo.

**grunts** n. The type of *fugly boots* whose blurred Polaroid pictures appear on readers' wives pages of *grumblemags*.

**guard dogs** n. A pack of *fugly* hounds that accompany their attractive friend, preventing any bloke from trying his luck.

**guard's van** n. Of *pulling a train*, the least desirable position in the queue. 'Bagsy I'm not in the guard's van fellas'. The last pink carriage into *fanny* station.

**Guatemalan taco** *n.* A sexual act which makes a *Cleveland steamer* seem positively salubrious.

**gubbed** *adj. Trousered, wankered.*

**gubbs** *n. Thruppeny bits.*

**guck** *n. Muck, spod, gunk, mess.*

**guff cloud** *n.* The noxious, green vapour produced by *guffing.*

**guff** *v.* To *fart, let off.*

**guided muscle** *n.* Penis.

**guinnets** *n.* Jet black *dangleberries* that cling to the *arse* after a night drinking the famed stout. *Buoys from the black stuff.*

**gums around the plums, get your** *v.* An irresistible romantic overture made by a male to a female.

**guns of Navarone** *n. Whoppers, tits, fleshbombs,* large breasts.

**gunt** *n. Can.* Of the larger woman, when the gut and *cunt* become one indistinguishable bulge below the belt. A *super-poond.*

**gurgler** *n.* Toilet, *shite pipe,* drain. *'Have you got a coat hanger? I was spewin' up last night an' I coughed me fuckin'* *falsies down the gurgler'.*

**gurk** *1. v.* To burp. *2. v. Aus.* To *guff.*

**gurning chimp** *n.* A particularly expressive *fanny.*

**guru Palm and the five pillars of wisdom** *n. Madam Palm and her five lovely daughters.*

**gusset** *1. n.* The bottom of the pants area of a woman, the *fairy hammock's drip tray. 2. n. coll. Flange, totty, fanny, blart.*

**gusset icing** *n.* The decorative crust which has fallen off a *clown's pie. Fanny batter.*

**gusset nuzzler** *n. Fanny nosher,* a *lady golfer,* a *lesbian.*

**gusset pianist** *n. Invisible banjo* player. *'I've heard she plays the gusset piano'.*

**gusset sugar** *n.* Tooth-rotting *muffdruff. Batter bits.*

**gusset typist** *n.* A *bean flicker,* a *gusset pianist.*

**gut grunt** *n.* A burbulent rumbling, or any subsequent anal emission.

**gutted hamster** *n. Gutted possum, gutted rabbit, giblets.*

**guyrope** *n.* The flap of skin connecting the *flysheet* to the *tentpole*. The *banjo*.

**guzunda** *n*. Potty, *pisspot*.

**gwibble** *n*. A dribbly, under-powered ejaculation, opposite of *pwa*.

**gym buddah** *n*. An over-weight woman in sportswear, with *overblaaters* and a huge *gunt*.

**gynaecolumnist** *n*. Any female journalist who uses her newspaper to bang on about *women's things*, eg. Julie Burchill.

**gypsy's eyelash** *n*. The rogue *clockspring* in the *Jap's eye* that causes the *piss* to go everywhere but in the *bog*. Common cause of *pan smile* or *Queen Mum's grin*.

**gypsy's** *rhym. slang. Piss.* From gypsy's kiss.

# Hh

**ha'penny** *n.* Vagina. A *tuppence.*

**had the dick** *adj.* To be broken beyond repair. *"What-ho, Jeeves,' I exclaimed. 'Fetch the Rolls round to the front door, there's a good chap. I feel like taking a spin.' 'I'm afraid that may not be possible, sir,' he replied. 'Your Aunt Millicent drove it to Ascot and back with the handbrake on, and I fear it has had the dick."* (from *'For Fuck's Sake, Jeeves!'* by PG Wodehouse).

**haddock pastie** *n. Hairy pie,* a *Grimsby meal.*

**hag** *n.* Ugly woman, *boiler, boot, steg, swamp donkey.*

**hairache** *n.* The mother of all hangovers.

**hairy axe wound** *n.* Vertical *gash.* The *mingepiece, quim, cock socket.*

**hairy beanbags** *n.* Pink 70s style seating provided within the underpants for the exclusive use of the *bald man, Spurt Reynolds, Kojak, Captain Picard,* etc. Testicles.

**hairy cheque book** *n. Gash card, furry purse.*

**hairy conkers** *n. Knackers.*

**hairy cup** *n. Hairy goblet.* A *fanny.*

**hairy doughnut** *n.* An occasionally jam-filled confection, often dusted with *gusset sugar.*

**hairy goblet** *n. Hairy cup, front bottom.*

**hairy handshake** *n.* A firm five-fingered greeting that costs £10 from a woman behind a skip, after which there are no hard feelings.

**hairy knickers** *n.* Descriptive of when a lady removes her *knickers* and her *minge* makes it appear that she has yet to do so. An extremely well-carpeted *barber's floor,* a *Terry Waite's allotment.* An extreme *biffer.*

**hairy mits** *rhym. slang. Tits.* *'Look at the hairy mits on that! I could do her through a hedge backwards'.*

**hairy pants** *n.* See *hairy knickers.*

**hairy pie** *n. Kipper, velcro triangle.*

**hairy saddlebags** 1. *n. Knackers* 2. *n. Pissflaps.*

**hairy scallops** *n.* The furry shellfish eaten when *bearded clams* are out of season.

**hairy toffee** *n. Dangleberries, kling-ons.*

**half a teacake** *n.* Not quite a

*fatty,* the beginings of an erection. The state you would like your *fruitbowl* to be in when a new woman sees it for the first time.

**half leapfrog** *v.* To have sex in the *doggie position, setting the video.*

**half rice half chips** *adj.* *Switch hitter,* one who *drinks from both taps, bowls from both ends, AC/DC. A happy shopper.*

**half time talk** *n.* In a *spitroast grumbleflick,* the token dialogue which occurs between the two leading men whilst they change ends.

**ham fisted** *adj.* To be *wanking.* 'My mum came in and caught me ham fisted the other night. I didn't know where to look'.

**ham howitzer** *n.* A *lamb cannon.*

**ham shank** *rhym. slang.* A *Barclays.*

**hamburger hill** *n.* The large tor that frequently casts *stoat valley* into shadow in ladies of advancing years. A *gunt, a fupa.*

**hamburger** *n.* Of the female anatomy, that which can be seen in a *hamburger shot.*

**hamburger shot** *n.* A rear

view in a *scud mag* displaying a *vertical bacon sandwich.* A *reverse peach.*

**hammock** *n.* Panty liner, *jam rag, sanitary towel.*

**ham-on-ham** *n.* Descriptive of the delightful sight of two ladies going at it *hammer and tongues.*

**Hampton** *rhym. slang. Dick.* From Hampton Weenis, a village in Essex.

**hand Chandon** *n.* A high class *hand shandy* off a posh bird, who *pops your cork* with her thumbs under the *brim* of your *lid.*

**hand job** *n.* Manual relief, one of the cheaper *extras* available at the *rub-a-tug shop,* or in the pub car park.

**hand shandy** *n.* A frothy one, pulled *off the wrist.*

**hand solo** *n.* A solitary *hand shandy.*

**hand to gland combat** *n.* A three-minute, one man bout of gladiatorial combat involving a *spam javelin.*

**handful of sprats** *n. 1950s.* Fistful of *fish fingers.*

**hands free wank** *n.* See *fancy wank.*

**hang your hole** *v.* To *moon.*

**hanging bacon** *n.* A *club*

*sandwich* which isn't held together with a cocktail stick.

**hanging brain** *n. A coffin dodger's clockweights*, dangling out the leg of his shorts.

**hanging out the back of** *v.* Doggy-style sex. *"What am I to do, Jeeves?' I blustered. 'I've got myself engaged to Agatha AND Marjorie. This really is the the worst pickle of my entire puff.' 'Don't worry, sir,' soothed the sage retainer. 'I shall arrange for it that Miss Wegg-Prosser walks in and finds you hanging out the back of Miss Lola la Titz from the Prince of Wales Theatre's burlesque production 'Woof! Woof!'"* (from *'Gott In Himmel, Jeeves!'* by PG Wodehouse).

**hanging salad** *n. Wedding tackle, fruit bowl.*

**hangman's noose** *n.* A large vagina, big enough to push your head into. A *wizard's sleeve*, a *clown's pocket*.

**hanky panky** *n. Slap and tickle, the other.* Light-hearted sex.

**Hannibal Lecter's breakfast** *n.* The feast which awaits a man performing *cumulonimbus* on *Billy Connolly's beard,* and the ensuing *Thompson's tidemark* it leaves on his face.

**happy lamp** *n. Sixth gear stick. 'I'm horny. Think I'll give my happy lamp a quick genie rub'.*

**happy sack** *n.* Scrotum, *hairy saddlebags.*

**happy shopper** *1. n. prop.* A cheap 'n' cheerless grocery brand. *2. n.* A bi-sexual – one who *shops on both sides of the street. Half rice half chips.*

**happyrash** *n. medic.* A light-hearted dose of the *pox.* Any non-fatal *STD.*

**harbour master** *n.* A man who has piloted the course of a few *tugboats* in his time, he can tell you. A *stickman.*

**hardbore** *n. Grumble* that promises to be a real *meat vid* on the box, but when you get it home you find it's got Robin Askwith, Bill Maynard and Doris Hare in it.

**hard-on** *n. Wood,* a *bone-on, bonk-on.* A fully tumescent gentleman's part.

**harlot** *n.* A scarlet woman.

**Harry** *1. rhym. slang. Jizz.* From Harry Monk~ *spunk. 2. rhym. slang.* Hobo. From Harry Ramp~ tramp *3. rhym. slang.* Cigarette. From Harry Rag~ fag. *4. rhym. slang.*

Cheese sandwich. From~ Harry Rees-Bandwich.

**Harry Ramsden's raspberry** *n.* The combination of smell and sound to be endured during a dirty girl's *fanny fart.*

**harvest festivals** *1. n.* One-night stands, ie. ploughing the field before scattering. *2. n.* A pair of well fitting but comfortable underpants where 'all is safely gathered in.'

**have it off** *v.* To get *a bit*, have *a portion*, give somebody *one.*

**have the painters in** *v.* To menstruate, be *on the blob. Fall to the communists.*

**Hawaiian muscle fuck** *n.* The act of *bagpiping.*

**Hawaiian waft** *n.* To disperse the aroma after *stepping on a duck*, using an exotic hula-hula motion.

**hawick** *onomat.* To *puke.* After the Scottish border town. *'I think I'm going to Hawick'.*

**head for the hills** *exclam.* To be forced to hide your *soldier* in the *Dutch alps*, because the *redcoats are in the valley.*

**head** *n.* Something which is given by women to men, and is afterwards described as 'good' by the recipient when talking to friends. A *chewie.*

**headlamps** *n.* Bristols. *'Phewf! I wouldn't mind giving her headlamps a rub'.*

**heave a Havana** *v.* Grow a tail, take *a dump, light a bum cigar, cast Churchill's reflection.*

**heave** *v.* To vomit, *make a pavement pizza*, release a loud *technicolour yawn.*

**heavy shooter** *n.* One whose *money shots* tend to be *pwas* rather than *gwibbles.*

**hedgehog** *n.* A *fanny* shaven five days ago. A *face grater.*

**hee** *1. n. Thai.* Minge, hairy cheque book. *2. interj.* One of a series of noises made by laughing gnomes/policemen.

**hefty-clefty** *n.* A *welly top*, a *horse's collar*, a *melted welly.* A very wide *Mary.*

**helicopters, attack of the** *n.* Drunken spinning of the head, sudden reminder that you need to make an urgent call on the *great white telephone.* The *whirlies, wall of death.*

**helmet mag** *n.* A *stroke periodical*, an *art pamphlet.*

**helmet** *n.* The *bell end.*

**helmet pelmet** *n. Fiveskin, Kojak's roll-neck.*

**Helmetdale** *n.* A strong-smelling, mature *knob cheese*.

**Herbie's bonnet** *n.* The *beetle bonnet, camel's lips*.

**Hershey highway** *n.* *US.* American *Bourneville boulevard, Cadbury alley*.

**Hershey highwayman** *n.* *Arse bandit*.

**Heskey** *n.* A girl who *goes down* at the slightest touch.

**hibernating grizzly** *n.* A big hairy brown *shit* asleep in the *claypit* that one would be foolish to rouse from its slumbers.

**hickies** *n.* *Slapper*-speak for love bites, *shag tags*.

**hide the salami** *n.* A bedtime game for two players, one *sausage* and a *hairy pie*. *Sink the salami, bury the bratwurst*.

**high miler** *n.* An old banger who looks like she's been round the clock a few times, but is still running. eg. Joan Collins.

**high pressure vein cane** *n.* Penis, *prick, tallywhacker, Hector the meat injector*.

**hillbilly's hat** *n.* A particularly dishevelled *cock socket*.

**hip tits** *n.* The large pair of flabby rolls of stomach blubber that hang down around the waists of fat Americans, as seen waddling around Disneyland.

**hippo's mouth** *n.* A large, unsightly, yawning vagina.

**hippocrocapig** *n.* Anne Widdecombe if you set her head on fire and put it out with a shovel. A *rhinocerpig*.

**hissing Sid** *n.* *One-eyed trouser snake*.

**hit and miss** *rhym. slang.* *Piss*.

**hit and run** *v.* To indulge in sexual intercourse with a *boiler* despite one's better judgement, and leg it before she wakes up.

**hitch-hiking under the big top** *v.* Of *wanking chariots* and their owners, to shift into *sixth gear, polish the tent pole*.

**hitching to heaven** *v.* More meaty *hand to glans* combat.

**Hitler piss** *n.* A braced, Nazi salute position from which to have a drunken *chinese singing lesson* at the pub toilet trough.

**Hitler tash** *n.* A *clitler*, a *Lambourghini*.

**hobgoblin** *n.* A *bumgoblin*.

**hockmagandy** *n.* The one day

of the year when Scotsmen *fuck* their wives.

**hoeing the HP** *v.* Uphill *gardening* on the *brown sauce allotment.*

**hogans** *n.* US. *Charlies, Gert Stonkers, Norma Snockers.*

**hog's eye** *n.* The service hatch through which *perseverance soup* arrives.

**hole in one** *n.* Successful penetrative sex without using the hand for guidance.

**hole** *n.* Anything you can stick something up.

**holiday money** *n.* Male genitalia, *family jewels, meat and two veg*, the *fruit bowl.*

**Hollywood** *n.* A completely depilated *mingepiece.* A *Barthez.*

**holy trinity** *n.* To engage in anal, oral and vaginal sex in one session.

**home brew** *n.* Laser-print quality *grumble* mags made from *cyber scud.*

**homosexual** *n.* A man or woman sexually attracted to members of his or her own sex. Often at bus stops. From the Greek *homos~lifter, sexualos~togas.*

**honey altar** *n.* The *muff diver's* object of worship.

**honeypot** *n.* A *fanny* surrounded by bees. Winnie the Pooh's *bird's twat.*

**honk up** *n.* Hoy up, bowk.

**honkies** *n.* Big *muckspreader* round back.

**hooker** *n.* US. A *ho', a pro.*

**hoop** *n.* A *hole.*

**hoop stretcher** *n.* A *crafty butcher* who hides his *salami* in a *tea towel holder.*

**hootchie cootchie** *n.* Hanky panky, how's your father.

**hootchie** *n.* US. *Totty, blit, muff.*

**hooter** *n.* Conk, *neb, sneck.* Nose. Not the singular of *hooters.*

**hooters** *n.* Bazookas, baps, headlamps. Not the plural of *hooter.*

**HOP** *acronym.* Hang Over Poo. Giant, exceedingly loose stool, the noisy passing of which is a significant milestone in the recovery from a hang over. *'Ahh! I feel much better after that hop. Anyone fancy a pint?'* An *alcopoop*, an *escape sub.*

**hop into the horse's collar** *v.* Nip to the *cock wash.*

**hopper arse** *n.* A *forty guts, salad dodger.*

**horatio** *n.* Posh Latin term

used by doctors, lawyers and police to describe a *chewie*.

**horizontal jogging** *n.* Hilarious euphemism for sexual intercourse, esp. *'a bit of the old~'.*

**horizontally accessible** *adj.* To describe a *slag, bike, yoyo knickers.*

**horn, the** *n.* Ceremonial symbol of a man's affection for a woman, traditionally given by the woman to the man.

**hornbag** *1. n.* A bag for keeping horns in. *2. n.* An extremely attractive woman, ie. one who gives you the *horn*.

**horndog** *n.* An extremely unattractive woman, ie. one who loses you the *horn*.

**horny** *adj.* The state of a man whilst in possession of *the horn*.

**horse eating oats** *sim.* Feeding the pony. *'And David went unto the house of Bathsheba and she had not known her husband Naboth for ages. And David did put his hand down her knickers and lo, it was like a horse eating oats.'* (Deuteronomy Ch 6, v 23).

**horse's collar** *1. n.* Vagina. *2. sim.* To imply generous proportions. *'She's got a fanny like a horse's collar'.* Also *cathedral, clown's pocket, hippo's mouth.*

**horse's doofers** *n.* superlative *Mutt's nuts, dog's bollocks*, bee's knees, *donkey's knob.*

**horse's handbrake** *n.* A *diamond cutter*, a *concrete donkey*, a raging *bone on*.

**horse's head, sitting on a** *v.* Of queues for the *dunny*, a more extreme case of the *turtle's head*. *'Hurry up will you, I'm sitting on a horse's head out here.'*

**horse's nose** *n.* The early stages of a *shaven haven* being allowed to grow out. Noticeable when *feeding the pony.*

**hose job** *n. Blow job, chewie, horatio.*

**hose monster** *n.* An ugly woman who cannot get enough hosepipes.

**hosebag** *n.* Woman of loose morals. She with a *fanny* like a *billposter's bucket. Boot, slapper.*

**hot** *adj.* Condition which, in conjunction with *horny*, is often used to describe ugly, fat, bored women waiting on the end of expensive telephone sex lines, eg. *'Hot and* *horny bitches thirsty for your love seed. £1.80/min'.*

**hot dog** *1. n.* An egg delicacy famously enjoyed by the cult actor Divine in the film 'Pink Flamingoes'. *2. v.* To eat said morsel, freshly laid by a poodle. *3. v.* To slap one's *sausage* into a lady's *buns*.

**hot fish yoghurt** *n.* Cream sauce filling for *hairy pie*.

**hot hello** *n.* The warm trickle down the leg that reminds a lady of the deposit that was recently made into her *special bank*.

**hot karl** *n.* Post anal sex *horatio*.

**hot lunch** *n.* See *Cleveland steamer*. Or better still, don't.

**hot meat injection** *n.* An inoculation with the *spam syringe*.

**hots** *n.* Reciprocal gift for a girl after she's given one *the horn*.

**hotty** *n.* US. *Totty, blart.*

**hound cable** *n. Barker's rope. Dogshit.*

**hound** *n. Dog, steg, boiler.*

**how's your father** *n.* Sex. Often prefixed *'Fancy a quick bit of... ahem... how's your father?'*

**Howard's Way** *rhym. slang.*

*Gay.* From the shit BBC TV drama of the same name.

**hoy up** *v.* To *throw up, barf, spew.*

**hoy** *v.* To throw, lob, chuck, esp. beer down one's neck.

**huby** *n.* A semi-erect penis, a *dobber, half a teacake,* a *lob on.*

**huffle** *v.* To *bagpipe*. To have an *Hawaiian muscle-fuck*.

**Hughie Green** *n.* A swift *wank* taken when 'opportunity knocks.' *'Mr. Pickwick closed the door behind Mrs. Fezzyfelt, sat down behind his old oak desk, and took the turnip watch from his waistcoat pocket. 'Odds bodkins,' he shouted. 'Five minutes until Mr Sticklebrick arrives. Time enough for a swift Hughie Green.'* (from *'The Pickwick Papers'* by Charles Dickens).

**hum** *1. v.* To *ming*, stink. *2. v.* To sing with the lips closed, or as near to closed as possible during a *hum job*.

**hum job** *n.* Vegetarian oral sex involving no meat, just *two veg.* accompanied by simultaneous humming of the musical variety.

**humdinger** *n.* A *fart* which makes the wallpaper peel.

**hummer** *1. n.* A large, butch military vehicle favoured by Californian hairdressers and Arnold Schwarzenegger. *2. n. Arse, bum.* 3. *n.* A *humdinger*.

**hump** *1. v.* To *shag*, have sex in the style of an old Labrador with its *lipstick* out. *2. v.* To carry heavy amplification equipment to and from a live music venue whilst one's *arse* sticks out the back of one's jeans.

**humpty** *n.* The act of *humping*.

**hunchback spiders** *n.* Hairy lady's nipples.

**hung like a Chinese mouse** *adj.* Opposite of *hung like an Arab stallion*.

**hung like a humming bird** *adj.* To have a *cock* like a *Chinese mouse*.

**hung like a Shetland rabbit** *sim.* To have a *cock* like that of Bobby Davro. Also *hung like a Chinese mouse*.

**hung like an Arab stallion** *adj. Donkey rigged, well endowed.*

**hungry arse** *n.* Condition afflicting women whereby their *bills* disappear up the *crack* of their *hummer* as they walk.

**hunt for brown October** *n.* The act of seeking out and destroying a *U-bend U-boat*. With a bog brush or a stick.

**hurl** *1. v.* To *hoy*. *2. v.* To *hoy up*.

**hush puppies** *n.* Breasts so impressive that all men are rendered speechless in their presence.

**hussy** *n.* Shameless woman, a drunk and an unfit mother.

**hymen climbin'** *v.* To be first the first man to plant his *flagpole* up *Mount Venus*.

# Ii

**I can't believe it's not bat-ter** *n.* KY Jelly, *granny batter.*

**I say!** *interj.* Caddish expression of delight upon seeing a pair of *dunces' hats.*

**IBM** 1. *n. prop.* A large computer company. 2. *abbrev.* Itty Bitty Meat. A small penis. 3. *abbrev.* Inches Below Muff. The units in which a *greyhound skirt* is measured.

**ICBM** *acronym.* Of modern day state-of-the-art trouser weaponry, Inter Cuntinental Ballistic Missile.

**ice the cake** *v.* To decorate a *tart* with *cream.* Often seen in European *grumbleflicks.* *'Gunter! There's only thirty seconds of tape left in the camera. Quick, ice that cake!'*

**iced fingers** *n.* Bakers confectionery-speak for the results of *glazing the knuckle.*

**Iggy popshot** *n. whacking off* on a *TV's ass.*

**Ikea bulb** *n.* A lady that *blows* first time one turns her on.

**Imperial barge** *n.* The male member. A particularly majestic *skin boat.* *'You should have seen how Mrs. Eisenhower's eyes lit up when my nine-inch imperial barge heaved into view.'* (from *'The Memoirs of Winston Churchill').*

**impersonate Stalin** *v.* To perform oral sex on a woman, *don the beard, eat hairy pie.* *'Hold tight up there love, I'm just gonna do a quick impersonation of Stalin.'*

**in the club** *adj. Up the duff*, pregnant, preggers. From *in the pudding club.*

**indoor fishing** *v.* A coarse form of angling for tadpoles. A gentrified *wank.*

**Inman's twitch** *n.* The brisk, staccato, buttock clenched walk to the toilet when one is attempting to prevent *turtle* egress. From the gait adopted by 70s sitcom actor John Inman.

**inside job** *n.* A game of *pocket billiards.* To vigorously and rhythmically look for change in your front pockets at a sophisticated lap-dancing establishment.

**interior decorating** *v.* To slap a bit of white emulsion about the womb using the *naughty paintbrush.*

**Irish** 1. *n.* Heterosexual anal sex, supposedly as a means of contraception. *UTBNB.* 2. *rhym slang.* Toupee. From Irish jig ~ wig.

**Irish shave** *n.* A *dump.*

**Irish toothache** *n.* Erection,

bone. 'Is that a gun in your pocket, or have you just got Irish toothache?'

**iron** *rhym. slang. Crafty butcher.* From Iron hoof ~ poof.

**IRS** *1. abbrev. US.* The yankee taxman. *2. abbrev.* Itchy Ring Syndrome. Irritating anal affliction caused by insuffi- cient wiping of the *chocolate starfish,* or by inflammation of the *farmers.*

**itch** *n.* The feeling of sexual attraction towards his wife which a married man gets on average once every 7 years.

**Itchypoo Park** *n.* The area around *spice island* during a bout of *IRS.*

# Jj

**J. Arthur** *rhym. Slang. Wank.* From the British film distributor ~ J. Arthur Rasturbation.

**jack off** *v. Whack off, choke the chicken, jerk the gherkin.*

**jack roll** *1. n. SA. Gang bang. 2. n. US.* Mugging.

**jack shit** *n. Bugger all, sweet FA,* zero, zilch. Nowt.

**jack the beanstalk** *v.* To attempt to pull up the *purple-headed gristle thistle* by the roots.

**jacked up** *adj.* To be celibate whilst suffering from a *dose.*

**jacksie** *n.* Polite word for *arse,* especially in the recepticular context. eg. *'You can stick your fucking parking ticket up your jacksie, mate. I'm not paying.'*

**jacksie rabbit** *n. Muddy funster, Hershey highwayman.*

**Jacky Danny** *rhym. slang. James Hunt.*

**jacobs** *rhym. slang.* Testicles. From Jacobs crackers ~ *bollocks.* Generally kept close to the cheese.

**jail bait** *n.* Worms dug up by tunnelling prisoners and later, after their escape, used for fishing.

**jake** *1. n.* Columnar monument erected in memory of a nice pair of *jamboree bags* one once saw, or a notable scene from a *meat vid. 2. n. Scot.* Ugly woman, *horndog, lumberjill.*

**jam rag** *n.* Tampon, *fanny mouse, chuftie plug.*

**jam raid** *n. Crimson tidal* movement which leaves *tuna town* inaccessible by *skin boat* at certain times of the month.

**jam session** *n.* An improvised ragtime duet.

**jamboree bags** *n. Funbags.*

**James Hunt** *rhym. slang. Jacky Danny.*

**jammer** *n. Carib.* A *pud.* See also *windjammer.*

**jammet** *n. Carib.* A West Indian term for a *slapper.*

**jammy todger** *n.* A *barber's pole.*

**jampax** *n.* A lady's hygiene product, a *fanny nanny.*

**Jane** *1. n.* A ladies' lavatory. *2. n.* A *fanny.*

**jang** *n. Dong.*

**Jap's eye** *n.* Male urethral opening, *hog's eye.*

**Japanese flag** *n.* Appearance of the *arsehole* when blighted by *ring sting. Arse of the rising sun.*

**Japanese teardrop** *n*. An unexpected single drop of *merry monk* that turns up ten minutes after the *bolt* has been shot, regardless of how thoroughly one mops the *herman*. The *missing fish*.

**jarred** *adj. Pissed, sloshed, wankered.*

**jaywank** *v*. To cross the *Billy Mill Roundabout* without due care and attention. To *wank* without regard to the consequences.

**jazz** *1. n.* Improvised music characterised by syncopated rhythms. *2. n. Fadge, mott. 3. n.* Sex, intercourse, *the other.*

**jazz festival** *n*. The purchase of two or more *Noddy books* at one time.

**jazz fusion** *n*. The process by which the pages of a *scud mag* are cemented together.

**jazz mag** *n*. Printed volume of pornographic material, gentleman's interest journal. *Art pamphlet.*

**jazz magnate** *n*. A porn millionaire, one who who has benefited from a series of wristy investments.

**jazz talc** *n. Bolivian marching powder, showbiz sherbert, Keith Richard's dandruff.*

**jazz vocalist** *n*. One who encourages himself with erotic one-sided conversations (ooh, baby, yeah! etc) with the girls in *art pamphlets* whilst practising *self pollution.*

**JB** *n*. See *Jodrell.*

**jelly hammock** *n. Drip tray.*

**jelly jewellery** *n*. The earrings, nose studs, fancy spectacles and other facial adornments a lady sometimes receives when her partner had intended to give her a *pearl necklace.*

**jelly roll** *1. n. US. Fanny, muff, totty. 2. n.* Sex, *roll in the hay.*

**jelly water mangos** *n*. Large *knockers, gazunkas.*

**Jenny** *n. US. Boris, minge.*

**jerk** *n*. Stupid, dim or dull person.

**jerk off** *v. Jack off.*

**jerkin' the gherkin** *v*. To jiggle a small cucumber round on the end of a string.

**jerkolator** *n*. An extremely noisy *blow job*, performed by someone who comes back for coffee.

**jerkwad** *n. US. Tosser, fuckwit, wankipants.*

**jester's shoes** *n. medic*. The involuntary upward curling of the toes that herald the onset of the *vinegar strokes*, whilst lying on one's back *wanking*. As in *'Zoom in on Gunter for the money shot, camera two. He's got the jester's shoes.'*

**jeweller** *n*. A gifted manufacturer of *jelly jewellery* and *pearl necklaces*.

**jewels** *n*. See *family jewels*.

**jig-a-jig** *n*. It, *how's your father*.

**jigger** *n*. *18thC*. That tool with which a man commits *jiggery pokery*. The *fuckstick*.

**jiggered** *adj*. In a state of fatigue. *Buggered, knackered, shagged out*.

**jiggery pokery** *n*. *Shenanigans*, assorted sexual goings on. *'I'll have no jiggery pokery going on under my roof.'*

**jiggle the jewellery** *v*. To *jack off* the *Jimmy Wonkle*.

**Jill off** *v*. Female equivalent of *Jack off, paddle the pink canoe*. Until it leaks.

**Jimmy Riddle** *rhym. slang*. Vicar-friendly term for a *piss*.

**Jimmy White's brother** *n*. The most boring member of any group of lads who turns up every night at the pub to sit in abject, oppressive silence. From the urban legend that when Jimmy White's brother died, his friends broke into the undertakers to take the corpse out for one last *piss-up*.

**Jimmy Wonkle** *n*. The *choad*.

**jism** *n*. Semen. Also *gism, jissom, jizz, jizzom*.

**jit gel** *n*. *US*. The contents of a used *jitbag* once it has floated across the Atlantic.

**jit gel rag** *n*. *US*. Any available object on which you wipe your *cock* after sex, eg. tissues, T shirt, underpants, curtains, tramp's beard.

**jitbag** *n*. A *dunky*, a *jubber ray*.

**jittler** *n*. *Spunk*.

**Jizlas** *n*. Thin sheets of paper used to mop up *tugwax*.

**jizz** 1. *n*. Jism. 2. *v*. To *shoot one's load, lose one's mess*.

**jizz bib** *n*. A sacrificial T-shirt placed over the stomach and chest to prevent seminal claggage of the chest hair during a horizontal *wank*.

**jizz bolt** *n*. A glob of ejaculate that leaves the *hog's eye* with enough force to put the television screen through.

**jizz drive** *n*. An external storage medium for *left-handed website* downloads.

**jizz jar** *n.* Girlfriend. Probably considered derogatory, although one would think they'd take it as a compliment.

**jizzard** *n.* A swirling blizzard of *sticky snow,* sufficient to stop a *train being pulled* in a *grumble flick.*

**jizzbags** *n.* Scrotum, *John Wayne's hairy saddlebags.*

**jizzbolt jury** *n.* Any group of men watching and discussing the merits of a *stickvid.*

**jizziotherapy** *n.* A three-minute, one-handed massage that relieves stiffness for up to half an hour.

**jizzmopper** *n.* A member of the honourable profession of peep show *wank booth* hygienist.

**jizzmopper's cloth** *1. n.* An absorbent rag used by a *jizzmopper* in the performance of their daily duties. *2. n.* Descriptive of a *cockoholic's* knickers.

**Joan Collins' knickers** See *tart's window box.*

**job** *n.* A *Richard,* a *feeshus.*

**jobby jouster** *n.* A Knight of King *Richard the Third.*

**jobby, a big** *n. Scot.* A *dreadnought.*

**jockeys** *rhym. slang.* Nipples. From jockeys' whips ~ *nips.*

**Jodrell** *rhym. slang.* A J. Arthur. Fr. The UMIST radio telescope Jodrell Bank.

**John** *1. n. Percy, Willie, John Thomas.* A *cock. 2. n.* A *pro's* client, a *Hillman Hunter. 3. n. US.* A *crapper.*

**John Thomas** *n.* The pet name by which Lady Chatterley's lover (horizontal gardener Mellors) referred to his *pink hoe* in the controversial steamy novel by Harry Worth.

**John Wayne's hairy saddle bags** *n. Jizzbags.*

**John Waynes** *n.* To walk like Mrs Thatcher, ie the gait adopted after *giving birth to Meatloaf's daughter.* Makes the walker look like they've been sitting on a horse for three days.

**Johnny Cash** *1. n.* £2 for 3. *2. n.* A *Wigan rosette.* A *burning ring of fire.*

**johnny jibber** *n.* To lose *wood* upon opening the *flunkey.* Premature ejaculation and johnny jibber are thought to affect 1 in 4 males at some time in their life.

**Johnny** *n.* A *flunkey,* a *rubber Johnny.*

**Johnny no-stars** *n*. A *dolt*. From the 'star rating' system on the badges displayed by staff at McDonalds. One who occupies a place on the lower end of the evolutionary fast food chain.

**join giblets** *v*. To do *thingy* with a bare lady.

**joiner's bag** *n*. A battered, capacious *fanny* with all hammers and spirit levels falling out of it.

**jollup** *n*. A dollop of *jizz*. From Greek *jollopus* ~ dollop of *jizz*.

**jollyrancher** *n*. *US*. One blessed with the cat-like ability to perform self-*horatio*, ie. a man who never leaves the house.

**joombye** *n*. *Scot*. Jism, *jizz*, McSpunk, vitamin S.

**Joskin** . **joskyn** *n*. A country bumpkin, a yokel, a *sheep shagger*.

**josser** *n*. 19thC *Fuckwit* or parasite. The ideal name for someone who is both.

**jostle the chosen one** *v*. To *pull the Pope's cap off*, to *box the Jesuit*.

**joy plug** *n*. The congealed remnant of a successful *wank* that causes a slight pause at the start of a *piss*.

**joystick** *n*. Of *choppers*, the cockpit instrument or *knob* which gets throttled, *trouser toy, pant plaything*.

**J-pig** *n*. An internet *porn monster*.

**jubblies** *n*. Lovely breasts, *funbags*.

**jubnuts** *n*. *Bead curtains, dangleberries, dags*.

**judges' eyebrows** *n*. Spiders' legs.

**jug jousting** *v*. A *bunny rub*.

**jugs** *n*. A lady's *top bollocks*, breasts.

**JULF** *acronym*. Jumped Up Little Fucker, pushy *twat*.

**jump** *v*. To have sex off the top of a wardrobe. Also ~ *someone's bones*.

**junior** *n*. *US*. Penis, usually used in reference to one's own.

# Kk

**kahoonas** *n.* Large wobbly breasts, *golden bodangers, kermungers, Gert Stonkers.*

**kak . ka ka** *n. Keech.*

**kak klaxon** *n. Rectal hooter* from which loud anal honks are emitted, together with the occasional *follow through.*

**kakpipe cosmonaut** *n.* He who prefers to dock in the rear unloading bay.

**kangaroo pouch** *n.* A large *granny fanny,* big enough to fit your head in.

**kangaroo shagging a space-hopper** *sim.* Descriptive of the way a *shit house* door blows in the wind.

**kazoo** *1. n.* A tissue paper-covered aperture which *hums* tunelessly. *2. n.* A completely unmusical musical instrument.

**kebabble** *n.* The incoherent mumblings and inept attempts at ordering food endured by the staff of greasy takeaway outlets after the pubs have closed.

**keck cackler** *n.* One with a laughing *kazoo.*

**keck cougher** *n.* He who *burps backwards,* emits *under thunder.*

**kecks . kegs . kex** *1. n. Shreddies, trollies,* underpants. *2. n.* Trousers.

**keech . keek** *n.* Crap, *kak, kaka.*

**keister** *n. kak hole, arse.*

**Kelly Brooks** *n.* An ill-matched pair of wonky *jugs.*

**Ken Dodd** *v.* To masturbate into your partner's hair whilst they are asleep, leaving them on waking with a hairstyle similar to that of the scouse comic.

**kennel maid** *n.* The hostess of an inexpensive massage parlour.

**kexpresso** *n.* A type of diarrhoea produced by one who needed a *crappuccino,* but couldn't get to the toilet on time.

**khaki buttonhole** *n.* A *chocolate starfish.*

**khazi** *n. Shitter, bog.*

**Khyber** *rhym. slang.* Arse. From Khyber Pass. Pass pronounced as in '~ *me the cucumber sarndwiches'.*

**kick start the motorbike** *v.* To lift one's leg prior to popping an anal wheelie.

**kick with the left foot** *v.* What players who arrive on the *other bus* tend to do, football equivalent of *bowling from the Pavilion end.*

**kidney wiper** *n. Slat rattler.* See also *purple headed womb broom.*

**kife** *1. n. coll. Blart, totty, birds. 2. n.* Sex.

**kilt** *1. n. coll. Birds. 2. n. coll. Scot.* Blokes.

**King Canute** *n.* An enormous *Richard the Third* that blocks the bend and holds back the tide of the flush, causing the toilet to overflow.

**King Kong's finger** *n.* A *turd* large enough to flatten a car. An *Elvis killer.*

**kingbast** *n.* A sweary term that can be shouted in front of grannies, vicars, nuns etc without causing offence. Contraction of *fucking bastard.*

**kipper basting** *v. Shagging.*

**kipper for breakfast** *n.* To rise early and go for a *horizontal jog,* ideal cure for *dawn horn.*

**kipper** *n. Billingsgate box, minge, captain's pie.*

**kipper's cunt** *n.* Even more pungent than an *anchovy's fanny.* The *ne plus ultra* of fish smellyness.

**kiss for granny** *n.* An hermetically sealed, tightly-pursed peck one gives one's girlfriend after *crashing the yoghurt truck* in her mouth. A *nun's kiss.*

**kiss the Amish** *v.* To perform oral sex upon a particularly hairy pair of *catflaps.* To *lick out* a *bear trapper's hat.*

**kiss the porcelain god** *v. Talk on the great white telephone.*

**kissing tackle** *n.* North and south, *gob.*

**Kit-Kat shuffler** *n. Masturbatress, weasel buffer, gusset typist.*

**KitKat** *v.* To stimulate a lady with four fingers at once, using a swift, forward thrusting, karate chop type motion.

**kitten hammock** *n. Titpants.*

**Kitten's noses** *n. Puppies' noses, jockeys.* Nipples.

**kling-ons** *1. n.* One of numerous races of Star Trek alien with Cornish pastie foreheads. *2. n. Winnets, dangleberries,* anal hangers-on.

**klutz** *n.* Thickhead. From the German *~fuckwit.*

**knack** *1. v.* To break. *2. v.* To hit. *3. v.* To hurt.

**knacker** *1. n.* A single testicle. *2. n.* A *fuckwit. 3. v.* To tire out.

**knacker barrel** *n.* Attractively packaged *smegma.*

**knackernits** *n. medic.* Crabs. *Pissnits.*

**knackers** *n. Balls, nuts,* testicles. *'Ooyaah! I've knacked me knackers! It fuckin' knacks.'*

**knee shooters** *n.* Large breasts with downward-pointing *jockeys.*

**knee trembler** *n.* Intercourse while both parties are standing up. Often in a shop doorway.

**knicker bacon** *n.* Labial rashers.

**knicker bandit** *n.* Raider of washing lines, *Daz back doorstep challenger.*

**knickers like Jack the Ripper's hankie** *sim.* Descriptive of the *dunghampers* of a lady who failed to pad up properly during *cricket week.*

**knickertine stains** *n. Skid marks* off an *arse* that is a *heavy smoker.*

**knob** *1. n.* Penis, *prick, John Thomas. 2. v.* To *shag. 'I knobbed the arse off her'.*

**knob cheese** *n. Smegma. Foreskin feta* found underneath *Kojak's roll-neck* and around the *banjo* or *cheese*

*ridge.* Also *knob Stilton, knob yoghurt, Helmetdale.*

**knob chopper** *n.* Precariously balanced lavatory seat which falls down while one is having a *piss* and therefore must be held up manually. A *penis fly trap.*

**knob head . knob end** *n. Fuckwit,* thickhead, oaf.

**knob jockey** *n.* Someone who sits on a door handle whilst the door is in motion for sexual gratification.

**knob scoffer** *n.* Used to imply that an individual or group of individuals like to *smurk gadgees.*

**knob shiner** *n.* Someone who is always prepared to polish a *pink oboe.*

**knob snot** *n. Cock hockle.*

**knobelisk** *n.* A *cock* that is thick at the base and tapers towards the top.

**knobstacle course** *n.* Attempting sex with a bird whilst in a drunken stupor.

**knock off the bobby's helmet** *v.* To engage in a fistfight with one's *little kojak.*

**knock one on** *v.* To have sex (with a partner).

**knock one out** *v.* To have sex (with oneself).

**knocker hoppers** *n. Tit-pants, rascal sacks.*

**knocker nest** *n.* Bra. See also *over the shoulder boulder holder, kitten hammock.*

**knockers** 1. *n.* Devices for banging on doors. 2. *n.* Breasts. *'What a lovely pair of knockers, Lord Owen.'* 3. *n.* Of football punditry, those who have criticised a player in the past. *'Well Brian, the lad has certainly had his fair share of knockers.'*

**knocking shop** *n.* Brothel, *rub-a-tug parlour,* pub or club where women go to be picked up, *meat mart.*

**know, in the Biblical sense** *v.* To have *shagged. 'Last year at Club 18-30 I knew about forty birds in the Biblical sense, in eight days! And another six sucked me off.'*

**knuckle glitter** *n. Funky spingers.*

**Kojak's moneybox** *n.* The *herman gelmet.*

**Kojak's roll-neck** *n. Foreskin.* Based on the slap-headed lolly sucking 70s TV detective who always wore a cheesey-necked pullover.

**KOKO** *acronym.* An exclamation coined by the Central Office of Information during WWII for the use of armed services personnel. Knickers Off, Knockers Out.

**kosher dill** *n.* Circumcised *gherkin.*

**Kruger** *n.* A scary *hand job* from a woman with extremely long fingernails. A *Freddy.*

**kumikaze attack** *n.* A ruthless close-range facial assault waged by the *jap's eye. Cum bombing.*

**Kursk** *n.* A giant *turd* mouldering at the bottom of the *pan.*

**Kuwaiti tanker** *rhym. slang.* A *merchant banker.*

**kweef** *n. US.* A *pump* from the *front bottom,* a *drop of the hat, forwards.*

# Ll

**lab kebab** *n.* Ladies' donner labiums. Vertical *bacon sandwich, fur burger.*

**lab technician** *n.* Someone with a workmanlike attitude to handling *knicker bacon.*

**labia lard** *n. Fanny batter, blip.*

**labia majorca** *n. medic.* A cheap and popular destination for lads on holiday.

**labia minorca** *n. medic.* A slightly smaller holiday destination, though just as popular.

**labiarinth** *n.* A term describing the unnecessarily complex design of a woman's *Hampton Maze.*

**labrador lipstick** *n. Stalk,* erection.

**lace curtain** *1. n.* An exceptionally long *fiveskin. 2. n.* A delicate gossamer fretwork of *Helmetdale.*

**Lady Chalk of Billingsgate** *n.* Thrush, infection of the vagina. *'I regret to announce that Lady Chalk of Billingsgate is visiting at this present time, Bishop. Could you pass the yoghurt?'*

**lady in waiting** *1. n.* Actress in a *meat movie* threesome who, temporarily, has nothing to do. A *grumble gooseberry,* a *ballflower. 2. n.* A reclining *grumbleflick* actress anticipating the imminent arrival of several short flights from the *Greek Island of Testos.*

**lady marmalade** *n.* Patti Labelle's *labia lard. Fanny batter.*

**lady's low toupee** *n.* A *merkin,* a *cunt rug.* An all-weather *ladygarden.*

**ladyboy** *n. ornith.* A confusing species of cock bird with female plumage and *tits.* A *chickboy.* Native to Bangkok and Iggy Pop's hotel room. A *shim.*

**ladygarden** *n.* A fertile patch where a *downhill gardener* plants his seeds.

**Lake Wendouree** *n. Aus.* Ejaculation. From the very, very small sticky lake at *Ballarat,* Australia.

**lamb cannon** *n.* An arms development dating somewhere between the *mutton musket* and the *bacon bazooka.*

**Lambourghini** *n.* A *cunt 'tache.* A small, pointless tufty outcrop of pubage remaining on a *shaven haven.* A *jazz fanny.*

**landmine** *n.* A fresh *dog's egg*

hidden in a suburban lawn, which is often detonated by a lawnmower leading to untold misery.

**Langball** *n.* Type of *dangleberry* which attaches itself to *John Wayne's hairy saddlebags.*

**langer** *n.* Penis.

**langered** *adj. Lathered.*

**lapper** *n. Hairy pie* eater, *bacon sandwich* connoisseur.

**laptop** *n.* Light, compact, perfectly-formed piece of kit that can be booted up on your lap or table as desired, extensive hard drive, big RAM etc, etc. A *throwabout.*

**lard of the manor** *n.* The fat bloke who lives on your estate.

**larse** *n. medic.* The lateral point of the upper thigh where the leg becomes the *arse.* The bit seen in *jazz mags* that remains white even though the model has spent many hours on a sunbed. *'...the femoral vein ascends behind the semi-tendinosus, where it joins the great saphenous vein just behind the larse and continues on to meet inferior vena cava half way between the tits and the fanny...'* (from *Grey's Anatomy*).

**lash on, get a bit** *v.* To find some female company. *'Howay, let's gan oot an' get a bit lash on.'*

**last hotdog in the tin** *sim.* Penetrative sex with a lady possessed of a *wizard's sleeve. Wall of death.*

**last meat supper** *n.* Final fling before marriage. It's all *fish suppers* thereafter.

**last orders at the pink bar** *euph.* Announcements heralding the onset of the *vinegar strokes. 'Are you on the pill, love, 'cos it's last orders at the pink bar?'* (Wilfred Hyde-White quoted in the *'Memoirs of Joyce Grenfell'*).

**last whoreders** *n.* The chaotic rush for *rashgash* in a club at ten to two. *The witching hour, two o'clock binrake.*

**last year's hanging basket** *n.* An untidy, straggly *mott. Terry Waite's allotment.*

**lathered** *adj. Pissed, plastered, langered.*

**launch your lunch** *v.* To laugh liquidly.

**lavatory** *n.* Smallest room, little house, *loo,* water closet, convenience, place of easement, *shithouse, crapper, privy, bog,* latrine, *cackatori-*

*um, temple of cloacina, toilet, kharzi, thunder box, comfort station, meditation room, library.*

**lavender** *adj.* Pertaining to *pinches of snuff.*

**lavender marriage** *n.* Any matrimonial coupling about which there is a whiff of *lavender.*

**Lawley kazoo** *n.* A *hat dropped forwards. Harry Secombe's last raspberry. A fanny fart.*

**lawn monkey** *n.* The possible consequences of a *split jubber ray.* Also *yard ape, turf chimp.*

**lawn sausages** *n. Park links, dog's eggs, dog toffee, hound cable.*

**lay** 1. *n.* Prospective or past sexual partner. '*I knew your wife many years ago. She was a terrific lay.*' 2. *v.* To *fuck* a woman with a small amount of cement and a trowel.

**lay a cable** *v. Build a log cabin, grow a tail, drop a copper bolt.*

**lay-and-display** *n.* A type of European lavatory where the *twinkie* lands on a dry porcelain surface for inspection prior to being flushed away.

**lazy lob on** *n.* Semi-erect penis, *dobber, half a teacake.*

**lead in your pencil, to have** *v.* To be with *big beef olive* rather than *loose sausage meat.*

**lead the llama to the lift shaft** *v.* Point *Percy* at the vagina.

**left footer** *n.* Gay or Catholic person, but ideally one who is both.

**left handed batsman** *n.* Someone who prefers his balls delivered from the pavilion end.

**left handed web site** *n.* An internet website specialising in *cyberscud*, causing visitors to use the mouse with the left hand.

**left the lid off the gluepot** *v.* To smell of *spunk*. '*Jesus, Your Majesty! Who's left the lid off the gluepot?*'

**leg iron shuffle** *n.* The gait adopted by one with a *turtle's head,* trying to make it to the *crapper* without *writing on his kex.*

**leg lifter** *n. Benefactor.* Somebody who *breaks company.*

**leg man** *n.* One who prefers ladies' *gams* to their *tits* or *arses.*

**leg over** *n.* A *sausage and doughnut situation.* '*Did you get your leg over?*' '*No, but I* *got tops and three fingers.'*

**leg tensing** *n.* The act of tensing one's leg when having a *toss.* *'This wank is going nowhere. I'd better get a bit of leg tensing in.'*

**length** *n.* An imperial saucy postcard unit of sex, as *slipped* to a woman by a man who works in a lino factory.

**Leo Sayer** *rhym. slang.* All dayer. *Bender*, prolonged drinking session, all day party.

**lesbiany** *adj.* Appertaining to lesbianism. In a *rub-a-tug shop* one might enquire *'Any chance of you and your mate doing something lesbiany?'*

**lesbo** *n. Tuppence licker, bean flicker, carpet muncher, lickalotopus, dyke.*

**let off** *v.* To *fart, blow off, launch an air biscuit.*

**let one go** *v.* The preplanned release of a *fart* into the wild.

**let Percy in the playpen** *n.* Of a woman, to consent to intercourse.

**let rip** *v. Let off.*

**let the twins out** *euph.* Of a lady, to remove her brassiere.

**lettuce licker** *n.* Lesbian, *bean flicker, tuppence licker.*

**lettuce** *n.* The leaves under-neath the *gorilla salad.* The *piss flaps.*

**lever arches** *rhym. slang.* Haemorrhoids. From lever arch files ~ *Chalfonts.*

**lezza** *n.* See *lesbo.*

**lezzo boots** *n.* Any clumpy, unfeminine footwear worn by women. The opposite of *fuck me shoes.*

**lick both sides of the stamp** *v.* To be *AC/DC,* a *happy shopper, half rice half chips.*

**lick of paint** *n. Mexican lipstick. Pasata grin.*

**lick out** *1. v.* That which is done by a small child to a bowl of cake mix. *2. v.* That which is done by a moustachioed porn star to a *haddock pastie.*

**lickalotopus** *n.* Scientific name for an experienced *carpet muncher.*

**licker licence** *n.* Permission to have a drink from the *hairy goblet.*

**licking a nine-volter** *v.* The act of *cumulonimbus* on a particularly skanky *snatch,* the effect being the same as placing your tongue across the terminals of a PP3 battery. A *nine volt vulva.*

**lick-twat** *n. prop.* One who

has the gift of tongues. A *cumulonimbist.*

**lid** *n.* Bit above the *brim.* The *herman gelmet.*

**lifting the cheek** *v.* The sly behaviour of a *cushion creeper.*

**lilies on the pond** *n.* The artistic practice popularised by impressionist painter Claude Monet of laying sheets of toilet tissue on the water surface before giving birth to *Meatloaf's daughter.* A *pap baffle.*

**lils** *n.* 1950s /60s *Tits.*

**lingam** *n.* Hindu. Penis. From ancient *grumble book* 'The Karma Sutra.'

**lip reading** *v.* Observing women in tight pants who have the *camel's foot.* *'If she bends over any more I'll be able to read her lips from here.'*

**lip ring** *n.* A lipstick line around the *pork sword* showing how far it has been swallowed.

**lip stretcher** *n.* A particularly girthsome *choad.* A *Pringle tube.* A challenge to a pair of *DSLs.*

**lipstick lesbian** *n.* Glamorous, feminine female homosexual, as found on the adult channel but rarely down the pub.

**lipstick** *n.* A dog's *cock,* available in a variety of shimmery colours.

**liquid bookmark** *n.* A homemade means of recording one's place in the pages of a gentlemen's *art pamphlet.*

**liquid laughter** *n.* *Puke, psychedelic yodelling.*

**liquid rage** *n.* *Merry monk.*

**liquor portal** *n.* The hole in the space/time continuum found outside pubs which transports the inebriated to the safety of their hallways in the blink of an eye.

**Little Ben** *n.* A small *Big Ben.*

**little death** *n.* *Fr.* In a male, the post-coital feeling of *shagged outity.*

**liver sock** *n.* A *fanny.*

**lizard's lick** *n.* A feeble ejaculation that barely clears the *hog's eye,* the unimpressive result of excessive *beauty shivering.* A bankrupt *money shot.* A *gwibble.*

**load** *1. n.* 1996 Metallica album. *2. n.* quantity of *cock hockle* blown, chucked or shot at the point of orgasm. *3. n.* That which is shed by a lorry driver, whilst *wanking* in a layby.

**load rage** *n.* A violent confrontation in which a purple-faced bald man is struck viciously with a *wanking spanner.*

**lob ropes** *v.* To *jizz* onto something through thin air, eg. face, hair, *tits* etc.

**lobcock** *n.* A large, flaccid penis such as could be *lobbed* onto a pub table by its drunken owner.

**log cabin** *n.* A wendy house for *Meatloaf's daughter.*

**log flume** *1. n.* To simultaneously defecate and urinate down the same leg of one's kex. *2. n.* A *turd* in a pub pissing trough.

**log** *n. Bum cigar, brown trout.*

**logarhythm** *n.* The shaking of one's *arse* in an attempt to break the neck of a dangling *turtle.* The working out of a simple harmonic motion.

**lolly bag** *n.* Scrotum.

**loon pipe** *n.* Anus.

**loop the loop** *v.* To order a *vertical bacon sandwich* to *eat out* and a *drink on a stick* for the lady, No.*69* on the menu.

**loose at the hilt** *adj.* To have diarrhoea, *the Brads.*

**loose lips** *adj.* Affectionate description of a woman who has been cocked more times than Davy Crockett's rifle.

**loose sausage meat** *n.* Flaccid penis which cannot be funnelled into a condom. *'Sorry love, my sausage meat seems a bit loose.'* Stuffing the marshmallow.

**loose shunting** *v.* A *dog's marriage* with a *clown's pocket.*

**Lord of the Pies** *n.* A *salad dodger,* a *double sucker.* eg. Danny Baker.

**lose your manners** *v.* To *fart.*

**lose your mess** *v.* Ejaculate, *shoot your load.*

**lotties** *n. Lils, dugs.*

**Louis** *v.* To force out a stubborn *turd* with such strain that one pulls a face like Louis Armstrong going for a top E.

**love bumps** *n. Funbags, guns of Navarone.*

**love juice** *n.* That liquid produced in the *Billingsgate box* upon which the *skin boat* sails. Often referred to as luv jooz in 1970s *scud literature. Blip, moip.*

**love palace** *n.* The *cunt.*

**love puff** *n.* Gentle, romantic *air biscuit* launched in the direction of one's partner in bed, often the morning after a *Ruby,* in an attempt to cement the intimacy of the moment.

**love sausage** *n.* Big pink *banger* served with *hairy love spuds.*

**love socket** *n.* Vagina, entry point for the *main cable.* Also *rocket socket, serpent socket, spam socket.*

**love spuds** *n.* Root vegetable found in the *shreddies.*

**love torpedo** *n.* Penis.

**love truncheon** *n. Love torpedo.*

**love tunnel** *n.* That place in which *Percy* the small engine shunts his *load.*

**low hanging fruit** *1. n. polit.* Funding which can easily be cut during a budget. *2. n. Nads* that hang out of low-cut shorts.

**LRF** *abbrev.* Low Resolution Fox – a female who appears to be attractive from a long distance, but is in fact unbelievably ugly close up.

**lucky Pierre** *n.* In *botting* circles, the busiest *botting* link in a three man *bum chain,* the filling in a *shirt lifter* sandwich. A *botter* who is simultaneously a *bottee.*

**lumberjill** *n.* A hatchet-faced woman that fells one's *wood.*

**lunchbox lancer** *n. arch.* Medieval term for a *cocoa shunter. 'Fear not the French, for their knights are without heart, and their King without wisdom. But keep thine backs as to the wall, for amongst their number thou shalt find more than a few lunchbox lancers, I can tell you.'* (from *'Henry V part III'* by William Shakespeare).

**lunchbox** *n.* In British tabloid journalism, that conspicuous bulge which appears in athlete Linford Christie's shorts.

**lunching at the Lazy Y** *v. Dining out* cowboy style, on *hairy pie,* beans and coffee.

**lung butter** *n.* Phlegm, *green smoking oysters.*

**lung warts** *n. Stits, fried eggs. Parisian breasts.*

**lychees** *n.* A sweeter, more exotic *knacker*-speak alternative to *plums.*

# Mm

**M32** *n.* A *titfuck*, ie. the most direct route for *coming* into the *Bristol* area.

**mac in the bath, I wouldn't wear my** *exclam.* Expression of a gentleman's unwillingness to don a prophylactic sheath on his *cock* end. In the same vein as *'I wouldn't wear my wellies on the beach.'*

**mack** *n.* Penis, *tadger.*

**mackerel** *1. n.* Pimp, controller of prostitutes. A *tart farmer. 2. n.* The *tarts* he farms.

**mad as a lorry** *adj.* About as *radge* as it is possible to be.

**Madam Palm and her five sisters** *n.* A *wank. 'I'm nipping off to bed with Madam Palm and her five sisters.'* See also *Palmela Handerson.*

**magic sheet** *n.* An enchanted blanket, often seen in American TV movies which clings to an actress through some invisible force, covering her *knockers.*

**magicking the beans** *v.* Gareth Hunt's *wanking* action.

**mailed and sent** *rhym. slang.* On *the other bus.*

**main cable** *n.* One's live seed feed into the *love socket.*

**make a bald man cry** *v.* Masturbate. *'Have you seen Kylie's arse on the front page of the FT today? It's enough to make a bald man cry.'*

**make babies** *v.* To go *bone jumping*, to fornicate.

**make like a Chinese helicopter pilot** *v.* Masturbate, *grin like a wanking Jap* whilst *polishing the joystick.*

**make your shit hang sideways** *v.* To be annoying. *'That Matthew Kelly really makes my shit hang sideways.'*

**mambas** *n.* Mammaries, *mumbas.*

**mammaries** *n.* Mammary glands, *swinging pink milk churns, knockers.*

**mammary dandruff** *n.* Morning-after residue from a *sausage sandwich*, remains of a *pearl necklace.*

**man eggs** *n.* Sperms.

**man fanny** *1. n.* A changing room entertainment whereby a bare gentleman impersonates a bare lady. A *cockafanny. 2. n.* A risible goatee beard sported by polytechnic lecturers and forty-five year olds who have just bought a motor bike.

**man mayonnaise** *n.* Gentleman's relish, *hanging salad cream.* Semen.

**man of the cloth** *n*. Our *farter*, who, despite fervent prayer, finds that he has besoiled his raiments. A *through-follower*.

**man overboard** *n*. A *bald man in a boat* whom you fear has become detatched from his mooring, but which turns out to be a pellet of compressed toilet paper.

**man trap** *n*. Female genitals, *hairy love pit, one-eyed trouser snake snare*.

**mandruff** *n*. Flakes of dried *lovepiss* found on one's wife's head and shoulders.

**manfat** *n*. Semen. Also *man milk*.

**mangina . mange** *n*. The badly-sewn Cornish pasty-like seam running along the underside of the scrotum that stops one's *clockweights* falling out.

**manging** *adj*. *Minging*.

**mangos** *n*. See *jelly water mangos*.

**manhood** *n*. In British tabloid journalism, the penis.

**mannery glands** *n*. A portly gentleman's dugs. *Bitch tits*.

**manshee** *n*. One who could conceivably be a man or a woman.

**map of Africa** *n*. The cartographical stain left on the bed sheet and often the mattress below after an exchange of bodily fluids. Also *map of Ireland*.

**mapatasi** *n*. *Aus*. *Minge*. From 'Map of Tasmania', the small hairy island that smells of fish off the south east coast of Australia.

**marabou stork** *n*. A *fixed bayonet, the old Adam*. An erection.

**maracas** *n*. *Knackers, clackers*, those that swing beneath *tallywhackers* making a rattling sound.

**marge** *n*. A loose woman. origin. Margarine, which 'spreads easily'. Also *Flora*.

**margold** *n*. The common male ability to do five *pop shots* in two hours. To do a margold. After a boast by *grumble* thespian Bill Margold on Channel 4 's 'After Dark.'

**Marianas trench** *1. n*. The deepest recorded sub-marinal depression on Earth, found in the Pacific ocean and reaching a depth of 35,839 feet below sea level. *2. n*. A *fanny* like a fucking bucket.

**marks of Mecca** *n*. Carpet burns on the knees caused by

excessive worship at the *hairy temple.*

**marks out of two?** *interog.* From one ogling male to another, to cue the reply *'I'd give her one.'*

**Marley arse** *n.* Accumulated *winnitage,* leading to *anal dreadlocks.* To let your *tagnuts* go.

**marmalade madam** *n. 17thC. Tom, doxy, flapper, laced mutton.* A *ho'.*

**Marmite driller** *n.* Workman on the *Marmite motorway.*

**Marmite motorway** *n.* Anus, *arse, back passage.*

**Marmite stripe** *n.* Brown stain or *skidmark* found on unwashed *shreddies. Russet gusset.*

**Mary** 1. *n. Sponge, pillow biter, angel.* 2. *n. Bean flicker, carpet muncher.* 3. *n.* A *liver sock.*

**Mary Chipperfield** *n.* A *wank* ie. *spank the monkey.* From the famous circus chimp dominatrix of the same name.

**Mary Hinge** *n.* Spooneristic *biffer.*

**Mary Poppins' bag** *n.* A surprisingly roomy *fanny.* A *clown's pocket.*

**mash** *v.* To fondle a ladies *chest spuds* as if testing them to destruction.

**massage parlour wank** 1. *sim.* Something that is performed quickly and efficiently. *'And the wheel change and refuelling was performed like a massage parlour wank by the Ferrari mechanics and Schumacher should exit the pit lane still in the lead.'* (Murray Walker, *Belgian Grand Prix*). 2. *sim.* Something that is expensive and over too quickly, eg. the Pepsi Max ride at Blackpool.

**masturmentary** *n.* TV programme with a high *tit* and *fanny* count with a token bit of information thrown in to justify its showing. eg. a behind the scenes look at the porn film industry. The staple fare of late night channel 5.

**mayor's hat** *n.* A *fanny* often eaten by goats.

**McArthur park** 1. *n.* A 70's maudlin ballad by Richard Harris. 2. *n.* A particularly evil *dropped gut* that gives the impression that 'something inside has died'.

**McSplurry** *n.* The type of *grimshit* one experiences after dining for a week solely at a fast food restaurant. *Bubblepoo.*

**McSuck** *n.* An *horatio* delivered with a force equivalent to that required to drink a newly poured McDonald's Thick Shake.

**me** *n.* Personal pronoun used at the end of a sentence to emphasise preference. *'For all these wenches are beauteous fair, and I doth admire them all, me.'* (from *'Romeo and Juliet'* Act III, Scene 2, by William Shakespeare).

**meat and two vag** *n.* A *three-some* involving two ladies and a smiling man who keeps pinching himself.

**meat and two veg** *n.* A gentleman's *undercarriage.* A *pork sausage* and *love spuds.*

**meat flute** *n. Pink oboe.*

**meat injection** *n.* An inoculation against virginity.

**meat market** *n.* Bar or club where *birds* with short skirts and blotchy legs dance with their handbags, waiting for a *pull.* A *meat rack, buttock hall.*

**meat movie** *n. Grumble flick.*

**Meatloaf's daughter** *n.* A big boned *mud-child.* A *dreadnought.*

**mechanical dandruff** *n.* Royal Air Force *crabs.*

**Melbourne** *n.* A soft *cock.*

**melching** *v. Minge felching.*

**melon farmer** *exclam.* The BBC-authorised, poorly-dubbed version of *Mother Fucker* used in films such as 'Die Hard' and the entire 'Beverly Hills Cop' series. Also *ever-loving, muddy funster.*

**melons** *n.* Female breasts. A large 'pear'.

**melvin** *v.* To grab by the *balls.*

**Melvyn** *1. rhym. slang.* A cigarette. From Melvyn Bragg~ fag. *2. rhym slang.* Sexual intercourse. From Melvyn Bragg~ shag. *'Me and the missus always light up a nice Melvyn after we've had a quick Melvyn.'*

**men in the rigging** *n. naval.* Small *tagnuts* trapped in the hairs of sailors' *arses. 'Six months since leaving Tahiti and no sign of land. We ate the last of the breadfruit weeks ago. Water and toilet paper strictly rationed. Crew growing restless, complaining of scrofula, scurvy and men in the rigging. Lord help us.'* (from *'The Diary of Fletcher Christian'*, 1789).

**menage a une** *n. Fr.* A one-in-a-bed *romp.* A *wank.*

**men-stool cycle** *n.* The happy period of a man's life when his *shit* appears at the same time every day.

**merchant** *rhym. slang. Kuwaiti tanker.*

**merkin** *n.* Man-made *mapatasi*, a *stoat syrup*, *pubic Irish*.

**mermaid's flannel** *n.* Descriptive of a very, very, very wet *fanny*. Also *otter's pocket, clown's pie*.

**merry monk** *rhym. slang.* The happy result of *pulling the Pope's cap off.*

**Mersey trout** *n.* A sweetcorn-eyed brown scouse fish.

**mess** *n.* Semen, *gunk, cock hockle.* That which is lost when one *chucks one's muck.*

**Mexican lipstick** *n.* The embarrassing *Thompson's tide marks* often found after *eating out* with a lady who was *up on blocks*. A *pasata grin.*

**Mexican picnic** *n.* SVSA, a *drugs bust.*

**Mexican barbecue** *n.* SVSASO. A *drugs bust* with a *cock* in the mouth for good measure.

**Mexican screamers** *n. medic.* A gastroenterological disorder characterised by fiery liquid excrement. *Tijuana brass-eye, Mexican shat dance.*

**Mexican suicide** *n.* To die peacefully in one's sleep. *'It is announced with deep regret and sadness that Her Royal Highness Princess Margaret committed Mexican suicide at 6.32 this morning at St George's Hospital.'* (Buckingham Palace press release, 9th February, 2002).

**mezoomas** *n. Pink velvet cushions* on which the *family jeweller* prefers to display a *pearl necklace.*

**Michaels** *rhym. slang.* Piles. From the 1970s TV game show host Michael Miles. *'These nylon trollies don't half chafe me Michaels.'*

**Mickey** *n. Irish. Dick.*

**middle leg** *n.* Penis. Also *middle stump, third leg.*

**mid-loaf crisis** *n.* Anything that spoils the enjoyment of a good *tom tit.* eg. a doorbell or telephone ringing, a dawning realisation that there is no *bumwad*, or a policeman approaching the shop doorway.

**mighty wurlitzer** *1. n.* An enormous organ. *2. n.* Reginald Dixon's *cock.*

**mile 'I' club** *n.* Similar to the Mile High Club, but for the solitary traveller. To *spin one's own propellor* in an aeroplane toilet.

**milk of human kindness** *n.* See *liquid rage.*

**milk race** 1. *n.* Adolescent *wanking* game for two or more public school children. 2. *n.* A barrack room *toss-up* to decide who eats the last cream cracker.

**milk the cow with one udder** *v.* To be the only hand in the *farmyard area.*

**milk the snake** *v.* To practice *self abuse.*

**milkman** *n.* That which comes, bringing yoghurt in the mornings.

**milkman's bonus** *n.* An unexpected gift after delivering the *cream* to Mrs Brown. A *winnet on a stick, shitty dick.*

**milkman's gait** *n.* The walk adopted by someone who has *overshagged.*

**millennium domes** *n.* The contents of a Wonderbra, ie. very impressive when viewed from the outside, but there's actually *fuck all* in there worth seeing. Disappointing *tits.*

**milm** *v.* To cover something in jism. *'Oy, mum, I've milmed me kex.'*

**mince medallions** *n.* Dangleberries, kling-ons.

**miner's sock** *n.* A perspiring, debris-laden *fanny* after a hard day's graft.

**ming** 1. *v. Scot.* To emit a foul smell, to *hum. 'Hoots mon, it's minging in here!'* 2. *v.* To exude ugliness. *'In the 80s Peter Beardsley's perm was minging.'* 3. *n.* The bill, the *scuffers,* the *bizzies.* 4. *n.* A new marijuana cigarette made up from discarded ends. A tramp's spliff. 5. *n. prop.* The evil Emperor in 'Flash Gordon.'

**Ming the merciless** *n.* An exceptionally foul-smelling *fart.*

**minge binge** *n.* The frantic fish-eating spree of the *gash gannet.*

**minge mat** *n. Mapatasi, velcro triangle.*

**minge** *n. Fanny, quim.*

**minge winker** 1. *n.* Striptease artist. 2. *n.* She who flashes her *gash,* eg. whilst folding her legs.

**minglewank** *n.* A surreptitious *tug* performed through the trouser pocket in a crowded place, eg, on a tube train, in a supermarket, at a funeral.

**mini series** *1. n.* A troublesome *log* that requires several flushes to see it off. *2. n.* A pile of *shite* starring Jane Seymour.

**minihughie** *n.* A mouthful of *spew* that can be discreetly swallowed back down. The *vurp's* big brother.

**mink** *n.* A more up-market name for the wife's *beaver.*

**minky** *1. n.* A French monkey. *2. n.* A species of whale. *3. n.* A *hornbag.* An attractive female.

**minnie moo** *n. Minge.*

**minute man** *n. medic.* One afflicted with the hilarious and shameful condition of premature ejaculation. A *two push Charlie*, a *point and squirt merchant.*

**Miss Lincolnshire** *n.* Any woman with *spaniel's ears.* 'And this year's Miss Lincolnshire is... Patsy Kensit.'

**missionary impossible** *n.* A lady with a *lovely personality* who can only be *poked* in the *doggy position.* A *lumberjill*, a *bobfoc.*

**Mobe** *n.* Abbreviation of Moby Dick. An epic *turd*, longer than a mini series, which

may require harpooning with the lavatory brush to see it off.

**mobile throne** *n.* A portable *shit house* that everyone avoids at pop festivals because the floor is two inches deep in *turds.*

**mohair knickers** *n.* Large, unruly *minnie moo*, one with *spiders legs.* A *biffer.*

**moip** *n.* Female genital lubrication. *Froth, fanny grease, vagoline.*

**moist and meaty** *adj.* Alliterating adjectives used extensively to describe the female and male genitals respectively, as well as dog food.

**mole at the counter** *euph.* A mammalian *turtle's head.* "From the imprint of his shoes, Watson, I deduce that our quarry is a left-handed doctor of unusually short stature, who has known prosperity but has lately fallen on hard times. And by the short, irregular length of his stride, it is apparent that he has a mole at the counter,' said Holmes.' (from 'The Case of the Speckled Bowl' by Sir Arthur Conan Doyle).

**money shot** *n.* The moment in a *bongo flick* where the

leading man makes a small deposit from *Kojak's money box*, usually into the leading lady's face. A *pop shot*.

**monk's cowl** *n.* A *wizard's sleeve*.

**monk's hood** *n.* A voluminous *Jacky Danny*. A *wizard's sleeve*, a *hippo's mouth*.

**monkey feather** *exclam.* Bizarre substitute for *m******f***** dubbed into Eddie Murphy films on BBC1 to avoid offending some stupid old cunt. Also *mother father, money farmer, melon farmer, muddy funster*.

**monkey** *n.* Vagina. *'Does the monkey want a banana?'* A *toothless gibbon*.

**monkey's chin** *n. Twix lips, beetle bonnet*, a prominent *mound of Venus*.

**monkey's fag break** *n.* Like slipping out for five minutes for a fag, but substituting the cigarette for *self abuse*. A *wank* at work.

**monkey's forehead** *1. n. velcro triangle, mapatasi. 2. n.* The front top bit of Sunderland manager Peter Reid's head.

**monkey's tail** *n.* A small lick of *turd* on the rear of the seat caused by sitting too far back

whilst *dropping the kids off at the pool.*

**monkey's toe** *n.* A nipple big enough to peel a banana. A *Westminster Abbey hatpeg*.

**Montezuma's revenge** *n. medic. Mexican screamers*, the *shits. Tijuana cha-cha*.

**moo** *n.* A name to call one's wife when one thinks the word 'cow' is too offensive. *'Where's me bladdy tea, eh? You fucking stupid old moo.'*

**mooey** *n.* A *sausage wallet*.

**moon** *v.* A rugby move, where the prop forward sprints around the defending back four to the rear of the bus and presses his naked *arse* up to the back window.

**Moonie** *1. n. prop.* A follower of the Rev. Ying Tong Yiddel-I Moon. *2. n.* An act of *mooning*.

**moose knuckles** *n. Can. Camel's feet, Ninja's toe*.

**moose** *n. Boiler, steg*. Often a feminist with hairy armpits.

**moped** *n.* Fat woman. Fun to *ride*, but you wouldn't tell your mates about it.

**more tea vicar?** *phr.* Faux-farcical attempt to distract clergyman after the launch of an *air biscuit*, now widely used to diffuse post *fart* tension. Other popular post flat-ulous remarks include; *sew a button on that, catch that one and paint it blue, good health!, pin a tail on that* and *there goes the elephant.*

**morgan** *rhym slang. Arse.* From Morgan Stanley Dean Witter ~ *shitter.*

**morning glory** *n.* The appearance of a *tent pole* first thing in the morning. A *dawn horn.*

**morning thunder** *n.* The first, usually very powerful *fart* of the day.

**moss cottage** *n.* The ideal home for *John Thomas.*

**mothball diver** *n.* One who savours *granny's oysters.*

**Mother Hubbard's dog** *sim.* Descriptive of an underused *minge*, ie, drooling and *gagging* for a *bone*. *'It's noo a score and seven years since her beloved Bonny Prince Albert passed awa'. Today, whilst oot aside the loch, Her Majesty confided in me that she missed his big wullie affy bad, and that most o' the time, her wee royal badger was akin tae Mother Hubbard's dog.'* (from *'The Life of John Brown, the Memoirs of a Royal ghillie'*).

**motion thickness** *n. Travel fat.*

**motor cycle kick stand** *n.* The morning erection that manifests itself whilst one is asleep on one's side, prevent-ing one from rolling over onto one's stomach.

**mott** *1. n.* A lady from Cum-bria. *2. n.* Part of a Norman fort from GCSE history. *3. n.* A *minge, mapatasi.*

**mound of Venus** *n.* Craggy outcrop above *salmon canyon* usually hidden by a dense covering of *bush*. A *beetle bon-net, monkey's forehead, grassy knoll.*

**mount** *v.* To *hop on* for *a bit.*

**mountbattens** *n.* Small frag-ments of shattered *turds* found floating in the toilet.

**mouse's ear, fanny like a** *sim.* A tight *minnie moo*. A *butler's cuff.*

**mouse's tongue** *sim.* Descrip-tive of a very small penis.

**mouth-to-muff** *n.* Lesbotic resuscitation technique. Also *quimlich manoeuvre.*

**Mr Brown is at the window** *euph.* To have the *turtle's head*. First used by Queen Victoria. *'Pray forgive us, Mr. Gladstone, but we cannot receive you at the moment.*

*Mr. Brown is at the window, and we fear we may papper our kex.'*

**Mr Happy's business suit** *n.* Condom.

**Mr Jones** *1. n. 19thC.* Penis. *2. n.* A butcher who frequently purports that 'they don't like it up 'em.'

**Mr Sausage** *n.* The excitable trouser man.

**Mr Whippy** *1. n.* Semi-viscous ice-cream that comes out a tap in a van. From 60p. *2. n.* Flagellation, corporal punishment dished out at *rub-a-tug shops.* From £25.

**Mr Whippy's in town** *euph.* Declaration that all is not well in the *chamber of horrors.*

**Mr. Bond** *n.* A particularly buoyant *turd* that returns to the surface of the water even after flushing. *'Ah, so we meet again, Mr. Bond.'*

**muck** *n. Mess, baby bouillon, load.* That which is *shot.*

**muck spreader** *n. Arse, bum.*

**mucksavage** *n.* A *bumpkin*, a *buffle*, a *cabbagehead.* A *joskin.*

**mucky** *n.* Any item of a pornographic nature, book, video, etc. *'Have you got any mucky*

*I can borrow?' 'Yes, but don't get any spragg on it this time.'*

**mud** *1. n.* Excrement. *2. n.* Excrement 70s pop group.

**mud button** *n. winnit, dangleberry, tagnut, clinker, etc.*

**mud hole** *n.* That *hole* from which one *blows mud.* A *crop sprayer, cable layer.*

**mud valve mechanic** *n.* A *brown pipe engineer.*

**mudchild** *n.* A *sweaty morph.*

**muddy funster** *1. n.* A *botter. 2. n.* A *melon farmer.*

**mudeye** *n. Arse, ringpiece,* one's old-fashioned plastic *tea towel holder.*

**muff** *1. n. Minge, fanny. 2. v.* To *shag*, have intercourse with. *3. v.* To fluff, miss an easy goal-scoring opportunity, eg. *'Oh fuck! Andy Cole has muffed it.'*

**muff diver** *n.* A footballer who misses an easy goal scoring opportunity, then falls over in an attempt to win a penalty kick.

**muff diver's dental floss** *n.* Female pubic hair.

**muff huff** *n.* Menstruation moodiness or PMT. A *period drama*, a *blob strop.*

**muff nudge** *n.* The light brushing of a female hairdresser's *beetle bonnet* against one's elbows when she leans forward to cut one's hair.

**muffia** *n.* A collection of criminal women, or women married to criminals.

**muffin** *1. n.* Flour-based bakery product. *2. n.* 1960s TV mule whose name remains a source of perpetual hilarity among the elderly and infirm.

**muffle** *v.* The female equivalent of *zuffle*.

**muffocation** *n.* The inability to breathe when a *dirty lady* is sitting on one's face.

**mug stains** *n.* Large, dark, flat *jockeys* that often appear during pregnancy.

**Mugabe** *n.* The frankly silly postage stamp-sized tuft of *muff turf* left above the *fannies* of certain porn actresses and *jazz mag* models.

**mullered** *adj. Langered.*

**mullet** *n.* Inbreds' haircut favoured by country and western singers and eighties footballers.

**mulligan** *n. Aus.* Penis.

**mumbas** *onomat.* Breasts. If *oomlaaters* made a noise, they would say 'mumbas' in a deep, fruity baritone.

**mumblers** *n.* Tight women's bicycle shorts through which you 'see the lips move but can't understand a word.'

**mumph** *onamat.* See *flub*.

**mumrar** *n.* The act of sneaking up behind your mother and shouting RAR!

**munch bunch** *n.* A gang of *dykes*.

**mung** *n.* Particularly runny type of *arse feta*.

**mungos** *n.* Great big sideburns as worn by Jerry Dorsey, lead singer of Mungo Jerry. *Bugger's grips, face fannies.*

**municipal cockwash** *n. Town bike, box of assorted creams, buttered bun.*

**muscle Mary** *n.* An extremely well-built *ginger beer.*

**musical vegetables** *n.* Baked beans, as eaten by cowboys and *trouser trumpeters.*

**musk mask** *n.* To wear a lady's *undercrackers* as a balaclava whilst having a right good *wank.*

**mustang** *n.* Of *shitty arses*, that stubborn *dangleberry* which cannot be shaken off.

**mutton musket** *n.* A smaller, more portable field weapon than the *lamb cannon.* Also *mutton bayonet, mutton dagger.*

**mutt's nuts** *adj.* Descriptive of something which is very good. The *dog's bollocks.*

**mystic smeg** *n.* See *wank séance.*

# Nn

**nadbag** *n. Nutsack, pod pouch, scrot sling.* The *jizzbags.*

**nadpoles** *n. Nadbag tadpoles. Spunks.*

**nads** *n. Knackers,* testicles, *plums.*

**nan's grin** *n.* A *shaven haven.* A *toothless gibbon,* a *Barthez.*

**nature's make-up** *n.* A range of black and blue eye cosmetics favoured by the wives of many British sportsmen.

**nauticals** *rhym. slang.* Piles. From nautical miles.

**navigator of the windward pass** *n. Rear admiral.*

**NBR** *abbrev.* No Beers Required. A good looking woman. Opposite of a *five pinter.*

**Neapolitan knickers** *n.* The disgusting state of a proper old *slapper's gusset.* Vanilla, strawberry, chocolate, the lot.

**necking turds** *v.* Descriptive of one suffering from halitosis. *'Excuse me, madam, I don't wish to appear rude, but have you been necking turds?'*

**neddies** *n. Nellies.*

**nellies** *n. Knockers, tits, neddies.*

**Neptune's kiss** *n.* The cold, wet smacker on the *arse* caused by *splashback.*

**nether eye** *n.* That single *unseeing eye,* situated in the *nether region,* which cries brown, lumpy tears.

**nether throat** *n.* In *farting,* the *poot chute, botty bugle.* *'Pardon me while I clear my nether throat.'*

**nettie** *n.* Outside loo, *clart cabin, shite house. Dunny, cludgie.*

**niags** *rhym. slang. Nuts.* From Niagra Festicles ~ testicles.

**nick bent** *adj.* Temporarily travelling on the *other bus* whilst staying at Her Majesty's pleasure.

**nick one to the wicketkeeper** *v.* To fail to avoid the follow-on whilst wearing white trousers.

**niftkin's bridge** *n.* Female equivalent of the *biffin bridge* or *barse.*

**night watchman** *n.* A *copper bolt* that has failed to flush away and is discovered the next morning.

**NIN** *acronym. medic.* Normal in Norfolk. Doctor's shorthand implying that your physical and mental characteristics indicate that your mother is possibly also your sister, cousin aunt, and perhaps even your father.

**nine-bob-note, as bent as a** *sim.* Gay.

**ninja's toe** *n.* Camel's foot.

**nip and tuck** *n.* The act of *nipping off* one of *Bungle's fingers* at the knuckle, with the result that the stump is retracted cleanly into the *bomb bay.* The correct response to a *mid-loaf crisis.*

**nipping Christian** *n.* A cutpurse, a thief.

**nipping the turtle** *v. Crimping off a length, shutting the bomb bay doors.*

**nipsy** *n. medic.* The pincerlike muscle just inside *Ena Sharples' mouth* that cuts one's *Bungle's finger* to length when contracted.

**no score drawers** *n.* Unflattering ladies' undergarments worn when the *pools panel are sitting* and the dividend forecast is low.

**nob** *1. n.* A hay clarse, hoitytoity person. A toff. *2. n.* A small piece of butter. *3. v.* To *fuck*, penetrate with the *knob.*

**Nobbies** *rhym. slang.* Haemorrhoids. From 1966 toothless footballer Sir Norbert Stiles ~ piles.

**nocturnal emission** *n. medic.* End result of a wet dream.

**Noddy book** *n. Bongo mag.*

**Noddy Holder's sideburns** *sim.* Descriptive of a particularly luxuriant ginger *bush,* the kind that Charlie Dimmock probably has.

**noddy** *n.* Condom, *French letter, cock 'holder'.*

**nodge** *v.* To observe the sexual activity of others. To *voy*, to *dog.*

**nodger** *n. Peeping Tom, voyeur.* A *merchant* who prefers 'live' *grumble* rather than the recorded variety.

**nookie** *1. n.* Sex, only a bit of which it is advisable to have at anyone time. *2. n. prop.* A humorous name for a ventriloquist's bear.

**nooner** *n.* See *funch.*

**nork hammock** *n.* Of female fashions, a halter neck top.

**norks** *n. Tits, knockers.* Also *norkers, norgs, norgers.*

**Norma Snockers** *n.* Wieldy *bojangles.* See also *Gert Stonkers.*

**Norman Cook** *n.* A measure of alcohol which after being drunk can make a *Fat Bird Slim.* Approximately two *St. Ivels.*

**norton** *n. Bearded clam.*

**NORWICH** *acronym. milit.* Cipher used on military correspondence – Knickers Off Ready When I Come Home. First used during WWI, when Norwich was known as Korwich.

**nosh off** *v.* To perform *philately* on a man.

**nosh out** *v.* To perform *philately* on a woman.

**notcher** *n. Biffin bridge.* The area of skin between the *clockweights* and the *starfish*, so called because it's 'notcher' *bollocks* and it's 'notcher' *arse.*

**nudger** *1. n.* Gay male. *2. n.* What a *nudger* uses to *nudge fudge.*

**nuggets** *1. n.* Testicles. *2. n.* Any inedible part of a chicken or turkey, when coated in batter or breadcrumbs. eg, the *nuggets.*

**number one** *euph.* A *penny, tinkle.*

**number threes** *n.* Vomit.

**number two** *euph.* A *sit down, tuppence*, a *duty.*

**nunga munching** *v.* The ganneting of *hairy pie*, the doing of *cumulonimbus.*

**nunnery** *n.* Elizabethan name for a *rub-a-tug shop* from an age when nuns were widely believed to wear *yo-yo knickers.*

**nurfing,** *v. Garbooning, nerding, pooning, shniffle-piffling, snaffling, snarfing, snarzing, snerking, snerdling, snerging.* The presumably very common act of sniffing ladies' bicycle seats.

**nut butter** *n.* A lightly-salted dairy product served hot from the male *churns* onto *baps.*

**nut chokers** *n.* Gentlemen's tight *shreddies, budgie smugglers.*

**nut custard** *n. Banana yoghurt.*

**nut sack** *n.* Scrotum, *nad bag.*

**nutmegs** *n. Balls* that hang down right between a footballer's legs.

**nuts** *1. n. Knackers,* scrotum and/or its contents. *'I'm going to shave my nuts'. 2. adj.* Mad. *'Shave your nuts? You must be nuts'. 3. n.* Things that monkeys eat. *'That monkey's nuts. I gave it some nuts and it's rubbing them on its nuts.'*

**nymph** *1. n.* The caterpillar of a dragonfly. *2. n.* A sexy young *bird.*

**nympho** *n.* Sex-crazed *bird* that's *gagging* for it 24 hours a day, 7 days a week. The sort who would *shag* a pneumatic drill and blow up the generator.

**NYPD blue** *n.* A *poke,* where the *pokee* assumes the position of someone being frisked by New York's finest, against the wall or on the bonnet of a car.

# Oo

**oats** *n*. A *portion* of that which one gets during sex with a Quaker.

**off the team** *adj*. To be forbidden from playing on the *furry turf*. To be in your missus's bad books.

**off your face** *adj*. *Ripped to the tits* on the demon drink.

**off your trolley** *adj*. Hatstand, mental.

**oil tanker** *rhym. slang*. *Onanist*.

**oil the bat** *v*. *Polish the pork sword, wax the dolphin*.

**oil the truncheon** *v*. To buff up the *bobby's helmet, collect kindling, wank*.

**oily loaf** *n*. A well-baked *turd*.

**OJ's glove** *1. n*. The state of the hand after *finger banging* a lady during *ragweek*. *2. n*. An extremely tight fitting *liver sock*.

**old holborn** *n*. The frayed edges of the *velcro triangle*, a *pant moustache. Spiders' legs*.

**old man** *n*. Penis. *'The old man's been out of work for six months. Most days we play pocket billiards to keep him occupied.'* Also *old fella*.

**old shocker, the** *n*. To surprise one's sexual partner by poking a cheeky *pinkie* up the *chuff* during intercourse. *"I say, Bertie. You'll never guess what,' gasped Piggy excitedly. 'I've just been in a clinch with Marjorie in the rose garden. Just as I got to the vinegar strokes, she popped me the old shocker. Quite took me aback, don't you know."* (from 'Now Start Humming, Jeeves' by PG Wodehouse).

**oldest toad in the pond** *n*. A particularly low, vociferous, grumbling *fart*, usually after eight pints of stout and a bar of Bournville.

**olivia** *v*. To have sex with several filthy tramps on a *piss*-stained mattress, all at once.

**omelette maker** *n. Sp*. A lesbian.

**on the bench** *adj*. After being *off the team*, to be optimistic that you may be given a late chance to score. To be in your missus's slightly better books. *'After the shameful episode with the exotic dancer I have alas been off the team these last six weeks. Today I bought my darling Victoria a bunch of flowers from the all-night garage, and I think I am on the bench.'* (from 'The Journal of Prince Albert').

**on the blob** *adj*. To be *riding*

*the menstrual cycle, to have the painters in, fallen to the communists.*

**on the bonk** *adj. Sergeant Sausage* when standing to attention.

**on the hoy** *adj. On the piss, on the razz, hoying* it down one's neck, and then back up again onto one's shoes.

**on the job** *adj. At it.* Busying oneself with one's partner's plumbing.

**on the nest** *adj.* To be treating one's *bird* to a big juicy *worm.*

**on the other bus** *adj.* Homosexual, *bowling from the Pavilion end.*

**on the pull** *adj.* Fishing for *kipper, on the salmon, on the sniff.*

**on the slipway** *adj.* Of stools and stool movement, to have the *turtle's head. 'Get out of that fucking bathroom will you, I've got a dreadnought on the slipway.'*

**on the sniff** *adj. On the pull, on the tap.*

**onanism** *1. n.* Incomplete sexual intercourse. *Vatican roulette. 2. n.* A posh word what the Queen might use for *wanking* and that.

**one cheek sneak** *n.* The stealthy approach to *shooting bunnies.* From a sitting position, lifting one *buttock* in order to slide out an aurally undetectable *air biscuit.* A *cushion creeper, leg lifter.*

**one eared spacehopper** *n.* Cliff Richard's genitals. A *panhandle* on someone with *DSB.*

**one eyed pant python** *n. One eyed zipper fish.*

**one eyed trouser snake** *n.* Gentleman's *pant python, sex serpent, cock.*

**one eyed Willie** *n.* Penis.

**one eyed Willie's eye patch** *n.* Condom, *English overcoat.*

**one eyed zipper fish** *n.* A *Cyclops, trouser trout.*

**one handed mag** *n. Jazz magazine, rhythm read, art pamphlet, a grumbular* periodical.

**one holed flute** *n.* A *pink oboe,* a *blue-veined piccolo,* a *purple headed* (insert wind instrument here).

**one in the pump, to have** *1. v.* To have the *hots* for a female. *'Phoar! I've got one in the pump for her, I can tell you.' 2. n.* Drinking parlance for a pint paid for but not yet poured.

**one** *n.* The SI unit of sex, given to a woman by a man. Equivalent to 0.6 of a *portion*, and 2.36 *bits*.

**one off the crossbar** *n.* To be just not quick enough in dropping one's *trolleys* after being caught short by an unexpected visit from *Mr. Whippy*. To *beskid* the waistband of your *shreddies*.

**one off the wrist** *v. Five knuckle shuffle, wank, hand shandy.*

**oomlaaters** *n.* Very large *chumbawumbas*.

**oomph!** *n.* Sex appeal. *'By crikey, that Thora Hird, she hasn't half got some oomph!'*

**oot on the tap** *adj.* Out *on the pull*, as opposed to *on the hoy*.

**open clam shots** *n. Full-on oysters, close-up pink.* Artistic/medical adult camera angle.

**open the hangar doors** *v.* Of an experienced lady, to prepare herself for sexual intercourse. *'Wisteria was powerless to resist. His eyes burned into hers like amethysts. His muscular arms enfolded her body as she felt herself being swept away in a hurricane of passion. Gently, Renaldo laid her down on the silken ottoman in front of the roaring fire. Then, as he pulled her knickers off, she lifted her legs and opened the hangar doors.'* (from *'The lady and the South American Footballer'* by Barbara Cartland).

**open your lunchbox** *v.* To float an *air biscuit* reminiscent in aroma of yesterday's egg sandwiches.

**opera house** *n.* A large vagina with heavy pink safety curtains.

**orchestras** *rhym. slng.* The testicles. From orchestra stollocks ~*bollocks*.

**oreo** *n.* An inverse *chocolate sandwich*.

**organzola** *n. Helmetdale, bell end brie. Knob cheese.*

**orgasm** *1. n.* A *fanny bomb*, a *stack blow. 2. v.* To *ring the bell, shoot one's load, chuck one's muck.*

**Oscar** *n. US. Dick,* penis.

**other, a bit of the** *n. Hanky panky.*

**otter's nose** *n.* When getting *tops and fingers*, that which is felt by the latter. *'I got a result last night. I touched the otter's nose.'* Something wet under the bridge.

**over the shoulder boulder**

**holder** *n.* Industrial bra, heavy lifting apparatus for *jelly water mangos.*

**overblaaters** *n.* Pendulous *oomlaaters* which rest on a big round gut.

**own goal** *n.* A *fart* so obnoxious, that even he who dealt it cannot stay in its presence.

**own up** *v.* In a *breaking company* situation, to identify oneself as the *benefactor.*

**owner operator** *n. Wanker*, a knight who wields his *pork sword* for pleasure, not for the benefit of fair maidens.

**oxygen thief** *n.* A senior citizen, a *coffin dodger.*

# Pp

**pace car** *n.* Of paying a sit down visit – the slow, unaerodynamic leading *turd* that once out of the way, allows the fast, souped-up *botrods* behind it to put their foot down into the first bend.

**packet** *n.* The contents of the *kecks* visible in relief at the front of the *trolleys*. Male equivalent of the *camel's foot*. *Darcy Bussell's footrest.*

**paddle the pink canoe** *v.* To *frig*. Weekend recreational pursuit of the *gusset typist*.

**paedo-smile** *n.* A particularly sinister grin, the type a kiddie fiddler might have.

**pagga** *n.* A free-for-all fight between anyone who wants to join in.

**pagga starter** *n.* A strong beer which breaks the ice at fights. *Supermarket smack.*

**paint the baby's bedroom** *v.* To slap a bit of *gonad gloss* around the vaginal walls.

**painting the ceiling** *v.* Hitch hiking with the big top removed, the *one handed snake* charming of the *pant python*.

**paisley removal** *n.* Pointing *Percy* directly at an area of *pebble dashing* in order to amuse oneself during a Chi-

nese singing lesson. See also *piss polo*.

**palace gates** *n.* *Fanny lips, beef curtains*.

**palm Sunday** *n.* A relaxing *day of wrist* spent in one's own company in the absence of other weekend commitments.

**Palmela and her five sisters** *n. prop.* The right hand.

**Palmela Handerson** *n.* ne's dream date to go out for a cruise in the *wanking chariot*.

**palmistry** *n.* A mystic art involving the palm of the hand and the *cock*. The skilled *palmist* is able to look a few minutes into the future and foresee a period of mopping up *jizz*.

**pan handle** *n.* An erect penis, *wood, stalk*, a *bonk on*.

**pan handle pipes** *n.* A Peruvian sex act, whereby a woman blows across the top of several men's *cocks* of differing length side by side. Presumably in a shopping precinct.

**pan of burnt chips** *n. orthodont.* Descriptive of dentition that leaves a lot to be desired. *'So in she comes with another fucking fishbone stuck in her* *craw. So she opens her mouth and it's like a pan of burnt chips in there. I know she's 102, but for Christ's sake, she should have had them out years ago.'* (from *'The Memoirs of Doctor Gladstone Gamble, Balmoral GP in Residence'*).

**pan scourer** *n.* A vagina covered in a coarser grade of *muff swarf. Brillo fanny.*

**pan smile** *n.* The crescent-shaped *piss*-bleached patch of carpet that grins yellowly around the base of the toilet. The *Queen Mum's smile.*

**panaconda** *n.* A South American *dirt snake* of enormous length, that suffocates its victims if they get too close.

**panda's eye** *n.* A *ringpiece.*

**pander** *1. v.* To act as a go-between in an act of sexual intrigue. e.g, to go and buy a hamster and some parcel tape for that odd couple in the flat below. *2. n.* A large, bamboo-eating mammel.

**panderer** *1. n.* One who *panders.*

**pant hamster** *n.* Natural prey of the *one eyed trouser snake.*

**pant moustache** *n.* Effect achieved when the *mapatasi* extends symmetrically beyond

either side of the *shreddies. Thigh brows.*

**pant stripper** *n.* Any fancy alcoholic drink that more or less guarantees free access to the *hairy pie.*

**pantilever** *n. Piss handle.*

**pants** *1. interj.* Exclamation of dismay. *2. adj&n.* Rubbish, *shit, pig's arse, bollocks.* *'You're talking pants!'*

**pantymonium** *n.* A flatulent charivari. A loud volley of *farts* causing havoc in the *undercrackers.*

**pap baffle** *n.* The scrunched up piece of bog roll placed in the pan which makes the person in the next cubicle genuinely believe that your *shit* doesn't make a 'plop!' when it hits the water.

**paper cut** *n.* Opposite of a *wizard's sleeve.* A *fanny* tighter than an *OJ's glove.*

**papper** *v.* To *shit. 'Oh no, I think I just pappered me trollies.'*

**paps** *n. arch.* Olde Worlde Tittes.

**parallel parked** *adj.* In bed together, having sex, to sleep with. *'Were you parallel parked with her last night?' 'Not half! I was in up to the bumper mate.'*

**parfume de plop** *n*. Acrid odour which accompanies a *twin tone* and heralds the arrival in the *bomb bay* of a *Peter O'Toole*.

**Parisian breasts** *n*. See *lung warts*.

**park and ride** *v*. Hurried intercourse in the back seat of a parked car. A *rear-end shunt*.

**park the custard** *v*. To vomit.

**park the fudge** *v*. To *shit*, pass a stool, *crimp off a length*.

**park the pink bus** v. To *slip* a lady a *length*. *'Time for bed. Come on, let's park the pink bus in the furry garage.'*

**park the tiger** *v*. To puke, *yodel*, let out a *technicolour yawn*.

**park your breakfast** *v*. Light a *bum cigar, lay a cable*.

**parlour** *n*. Place where one is only allowed on special occasions. The *bonus tunnel*.

**parp** *1. onomat*. A romantic foreplay technique whereby one squeezes a breast in the same way that a clown would honk a car horn. *2. n. onomat*. A *fart*.

**particulars** *n*. Of low budget British sex comedies involv-

ing police officers, ladies' underwear, *knickers*. *'Excuse me, madam, but I may need to take down your particulars.'*

**parts of shame** *n*. A God botherer's genitals.

**pasata grin** *n*. *Mexican lipstick, clown's smile*.

**passion cosh** *n*. A stout, six-inch, hand-held weapon. With all veins up the side.

**passion flaps** *n*. A more romantic alternative to *piss flaps*.

**passion pit** *n*. Bed, *fart sack, scratcher, wanking chariot*.

**passion wagon** *n*. Clapped-out van, usually a Ford Transit, with blacked-out windows and a *piss*-stained mattress and several empty beer cans in the back. Also *shaggin' wagon*.

**pastie baby** *n*. An ear-ringed neonate sucking on a *Greggs dummy*.

**pathfinder** *n*. An *air biscuit* that lets one know in no uncertain terms that it's time for a *tom-tit*.

**patty** *n*. A posh lady's *snatch* ie, what HM the Queen calls her *cunt*.

**pavement pizza** *n*. The contents of your stomach as they appear after *barfing* in the street. A *parked tiger*.

**peach stone** *n.* A hibernal scrotum.

**peanut brittle** *n. medic.* Condition of a hardened drinker whose only solid intake for some days has been items available at the bar. Symptoms include mental fragility and uncontrolled shaking. *'Harry froze as they spotted an unshaven Mr. Snape slumped at the bar of the Black Cauldron. 'We're done for now', he cried. 'No we're not,' replied Hermione. 'He's been drinking all weekend and he's completely peanut brittle."* (from *'Harry Potter and the Wizard's Sleeve'* by JK Rowling).

**Pearl Harbour** *n. prop.* A place where one's *jap's eye* commits atrocities.

**pearl necklace** *n.* Those globular consequences of having a *sausage sandwich* at the *Billy Mill roundabout* that so delight the ladies.

**pebble dash** *v.* To *crop spray* the toilet bowl with *clarts*.

**pecker** *1. n. US.* Penis. *2. n. UK.* Nose.

**pee** *1. v.* To *piss. 2. n.* Some *piss.*

**peel** *1. v* . To strip, pose nude. *2. v.* When so doing, to draw back the *beef curtains*. *'Crikey, have you seen Razzle? I never knew Joanne Guest was a peeler.'*

**peeling the carrot** *v. Spanking the monkey.*

**pelican's beak** *n.* A flappy double chin that is unpleasant to look at, eg. that of Thora Hird, Hugh Lloyd.

**pelt lapper** *n.* A lady in *comfortable shoes*, a *tennis fan.*

**penguin** *1. v.* Act performed by a prostitute whereby, upon receiving payment but before providing service, she pulls the gentleman's trousers around his ankles and runs off down the alley. From the resemblance of the client's gait to that of the flightless arctic bird as he attempts to give chase, much to the amusement of onlookers. *2. n.* The trouser ankled, cheeks apart waddle adopted by one who has been surprised after *dropping the kids off at the pool* by a lack of *bumwad.*

**penile dementia** *n. medic.* The effect a *panhandle* has on its owner in the company of a *hornbag*, causing him to temporarily forget about his wife and children.

**penis fly trap** *n.* A precariously balanced toilet seat which stays vertical for a few moments before dropping upon unsuspecting *helmets* in its path. A *knob chopper.*

**penis** *n.* The *Right Honourable Member for Pantchester.*

**pensioner's leg** *n.* A thin, pale, knobbly, varicose veiny penis.

**Percy** *1. n. UK.* Penis. *'I'm just off to point Percy at the porcelain.'* *2. n.* A small green 0-6-0 saddle tank steam train named after the late Rev. W. Awdrey's small, green penis.

**period drama** *n.* Moody and erratic behaviour of women at times of menstruation. A *blobstrop, tammy huff.*

**perpetual motion** *n.* A seemingly endless *shit.*

**Perry Como** *rhym slang.* An easy listening *crafty butcher.*

**perseverance soup** *n. Jap.* The tiny tears from the *hog's eye* which precede ejaculation. The clear secretion which lubricates the glans. That which comes out of the kitchen before the main course. *Dew on the lily.*

**personalities** *n.* Tabloid euphemism for breasts. *'My,*
*you've got a lovely pair of personalities'. Charms, assets, terrible arthritis.*

**petal dick** *n.* A gentleman drinker who requires the toilet before his fifth pint. A *shandy pants, shandy pandy.*

**Peter O'Toole** *rhym. slang.* A *Thora Hird.*

**Peter two pumps** *n.* An inexperienced *swordsman.* A *two push Charlie.*

**phallucy** *n.* Any statement made by a man about the size of his *choad,* eg. in the readers' letters page of a *grumblemag* or a small ad in a *greet and meat* mag.

**phantom farter** *n.* An anonymous *benefactor.*

**philosopher's stone** *n.* A *turd* that emerges after a couple of hours' intense concentration.

**phlegm brulee** *n.* A particularly creamy *docker's omelette* with a hard crust. Usually hocked up during a hangover.

**photo finish** *n.* A session of *horizontal jogging* in which both contestants break the tape at the same time. Also *dead heat.*

**Picasso arse** *n.* A lady's *chuff* in knickers so tight that she appears to have four but-tocks.

**Picasso face** n. Descriptive of a lady who is certainly no oil painting.

**piddle** 1. v. To *pee*. 2. n. Some *pee*.

**pie blight** n. *Muff druff.*

**piece of piss** n. An easy thing. 'Hey, this show jumping thing is a piece of piss' (Christopher Reeve), 'Hey, adjusting television aerials is a piece of piss' (Rod Hull).

**pieceps** n. Bulging stomach muscles made famous by for-mer Everton goalkeeper Neville Southall.

**pie-hider** n. A *gunt, bilge tank, muff pelmet.* The kind of overhanging gut that allows a lady to strip from the waist down whilst still retaining her modesty.

**pie-liner** n. A femidom.

**pieman's wig** 1. n. An artifi-cial hairpiece worn by a pur-veyor of pastry-enveloped foodstuffs. 2. n. An untidy *cunt-rug.*

**pig at the gate** euph. A *mole at the counter.*

**pig bite** n. A poetic term for the vagina. 'A daughter of the Gods, divinely tall/ And with a pig bite like a horse's collar.' (from 'A Dream of Fair Women' by Alfred Lord Ten-nyson).

**pig's toe** n. Beetle bonnet, camel's foot.

**pigboard** n. The rear wall of a metropolitan phonebox.

**pigeon's chest** n. The female swimsuit *lunchbox.* The *bee-tle bonnet, shark's fin.*

**PIK** acronym. Pig In Knickers. An extremely unattractive fleshy woman.

**pillicock** n. arch. A *cock.* From the pig's penis used in an early form of badminton.

**pillock** n. Tame, TV sitcom-friendly insult. Possibly derived from *pillicock.*

**pillow biter** n. One who bites their pillow, often in a moment of uphill horticultur-al delight. Also *mattress muncher.*

**pills** n. Pods, knackers, niags.

**pilot light** n. An ex-socialite now restrained by the *pink handcuffs,* ie. he never goes out.

**pinballing** v. To make progress home from the booz-er by a series of ricochets from one item of street furniture to the next. Accompanied by the ringing of bells and clunking noises.

**pinch a loaf** *v. Curl one off.*

**pinch of snuff** *rhym. slang.* A *crafty butcher.*

**pineapple** *rhym. slang. Spunk.*

**pink bat's face** *n.* A nocturnal, high-pitched *fanny.*

**pink cigar** n. Penis. *'Tell me Madam, do you perchance smoke the pink cigar?'* Not to be confused with *bum cigar,* except in Germany.

**pink Darth Vader** *n. Knob.* From the Star Wars character with a *bell end* helmet. From the same film; *shake hands with the Wookie, Hand Solo.*

**pink oboe** *n.* Penis. *'Tell me Madam, do you perchance play the pink oboe?'*

**pink pillows** *n.* Ladies' *love cushions,* bosoms.

**pink steel** *n.* Even harder than *wood.*

**pink ticket** *n.* Imaginary *vadge* visa issued to a husband when he spends the night apart from his wife. *'Eureka! I've got my pink ticket for the conference on Tuesday.'*

**pink** *v.* Of a lady, to make a

*fanny slug* on a window for the amusement and edification of passers by.

**pink velvet sausage wallet** *n.* Vagina, *muff.*

**pink, the** *n.* A really good eyeful of the female genitals, esp. in a *meat mag.*

**pinksmith** *n.* One who is expert in *fannycraft.*

**pintle** *n.* Olde Worlde Penis. *Pipe cleaner.*

**pipe smoker** 1. *n. US. Botter .* 2. *n.* A person who smokes a pipe.

**pirate of men's pants** *n.* Swashbuckling term for your jolly *Rogerer, cock,* penis.

**pirate's piss** *n.* The *piss* you have with one eye shut to improve targeting after a long night on the pop.

**piss** 1. *v.* To micturate. 2. *n.* Some micturation. 3. *adv.* Extremely. eg. ~poor, ~easy.

**piss flaps** 1. *n. Labia, beef curtains.* 2. *interj.* Exclamation of disappointment. *'Oh piss flaps! I never win the Lottery!'*

**piss it up the wall** *v.* To waste money on drink.

**piss it** *v.* To do something *piss* simple, *piss* easily.

**piss mist** *n.* The fine mist that

forms around a urinal trough at shin level when having a *gypsy's kiss*. Only noticeable when wearing shorts.

**piss on your chips** *v.* To put yourself at a long-term disadvantage through a foolhardy short-term action.

**piss polo** *1. n.* Game of skill whereby disinfectant tablets are pointlessly manoeuvred in a urinal trough by the participants' *piss* streams. *2. n.* A very unsuccessful flavour of sweet.

**piss pot** *1. n.* Lavatory bowl. *2. n.* Idiot, fool. *3. n.* Old-fashioned motorcyclist's helmet.

**piss proud** *adj.* To be the owner of a *dawn horn*, a *morning glory*.

**piss rusty water** *v.* To pass liquid *feeshus*.

**piss sauna** *n.* The all-enveloping fog of urine steam in an outside pub lavatory on a cold winter's evening.

**piss up** *n.* An ale soiree, social gathering of boozing companions.

**pisshead's labourer** *n.* A barman.

**pissing in the wind** *v.* Wasting one's time, attempting the impossible.

**pit fillers** *n.* Massive *thruppeny bits* which emigrate towards a bird's oxters when she's lying on her back.

**pit prop** *n.* Strategic structural member found in a *passion pit, tent pole, dawn horn.*

**pitch a tent** *v.* To get *wood* either beneath the bed linen, or conspicuously in your trousers.

**pizzle** *n. medic.* A sorry looking *penis,* like one would imagine the Pope has.

**placket** *n. arch.* A Medieval maiden's *cunt.*

**Planter's hum** *n.* The nauseating smell of *air croutons.* From the aroma of a freshly-opened bag of dry-roasted peanuts.

**plasterer's radio** *sim.* Descriptive of one heavily adorned with *jelly jewellery.* frequently found on Japanese and American cyber-scud.

**plastic cockney** *n.* A *mockney.* A posh person who affects to be an Eastender, eg. Ben Elton, Nigel Kennedy, Shane McGowan.

**plastic paddy** *n.* A posh person who affects to be Irish, eg. Shane McGowan.

**plate** *v. Vict.* 19thC *rub-a-tug shop* parlance for performing *horatio, giving head.* Half a crown in the old money.

**play the back nine** *v. Irish golf.* To use one's *wood* to play into the bunker, *get the dog in the bathtub.*

**play the B-side** *v.* To swap from the Missionary position to the *doggie* position. *'I got fed up with looking at her face while I was giving her one, so I flipped her over and played the B-side.'*

**play the pink oboe** *v.* To perform oral sex on a man, presumably with a thin reed sticking out of his *hog's eye.* Often used to denote homosexuality. *'I didn't know Michael Barrymore played the pink oboe.'*

**play the violin** *v.* To scrape your *bow* against a lady's *G-string.* To make sweet music with a lady after merely pushing the *driptray* of her *dunghampers* to one side.

**play the whale** *v.* To *spew.*

**playing chopsticks** *v.* A beginners' duet. Mutual masturbating.

**playing snooker with a piece of string** *sim.* Trying to *sink a pink* with a *marshmallow cue.*

**playing the bone-a-phone** *v.*

*Wanking,* pulling oneself a *hand shandy,* playing the *one string banjo.*

**playing the invisible banjo** *v.* George Formby-style female masturbation technique.

**playing the upside-down piano** *sim.* The overture to the second movement of *hiding the sausage. Ferkyfoodling.*

**pleasure** *v.* Tabloidese, to *suck* or *wank off.* To perform a lewd act on oneself or on someone else.

**plinth** *v.* Of males *on the job,* to manoeuvre oneself into a comfortable position for penetration.

**plonker** *1. n.* Penis. *2. n. Crap* put-down line from Britain's favourite tedious TV sitcom.

**ploughman's** *n.* The *barse, taint, notcher* etc. The area between the cheese and the pickle. *'Mr Kneivel's motorbike hit the last bus at an approximate speed of 120mph, before careering into several fruit machines and a tuppenny waterfall. He suffered severe internal injuries including fractured ribs, two broken legs and a fractured skull. He also ripped his* *ploughman's wide open on the petrol tank.'* (Doctor's report, Las Vegas County General Hospital, 1978).

**pluke** *n.* A facial spot. A *zit.*

**plum sauce** *n.* Ejaculate.

**plumbago** *n.* painful ache in the *Gladstones* caused by over-revving the *spunk* engines without releasing the *horse's handbrake. Lover's nuts.*

**plumber's bonus** *n.* A *U-blocker* of such proportions, it has to be dealt with by some-one who has served an apprenticeship. A *windfall.*

**plumber's toolbag** *n. Furry bicycle stand, mott.*

**plumber's wipe** *n.* The art of shoving one's hand into a lady's *driptray,* and rubbing backwards and forwards, in the same way that a plumber would wipe a recently-soldered joint.

**plums** *n. Knackers, balls,* testicles.

**plunker** *n. US. Johnny,* a jumpsuit for a plonker. A *Trojan.*

**Plymouth Argyles** *rhym. slang.* Piles.

**pobolycwm** *n. Welsh.* Literally *'People who like quim.'*

**pocket billiards** *n.* A game for one player, two *balls,* and a *cock.*

**pocket fisherman** *n.* He who plays with his *tackle* through his trouser pockets.

**pocket frog** *n.* A *fart, botty burp, anal announcement.*

**pocket pinball** *n.* A game where one's testicles are fired up into one's chest, where they ricochet from organ to organ whilst bells ring and one's eyes spin round.

**pocket rocket** *1. n* A small, but powerful motorbike. *2. n.* A small, but powerful *knob.*

**pod purse** *n.* Where the loose change for a *money shot* is kept.

**poe** *n.* The *fadge.*

**poe slap** *n.* A *fanny nanny.*

**pogie** *n. US.* Where American *plonkers* go dressed in their *plunkers.*

**pogue mahone** *exclam. Gael.* Kiss my *arse,* to be sure.

**point Percy at the porcelain** *v.* To have a *wee-wee.*

**poke holes in a cheap door** *phr.* Property of a *diamond cutter. 'When Elizabeth was near, D'Arcy's heart raced, and he got a panhandle that could poke holes in a cheap* *door.'* (from *'Pride and Preju-dice'* by Jane Austen).

**poke the spider's eye** *v.* To dig at one's *claypit* through one's underpants.

**poke** *v.* What *plonkers* do to *pogies.*

**pole vault** *n.* Vagina, *stench trench*, strong room where the *spam sceptre* can be safe-ly housed.

**police horse fart** *n.* An *air buffet* capable of dispersing an unruly mob.

**policeman's dinner** *n. US.* An *arsehole.*

**policewoman's treat** *n.* A bobby's *bob.*

**polish a turd** *met.* To fruit-lessly attempt to dress up something *shite*, eg. the relaunch of the Morris Mari-na as the Ital, or putting a baseball cap on William Hague.

**polish the lighthouse** *v.* To masturbate in the bath.

**POLO** *acronym. milit.* Code used on military correspon-dence prior to coming home from a posting abroad. Pants Off, Legs Open.

**polony party** *n.* A social gath-ering of two or more consent-ing adults where party games

include *hide the sausage, park the salami* and *split the kip-per*. And one's party bag would contain a slice of cake and a dose of the *clap*. An orgy.

**pompom** *n. Jam.* A furry thing waved by cheerleaders to entertain a crowd.

**ponce** *1. n.* A *pimp. 2. n.* Brian Sewell soundalike. *3. v.* To borrow something with no intention of giving it back, eg. cigarettes, garden tools.

**pong** *n.* The smell of a *poot.*

**pony** *rhym. slang. Shit.* From pony and trap ~*crap.*

**poo** *1. exclam.* A word spoken with fingers on nostrils to describe an unpleasant odour. *2. n. Shit.*

**poo fairy** *n.* Magical entity which regularly visits the female half of the population, resulting in the male half being under the handy illu-sion that ladies never need to *lay a cable.*

**poo packer** *n.* A *dinner mash-er*, a *marmite driller.*

**poo pipe pirate** *n.* Jolly *Rogerer, pirate of men's pants.*

**poo preview** *n.* An *air buffet*, an *Exchange and Mart.*

**poo tea** *n.* An unrefreshing brown infusion made by

allowing *logs* to brew in the pot for a long time.

**Poocomknockerphilication** *n.* *Cleveland steaming*, as performed by Ken Dodd.

**poof** *n.* A *woolly woofter*.

**poofter** *n.* A *Bertie woofter*.

**poomerang** *n.* A *turd* which is able to return from the U-bend with twice the force with which it was flushed away in the first place.

**poon** *n.* *Fanny, crumpet, toosh.* *'I guess, this means my poon days are over.'* (Abraham Lincoln after his inauguration in May 1776). *'Knickers off, this is poon city!'* (Bill Clinton after his inauguration in June 1993).

**poond** *n.* A *gunt*, a *fupa*. From the Geordie 'a poond o' tripe'.

**pooning** *v.* The act of sniffing ladies' bicycle seats.

**poontang** *1. n.* A *fanny*. *2. n.* Some *fanny*.

**poop catchers** *n.* *Knickers, dung hampers, bills.*

**poop chute** *n.* *Bumhole, arse.*

**poosex** *n.* A nice, innocent word for anal intercourse.

**poosticks** *n.* Game whereby lolly sticks are inserted into *barkers' eggs* by curious children. *'What are you doing?'* *squeaked Piglet excitedly. 'I'm pushing a lolly stick into a dog shit,' replied Christopher Robin.'* (from *'When we were very, very young'* by AA Milne).

**poot flute** *n.* *Trouser trumpet, singing ring, botty bugle, bumhole.*

**poot** *v.* To sound one's *botty bugle*, often after eating *musical vegetables*.

**pooter** *n.* The *bum* bellows with which you *poot*. The *poot flute*.

**poove** *n.* A *puff*, a *ginger beer*, a *pinch of snuff*.

**poovery** *n.* *Bottery* and everything associated therewith.

**pop her cork** *v.* To give a lady an orgasm. Presumably by pushing her *clit* up with one's thumbs.

**pop shot** *n.* Scene in a *grumbleflick* in which a male actor is required to splash his *population paste* for the camera, after being suitably prepared by the *fluffer*. See *margold*.

**pop your cherry** *v.* Lose one's virginity, *break one's duck*.

**popazogalou** *n.* A *chewie*, a *gobble*, a *blow job*. From the name of the landlord in the film 'Personal Services' who accepted payment in kind.

**Popeye eating spinach** *sim.* To engage in enthusiastic *cumulonimbus*. With a pipe in one's mouth. *'And the husband of Bathsheba did venture forth for Regal Super Kings that numbered two score and did leave Bathsheba alone in the tent. And David did enter the tent and did know Bathsheba. And David did kneel before Bathsheba, and lo, he did go at it like Popeye eating spinach.'* (from *'The Book of Clive'* Chapter 6, vv 3-5).

**poppycock** *n.* Nonsense, bollocks. From Dutch pappekak *~soft shit.*

**population paste** *n. Joy gloy,* semen, *spunk, Aphrodite's evostick.*

**porcelain tingle** *n.* The cold shock that occurs when one's *bell end* touches the lavatory pan when sitting on the *throne.* A *harprick.*

**pork** *1. v. Aus.* To *fuck.* *'I couldn't pork her because she had the painters in.'* *2. n. Aus.* The *cock.*

**pork prescription** *1. n. Cock,* to be swallowed twice a day before meals. *2. n.* Doctor's authorisation for a *meat injection.*

**pork sword** *n.* Penis, *bacon bazooka, lamb cannon.*

**porn flakes** *n.* The crusty bits found on the sofa/sheets the morning after a late night *scruff video* session.

**porn fuzz** *n.* Characteristic picture quality of an 18th generation *bongo vid.*

**porn glare** *n.* The cruel, frustrating shaft of light which partially obscures the spread-eagled bird on the double page spread of an *art pamphlet* as the victim strives for *vinegar.*

**porn horn** *n.* A three-quarters hard erection regularly seen being fed into the models in *scud films.* An *Indian rope prick.*

**porn mirage** *n.* A cruel trick of the light, whereby a *tug-hungry* adolescent spots some *grumble* under a hedge, which on closer inspection turns out to be an Argos catalogue or the Sunday Mirror TV guide.

**porn sacrifice** *n.* A poorly-hidden stash of low quality *grumble* designed to put your missus off the scent of the barely legal stuff.

**porn trauma** *n.* Upon reaching the *vinegar strokes* whilst watching an *art film* and finding the screen suddenly filled by a big, sweaty bloke with large sideburns, to be too late to stop and *gwibble* to a disappointing finish. See *vinegar Joe*.

**porn vortex** *n.* A whirling fifth dimension where time has no meaning, encountered when looking for *left-handed websites* on the internet. One could fall into a porn vortex and emerge ten minutes later to discover that three days have elapsed.

**pornbroker** *n.* The man at work who can be relied upon to lend you a bit of *mucky* to see you through hard times. A *pornmeister*.

**pornithologist** *n.* One who enjoys looking at pictures of birds rather than going out and looking at them in the flesh. A *cock twitcher*.

**pornorama** *n.* A magnificent, breathtaking array of *meat mags*, arranged in a vista to provide variety and spectacle whilst having a *tug*. A *wank crescent*.

**porridge gun** *n.* Tool for distributing *population paste* quickly and efficiently.

**PORT** *abbv.* A politically cor-

rect term for a bird with small *tits*. Person Of Restricted Tittage. eg. Jilly Goulden.

**portion** *n.* A large but nonspecific quantity of sex. *'I'd give her a portion, and no mistake.'* See also *one, length, a bit.*

**posh wank** *n.* A *mess*-free masturbatory manoeuvre undertaken whilst wearing a *jubber ray*.

**pot brown** *v.* To bury the *bone-on* in *kak canyon*.

**pot pink** *v.* To moor the *skin boat* in *cod cove*. See also *snookered behind the red, difficult brown*.

**potty-mouth** *n.* US. Someone who shows a lack of vocabulary. *'Fucking goddamit. Fucking chicken for fucking dinner again, mom. Why the fucking fuck can't we have fucking hot dawgs?' 'My, my, Rusty, where did you hear language like that? You're turning into a real little potty mouth.'*

**pouch** *n.* An ageing, saggy *mott* that hangs between the legs like a sporran.

**pound the pork** *v.* Of *pinksmiths*, to pummel a hot *pork sword* into shape. *Pound the pudding.*

**pox** *n.* Venereal disease, specifically syphilis.

**prairie dogging** *v.* Of an *arse*, to have a stool poking in and out. A moving *turtle's head*.

**pram fat** *n.* See *plum sauce*.

**pranny** *n.* Fool, *arsehole, twat*. A form of insult popular amongst The Troggs during the 1960s. Also *prannet*.

**pratt** *1. n.* An egg-bearing female fish. *2. n.* A *pranny, fuckwit, arsehole*.

**pre-cum** *n.* Substance often referred to in the letters pages of *jazz mags* but rarely mentioned elsewhere. *Perseverance soup, dew on the lily*.

**predator's face** *n.* A somewhat unsettling vagina. From the film 'Predator' starring Arnold Schwarzenegger.

**premature pinch** *n.* The snipping off of an unsmoked *bum cigar* when disturbed in the act, by an important telephone call for example.

**prepare yesterday's lunch** *v.* To go for a *shit*.

**press the devil's doorbell** *v. Flick the bean.*

**pressed ham** *n.* The effect achieved by pushing one's naked *buttocks* onto the photocopier at the office Christmas party.

**prick** *1. n.* A penis. *2. n.* A *twat, fuckwit,* fool. *3. n.* A life-threatening finger injury often suffered by fairy tale princesses.

**prick tease** *n.* A woman who teases one's *cock* by calling it names.

**prick-stick** *n.* A white DIY glue in a handy tubular dispenser used solely to stick the pages of an *art pamphlet* together.

**priest's hole** *n.* A *minge* that's a tight squeeze. A *paper cut*.

**pringle** *n.* Yet another word for one who sniffs bicycle seats.

**prison pussy** *n.* The anus.

**private fur** *n.* A lady's *secret squirrel*.

**privates** *1. n.* Inoffensive unisex term for genitalia invented by the Women's Institute in 1904. At the opposite end of the rudeness scale to *fuckstick, bollocks* and *cunt*. *2. n.* A double entendre enabling 'Carry-On' script writers to confuse low ranking soldiers with their *meat and two veg*.

**procrasturbation** *n.* The act of repeated, and often pleasureless *self-love* brought on by the need to stave off more weighty tasks. *'For heaven's sake, Lester, stop procrasturbating and get your tax return filled in.'*

**prune juice** *n.* Anal seepage.

**psychedelic yodelling** *n.* Vocal projection of your biscuits out your mouth.

**pube lunch** *n.* A tasty *bacon sandwich* with a token garnish of *gorilla salad*, served all day in a friendly atmosphere.

**pud** *n.* Penis. That which was always *pulled* by Ivor Biggun (aka Doc Cox of 'That's Life' rude vegetable fame), in his 'Wanking Song.'

**pudendum** *n.* Genital area. From Latin *pudes* ~meat pie & *dendum* ~two potatoes.

**pud-whapper** *n.* US. *Wanker*, obnoxious person.

**puff** *1. v.* To exhale cigarette smoke. *2. n. prop.* Magic dragon that lived by the sea. *3. n.* A lifter of shirts.

**pugwash** *n. Aus.* Cleaning of the teeth using *tapioca toothpaste* and a *naughty paintbrush*. A *blow job.*

**puh-seh** *n. US.* A grumbleflick fanny. *'Hmmmm, be-beh! I'm gonna get ma'self a liddle piece-a yo' puh-seh!'*

**puke** *v.* To *throw up.*

**pull** *1. v.* To tap, pick up members of the opposite sex. *'I went out on the pull last night'. 2. v.* To *wank*. *'Nowt pulled, so I went home, watched the free ten minutes of the Fantasy Channel and had a bit of a pull.'*

**pull a pint on the piss pump** *v.* To pour oneself a 5ml *hand shandy.*

**pull a train** *v.* To take turns at *stirring the porridge.* A *gang bang.*

**pull off** *1. v.* To manoeuvre a car away from the kerb. *2. v.* To drag a drunken friend away from a fight in which he has the upper hand, usually whilst shouting *'It's not worth it'* or *'Leave it, he's had enough.' 3. v.* To masturbate. *'Fucking hell! She went downhill skiing and pulled us both off at once.'*

**pull out and pray** *n.* A method of contraception that is also a test of faith. *Vatican roulette.*

**pull the Pope's cap off** *v.* To *bash the Bishop, box the Jesuit.*

**pull the turkey's neck** *v. Choke the chicken.* See *throttle the turkey.*

**pull your pud** *v. Wank*. See *pud*.

**pulling power** *n*. The strength of one's *fanny magnetism*.

**PUMA** *acronym*. Pants Up My Arse. To be suffering from cleftal discomfort. *Hungry arse*.

**pump action mottgun** *n*. Advanced rapid fire development of the *mutton musket*.

**pump up the jam** *v. Cranberry dip*. To *stir the paint*.

**pump** *v*. To *fart, poot, pass wind, shoot bunnies, drop a rose petal*.

**pumper's lump** *n. medic*. The condition of enhanced right forearm muscle due to excessive *wanking*.

**pumping up the tyres** *v*. Involuntary movement of the leg during the *vinegar strokes*. *Elvis's leg, Elvis tremble*.

**punk cock** **n**. A *choad* with multifarious piercings. A *knob* bejewelled with chains, rings and pop rivets.

**puppies** *n. Bubbies*. Affectionate euphemism for *tits*. See *two puppies fighting in a bag*.

**puppies' noses** *n*. Little cold, wet nipples.

**purple headed womb broom** *n*. See *purple headed yoghurt warrior*.

**purple headed yoghurt warrior** *n*. See *purple headed womb broom*.

**purple helmet** *1. n. Pink Darth Vader's* headgear, *bobby's helmet, German helmet, Roman helmet, bell end*. *2. n*. Any member of the Rover Aerobatic display team.

**purple pearler** *n*. Extendable icing tool for decorating pink blancmanges.

**push gas** *v*. To *poot*.

**push through** *n*. the consequence of buying 'Economy Brand' *bumwad*. *'Would you care for another scone, Father Brown', asked Lady Chelmshurst. 'Bless you, but thank you no', replied the small priest, blinking owlishly and proffering a smelly digit towards his hostess's nose. 'I've just been to lay a cable and fear I had a push through.'* (from *'Father Brown Points the Finger'* by GK Chesterton).

**pushing sauce** *v*. The stage of coitus immediately after the *vinegar strokes,* i.e, when the *yoghurt truck* has crashed and is in the act of shedding its load. Ejaculation. *'Bond* *and Fanny Akimbo made love on the silken sheets of the mini-sub's bed. Suddenly, the videophone crackled into life and the face of M appeared, seated at his familiar White-hall desk. 'Ah, there you are 007. We've had reports that Blofeld is planning to blow up China with a big ray gun,' he said excitedly. 'I'm afraid I have my hands rather full at the moment, sir,' replied Bond, raising a quizzical eye-brow. 'Call me back in about 10 minutes after I'd pushed me sauce and zuffled me charlie.'* (from *'Tops and Goldfingers'* by Ian Fleming).

**pussy** *1. n.* Of woeful British TV sitcoms set in quiet, over-staffed department stores, a much-stroked pet cat fre-quently referred to by Mrs Slocombe. *2. n.* Her *cunt*.

**pussy pelmet** *n.* Short mini skirt.

**pussy poof** *n.* A *todger dodger,* a *three wheeler,* a *friend of Valerie.*

**put the red lights on** *v.* Naval. To have a silent *wank* in bed so as not to disturb one's wife. Also *silent run-ning, American Beauty.*

**put to the sword** *v.* To make love to. *'From the Charing Cross Theatre where I saw Mr. Herbert give his Death of Icarus, to tea with the French Ambassador, and thence home to bed whereupon I put Mrs. Pepys to the sword before set-tling down to sleep.'* (from *'The Diary of Samuel Pepys'*).

**putting from the rough** *v.* Golfing equivalent of *bowling from the Pavilion end.*

**putz** *n.* A yiddish *prick.*

**pygmies' cocks** *n.* Erect nip-ples. *'She had jockeys like pygmie's cocks.'*

**pyroflatulate** *v.* To light one's *farts.* See also *afterburner, blue streak.*

**pyropastie** *n.* Excrement wrapped in newspaper, then set alight on a doorstep in the hope that the occupant will stamp it out.

**Pythagoras piss** *n.* The *piss* performed with one's fore-head propped against the lavatory wall, the body form-ing the hypotenuse of a right-angled triangle.

# Qq

**quack** *n.* Short, sharp *botty burp* often followed by an apologetic 'Oops!' See *step on a duck.*

**quail** *n.* A game young *bird.*

**Quaker, to bury a** *v.* To *lay a cable. 'Do come in, Mr. D' Arcy. Miss Bennet has just nipped upstairs to bury a Quaker. Would you care to wait in the drawing room until she has finished?'* (from *'Pride and Prejudice',* by Jane Austen).

**quandong** *1. n. Aus.* A difficult *lay,* a hard, as opposed to an easy, woman. One who wears armour-plated *knickers. 2. n.* A prostitute.

**quaynte** *n. Placket.*

**quaz** *n.* An ugly *wanker, bell end* ringer. Abbreviation of Quasimodo.

**quean** *n.* A gentleman homosexualist, a *pinch of snuff.* Original spelling of *queen.*

**queef** *n. Can.* A *Lawley kazoo,* a *hat dropped forward,* a *flap raspberry.* Also *kweef.*

**queen** n. See *queer.*

**Queensway** *n.* A regular mammoth rectal stock clearance where *everything must go!*

**queer** *1. n. pre-1960* ~**fellow**.

One exhibiting strange behaviour. *2. n. post-1960.* A *ginger beer.*

**quiche** *n. Taint, notcher, barse,* whatever.

**quickie** *n.* A swift bout of intercourse that one often fancies in the same way as one fancies a cup of tea. *'Oh, it's half time. Do you fancy a quickie, love?' 'Er...go on, then. But stick the kettle on first.'* A hurried *one.*

**quim chin** *n. Muff mouth, cunty chops.* A bearded fellow. *'Did you see Noel Edmonds on telly last night? What a stupid fucking quim chin.'*

**quim** *n.* Refined word for the *mapatasi* such as a gentleman might use at a hay clarse cocktail party. From the Welsh Cwm ~valley beneath the 13 amp fuse wire.

**quim pro quo** *n. Lat.* An ancient Roman bartering system where goods and services are exchanged for *gash.*

**quim strings** *n.* Imaginary internal female organs, resembling Coronation Street Deirdre's neck, that tighten in stressful situations. *'Bob Cratchit raised his glass. 'To Mr Scrooge, the founder of the* *feast', he said cheerily. 'Ha! Founder of the feast indeed', screeched his wife. 'Why, I'll no sooner drink a toast to him that I would the devil himself, the mean-hearted, penny pinching, tight arsed...' 'Now, now, Sara,' interrupted Bob. 'Don't go snapping your quim-strings. It's Christmas day, and we shall drink to Mr Scrooge."* (from *'A Christmas Carol'* by Charles Dickens).

**quimby** *n.* Middle person in a *threesome*, the filling in a sex sandwich. See also *lucky Pierre*.

**quiminals** *n.* Prison lesbians. *Queen bees.*

**quimle** *v.* To eat *hairy pie*. I will quimle, I was quimling, I have quimled, etc.

**quimwedge** *v.* To do *it* with a lady.

**quince** *1. n. Aus.* Mincing *quean. 2. n.* Something owls and pussycats eat with a runcible spoon.

**quoit** *n. Ring, hoop, rusty sheriff's badge, balloon knot, tea towel holder.*

**quornography** *n.* Soft core pornography, ie. no meat.

**quumf** *v.* To sit in waiting outside a public library in Blyth, for example, and sniff ladies' bicycle seats as soon as possible after their owner has dismounted and gone inside.

# Rr

**rabbit's tail** *n*. The split second flash of white cotton gusset caught in one's peripheral vision when a lady crosses her legs at the other side of a waiting room.

**rabid dog, fanny like a** *sim*. A *clown's pie*, *cappuccino twat*.

**rack** *n*. Female mammarial display, collectively the *tits, funbags*. '*She's got a lovely rack on her. Very well presented. And nipples like a fighter pilot's thumbs.*'

**radge** *1. v*. To become furious, to lose one's blob. *2. n*. A furious episode. '*This little bairn puked aall doon me goon, an I took a fuckin radge.*' (Mother Theresa of Calcutta). *3. n*. ~**y**. One who is predisposed to taking radges. *4. n. adj*. In a state of radge.

**radio rental** *rhym. slang. Radgy, hatstand*, mental.

**RAF** *abbrev*. Rough As Fuck. Particularly ugly or unattractive.

**rag and bone man** *n*. One who doesn't mind getting a *barber's pole* now and again.

**rag week** *1. n*. Seven days during which students get pissed and behave like *cunts* in the name of charity. *2. n*.

Time of the month when the *flags are out. Blob week*.

**ragman's coat** *n*. A *turkey's wattle*, a *raggy blart*, a *pound of liver*, a *club sandwich*. An untidy vagina.

**ragman's trumpet** *n*. A capacious *fanny. Big Daddy's sleeping bag*.

**rainbow yawn** *n. Puke, technicolour yawn, pavement pizza*, a *sung rainbow*.

**raisin bag** *n. Nut sack, John Wayne's hairy saddlebags*.

**raisin** *n*. Corn dot.

**rake the cage out** *v*. To *build a log cabin*, give birth to a *Richard*.

**Ralph** *onomat*. To vomit. Also *call Huey*.

**ram job** *n*. Vatican-approved, conventional heterosexual sex, as opposed to *blow job* or *hand job*. A *knobjob*.

**ram raiding on a scooter** *adj*. Descriptive of ugly women. '*She was a worthy woman, yette sore ugglie, with a face lyke shede been ramme-raidynge onn a scooter.*' (from '*The Miller's Tale*' by Geoffrey Chaucer).

**ram shackled** *adj*. To be engaged in the act of *botting*.

**RAM sleep**. *n. abbrev*. The

phase prior to deep sleep. Rapid Arm Movement.

**rammadanny** *n*. An enforced monthly *Jacky Danny* fast.

**randy** *n*. Cowboy version of *horny*.

**rantallion** *n*. *18thC*. One whose *shot pouch* is longer than the barrel of his *fouling piece*.

**rascal wrapper** *n*. French letter, blob, rubber Johnny.

**raspberries in syrup** *sim*. The consistency of *shit* after a night *on the pop*. The kind that makes you pull a face like Kenneth Williams going *'Ooh, Matron!'*

**raspberry** *rhym. slang*. Break wind. From raspberry tart ~*fart*. *'Did you just drop a raspberry?' 'No. He who smelt it, dealt it'. 'Ah! But he who denied it, supplied it'. 'Yeh, but he who made the rhyme, committed the crime.'*

**Rasputin** *n*. An unkempt vaginal or anal beard.

**rat arsed / faced** *adj*. *Shit faced.*

**rat catcher's bait box** *n*. An unpleasant tasting *fanny*. A *nine volter*.

**rat killer** *n*. A foul *turd* capable of killing any pipe-dwelling rodent within a mile of the S-bend.

**rat's cocks!** *exclam*. Expression of extreme disappointment. Drat, confound it, curses, etc. *"My God!' the boatswain cried. 'What has happened to the ship?' 'The Pequod has been stove in by a Leviathan, a Great White Whale!' replied the helmsman, scarce able to comprehend the enormity of his own words. 'Rat's cocks,' yelled Ahab. 'That's fucking torn it!"* (from *'Moby Dick'* by Herman Melville).

**razz** *v*. To *hoy up, puke*.

**Razzle** *n. prop*. An unpretentious, no-nonsense *jazz mag*. In its own words *'The magazine that makes your cock go big.'*

**Razzle stack** *n*. The fondly-remembered, and deeply erotic tableau in the said *art pamphlet*, featuring 6 vertically-arranged *quims*. Now sadly banned due to the near suffocation of the lowermost participant.

**reach around** *n*. In *botting*, pouring your partner a *hand shandy* whilst *ram shackled*.

**reading the paper** *v*. To examine one's used toilet tissue to catch up on the latest news of one's anal health. To peruse the *rusty bulletin*.

**readybrek glow** *n.* The fuzzy, red outline surrounding everyone on a 6th generation copy of a *stick vid. Porn fuzz.*

**rear admiral** *n.* A sailor who prefers to navigate the *Windward passage*.

**rear gunner** *n.* In aviation terms, a gunner who shoots one of his own side by firing his *lamb cannon* into their *bomb bay*.

**receiver of swollen goods** *n.* Someone involved in a transaction with a *botty burglar*.

**rectal retort** *n.* A witty *fart*.

**red ring** *n.* Inflammation of the *chocolate starfish* as a result of being *skittered*. See *Japanese flag*.

**red wings** *n.* Dubious honour bestowed upon one who eats *haddock pastie* during *rag week*.

**reggae like it used to be**. *v.* To masturbate. Wearing a bowler hat.

**release the chocolate hostage** *v.* To liberate *Richard the Third* after his incarceration in one's *chamber of horrors*.

**release the handbrake** *v.* To *drop a gut* into your hand and then present it into your friend's face for his olfactory delectation. A *cupcake*.

**release the hounds** *n.* To empty one's *arse*.

**remould** *n. Rubber, single finger Marigold glove, blob.*

**retch** *v.* To vomit, but with more noise and less *puke*.

**return fire** *n. Splashback.*

**return serve** *n.* The reappearance of a *turd* you thought you had seen the last of.

**reveille** *n.* An early morning *brass eye* fanfare delivered with military precision, that makes your company jump out of bed.

**reverse cowgirl** *n.* A *cowgirl* who has been bucked through 180 degrees, a sexual position much favoured by *meat vid* cinematographers as one can see it going in. A *fucking bronco*.

**reverse Doagan** *n. NZ.* A *chocolate hostage* released into the *chodbin* whilst sitting the wrong way round, leaving a breathtaking *skidmark vista* for the next unfortunate lady patron of the toilet.

**reverse peach** *n.* A rearward elevation of a lady's *parts of shame,* such that they resemble a ripe and juicy pink fruit.

**reverse thrust** *n.* The act of *getting off at Edge Hill.* The *interruptus* of one's *coitus.*

**rhino horn** *n.* A well-matted tarantula among *arse spiders.* Definitely not an aphrodisiac.

**rhythm mag** *n. Jazz mag, scud book, art pamphlet,* one handed reading material.

**rhythm stick** *n.* The late Ian Dury's *cock. Sixth gear stick, joy stick, copper stick, giggle stick, love truncheon.*

**rib cushions** *n. Dirty pillows.* Breasts.

**Richard** *rhym. slang.* A stool. From Richard the Third ~*turd. 'I've just given birth to a ten pound Richard. Ooh, my poor ringpiece!'*

**riddle of the sphincter** *n.* A mysterious *fart* that erodes your nasal cavities.

**ride the baloney pony** *v. US.* To *wank.*

**ride the great white knuckler** *v.* To knock out a bit of *jizz* on one's *bone-a-phone.*

**ride the porcelain bus** *v.* To have the *squits.*

**ride the waves** *v.* To poke an amply proportioned lady. See also *moped. 'It's not as bad as you might think, if you just slap the fat and ride the waves.'*

**ride** *v.* That which one does on a *bike.*

**riding the clutch** *v.* The hovering state between releasing the *pace car* and making *skidmarks* on one's underpants. Puts wear and tear on the *bum brake.*

**right hand cream** *n.* Hand and face moisturiser made from a special blend of *nut* oils.

**rigid digit** *n.* Erect penis, *bone, bonk-on.*

**rim** *1. n.* Circumference of the anus. *2. v.* To lick the *rim.*

**rim job** *n.* A *rimming,* a *trip around the world.*

**ring** *1. n. Hole, jacksie,* anus, *brown eye, chocolate starfish. 2. n.* The vagina.

**ring bandit** *n.* A *Hershey highwayman.*

**ring burner** *n.* An exceptionally hot curry prepared for the entertainment of the waiters and kitchen staff in Indian restaurants.

**ring master** *1. n.* Master of ceremonies at a circus. *2. n.* A *botter.*

**ring pirate** *n.* A *pirate of men's pants.*

**ring stinger** *n.* A *Ruby Murray* that induces *ring sting* and leaves one with an *arse* like *a Jap flag.*

**ring the bell** *v. Pop the cork,* detonate the *fanny bomb.*

**ring worm** *n.* A *shirt lifter's Jimmy Wonkle.*

**ringpiece** *n.* A *Samantha Janus.*

**ringtone** *n.* A *fart.*

**rinky dink** *1. n.* Stink, that unpleasant odour created by a *fyst, Richard the Third's BO. 2. adj.* Descriptive of the Pink Panther.

**rinse the lettuce** *v.* To wash the *beef curtains,* in situ as it were. Female equivalent of a *gentleman's wash.*

**ripped out fireplace** *n.* A *butcher's dustbin.*

**ripped sofa** *n.* A *badly packed kebab.*

**ripped to the tits** *adj.* A level of inebriation achieved using drink and drugs. Also *whipped to the tits.*

**ripping up rags** *sim.* Descriptive of the sound of a long drawn out *fart.*

**rising main** *n.* In pubic plumbing, the *tatty watta* supply pipe usually fed in through the vagina. The *main cable.*

**riveting stick** *rhym. slang. Dick.* From the jeweller's instrument.

**roadkill** *n.* A rather flat, dry, *hedgehog.*

**robbing the date locker** *v.* The burgling of *turds.*

**Robin Cook's beard** *n.* A sparsely-vegetated ginger *minge.* A *grated carrot,* a *council twat.*

**rock poodle** *n.* A heavy metallurgist, complete with long shaggy hair and puffed-up leather jacket.

**rocket polisher** *n.* An over-enthusiastic cleaning of the *pocket rocket* leading to detonation on the launchpad.

**rocket socket** *n.* Vagina.

**Rockfords** *rhym. slang. Arse grapes, Nobbies, Emmas, Michaels, farmers, ceramics, Chalfonts.* Piles. From the TV series 'The Rockford Files.'

**rocks** *1. n.* Masses of hard, stony matter, esp. extensive formation of such matter. *2. n.* Big, hairy *bollocks. 3. n.*

Those which are 'gotten off' whilst *on the job*.

**rod** *n*. Spam sceptre.

**rod walloper** *n*. One who *wallops* his *rod*.

**rodeo sex** *n*. A bedroom game where the couple adopt the *doggy position*. The gentleman then calls out an ex-girlfriend's name and sees how long he can stay on for. Also *bronco sex*.

**roger ramjet** *n*. A *botter*.

**roger** *v*. To *fuck*. Often in the past tense. *'I gave her a jolly good rogering.'*

**Rolf Harris eating a banana** *sim*. Descriptive of the close-up intercourse scenes in a very blurred, 200th generation *scruff video*.

**roll in the hay** *n*. What everyone wanted to do with Julie Christie in 'Far From The Madding Crowd.' And Donald Sutherland did with her in 'Don't Look Back.'

**roll the crevice** *v*. To attempt to wipe one's *freckle* with the coarse cardboard tube after exhausting the supply of *bumwad*.

**rolling the dice** *v*. *Feeding the ducks, spanking the monkey*.

**rollover week** *n*. A week when the *painters are in*.

**roly-poly** *adj*. Tabloid prefix for any celebrity who's the tiniest bit overweight. eg. *'Roly-poly actor Leonardo Di Caprio...'*

**Roman helmet rumba** *n*. See *Bologna bop*.

**romancing the bone** *n*. An evening in alone with a meal, a bottle of wine and some soft music, followed by a top shelf *stick vid*.

**romp** *v*. To chase a woman in a corset round and round a bedroom, lifting the knees very high, accompanied by 'BOING!' noises when leaping onto the bed.

**Ronson** *rhym. slang*. Arse. From Ronson lighter ~*shiter*.

**room clearer** *n*. Of flatulent emissions, a *fart* which registers one notch higher than *breaking company* on the sphincter scale. See also *fyst*.

**root . rootle** *v*. To make love to.

**rope the pony** *v*. To *wank*.

**rotoplooker** *n*. US. Penis, *chopper*.

**roughing up the suspect** *v*. What a vice squad copper tells his superiors he's doing when he's caught polishing his *bobby's helmet* in the seized porn store room.

**round up the tadpoles** *v.* To *wank, bash the bishop*.

**roundhead** *n.* A *pink Darth Vader* after the surgical removal of his *Kojak's rollneck*, a *yiddled whanger*.

**row the boat** *v.* A dual *tug* boat, multiple *wanking*. Nautical variation on the *downhill skiing* position.

**Roy Castle's last blow** *n.* A wimpering, pathetic *trouser trumpet* that sounds like it's feeling very sorry for itself.

**rub-a-tug shop** *n.* Brothel, bordello, house of ill repute. Massage parlour supplying a rub down and a *tug off*.

**rubber gash** *n.* Sailor's favourite. A plastic *fanny* which the manufacturers claim is 'better than the real thing.' £8.99.

**rubber Johnny** *n.* A *blob*, contraceptive, *a jubber ray*. Also *rubber*.

**rubics** *rhym. slang. Gorilla salad.*

**rug munchers** *n. Fanny noshers.*

**rump gully** *n.* Viewed from *biffin bridge*, the gradually sloping valley beyond *kak canyon*.

**rump ranger** *n. Chocolate cowboy.*

**Rumple Foreskin** *n.* Penis, *John Thomas, junior.*

**rumpo** *n. Rumpy pumpy.*

**rumpy pumpy** *n.* Lightweight sexual shenanigans, slightly more erotic than *how's your father*. US equivalent *hoochie-coochie*.

**runs, the** *n.* What English cricketers get when they face fast bowlers.

**russet gusset** *n. Skidmarks* or *dangleberrian* deposits on the *shreddies*. *Marmite stripe, starting grid at Brands Hatch.*

**rusty sheriff's badge** *n.* Ride along *biffin bridge* from *John Wayne's hairy saddlebags* and there it lies, right in the middle of *kak canyon*. Just before you reach *rump gully*.

**rusty water** *n.* See *piss rusty water*.

# Ss

**S and M** *n. Rub-a-tug shop* parlance for sado-masochism. *Mr Whippy.*

**sack artist** *n.* Womaniser, gigolo, *fanny rat.*

**saddle bags** 1. *n.* Labia, *piss flaps.* 2. *n.* Scrotum.

**Safe** *n.* See *French safe.*

**salad dodger** *n.* A contumelious epithet for a fat bastard. One who at a buffet sidesteps the lettuce and celery and heads straight for the pork pies. *"Contrarywise', continued Tweedledee, 'if it was so, it might be; and if it were so, it would be; but as it isn't, it ain't. That's logic'. 'That's not logic, that's bollocks, you salad dodger."* (from *'Through The Looking Glass'* by Lewis Carroll).

**salami slapper** *n.* He who tolls upon his own *bell end.* A *wanker.*

**Sally Gunnell** *n. prop.* A motor trade term to describe a used car, ie. not much to look at but a fucking good runner.

**salmon** 1. *rhym. slang.* Sexually excited. From salmon on prawn ~*the horn. 'I saw Pam Anderson's video on the internet last night. It didn't half give me the salmon, I can tell you.'* 2. *rhym. slang HMP.*

Tobacco. From salmon and trout ~*snout. "Ere, you don't half give me the salmon, Lord Archer. Fancy giving me a blow job for an ounce of salmon?'*

**salmon canyon** *n.* Piscine pass leading to *tuna town.*

**salmon handcuffs** *n. Pink handcuffs.* Invisible restraints that keep a gentleman from seeing any of his friends. *Pussy whipped. "This is quite rum do, Jeeves', I exclaimed. 'I've met Piggy for cocktails every Friday for ten years. Where the pip can he be?' 'If I may be so bold', intoned Jeeves in that way of his, 'he has recently taken up with a soubrette from a London show, and I fear she has slapped the salmon handcuffs on the poor cunt."* (from *'What the Fuck, Jeeves?'* by PG Wodehouse).

**saloon doors** *n.* A pair of well used, swinging *fanny flaps* that one swaggers into, only to be thrown out of three minutes later.

**salsa dip** *n.* A splash about in the *crimson waves.*

**salt** *n.* 1960s Mod term for a *bird.*

**Samantha** *rhym slang.* A *ring piece.* From Samantha Janus.

**Samurai** *n.* A fearsome, ceremonial *pork sword.*

**sand hole** *n.* Of crowded beaches, the hole caused by sunbathing on one's stomach in order to conceal a *Jake.*

**sarson's nose** *adj.* The condition of the *old fella,* post *vinegar strokes* after leaving a *salty dressing* on the *pink lettuce salad.*

**satiscraptory** *adj.* Descriptive of something of a poor, but adequate standard, eg. BBC local radio, high street burger-chain fast food.

**sauce** *1. n.* Booze, usually in large quantity. *'That Keith Chegwin didn't half hit the sauce, you know.' 2. v.* To seduce. *3. n.* Cheek. *'He asked to borrow me motor, an then said could I bring it round and make sure the tank was full. What a fucking sauce!'*

**sausage and doughnut situation** *n.* Heterosexual intercourse. *'Houston, this is Challenger. Sorry about that loss of communication. The first officer and I encountered a sausage and doughnut situation. All systems now normal.'*

**sausage grappler** *n.* A *salami slapper.*

**sausage jockey** *n.* Passive male homosexual, anyone who sits on a sausage and bounces up and down. A *sausage rider.*

**sausage kennel** *n.* A male homosexual's *bottom.*

**sausage pizza** *n.* Closest thing to a *sausage sandwich* that *Miss Lincolnshire* is able to provide. A *diddy ride* on a lady with *stits.*

**sausage sandwich** *n.* A juicy *salami frotted* between two pink *baps,* the end result of which is a *pearl necklace. Dutch.*

**sausage supper** *n.* Female equivalent of a *fish supper.*

**sausage wallet** *n.* A wallet for putting sausages in. A *fanny.*

**SBD** *abbrev.* Of *farts* and *farting,* Silent But Deadly. A subtle release of fatally pungent *botty gas.*

**SBV** *abbrev.* Of *farts* and *farting,* Silent But Violent. Minging *fizzle* from the *fart fissure.*

**scads** *n. Kicksies, dunghampers, thunderbags.*

**schizophrenic face** *n.* Of a lady, to have stunningly beautiful eyes, but a nose like Ricky Tomlinson's.

**schlong . schlonger** *n. Yiddish.* Large *putz.*

**schlong shed** *n.* Condom, *stopcock, stiffy stocking.*

**schmeckie** *n.* Opposite of a *schlong.*

**school dinners** *1. n.* A foul, brown mess, served in a large white bowl, the smell of which makes you heave. *2. n.* A toilet full of *shit.*

**scoobysnack** *n. Oral sex* involving a dog and a very tall sandwich.

**scooter** *n. Arse.* From Dutch schoeter ~*shitter.*

**Scottish bedwarmer** *n.* A *fart*, anal announcement.

**Scouser's key** *n.* A crowbar, hammer, half a brick or anything used to open someone else's back door.

**scranus** *n.* The *barse* again.

**scratcher** *n.* Bed, *fart sack.*

**scratter** *n. Halifax.* A person of limited finances and breeding, eg. 8 Ace. Also *ronker.*

**screamer** *n.* Raving *poofter.*

**screw** *v.* To have sex piggy-style, rotating clockwise due to a corkscrew-shaped *cock.*

**screwnicorn** *n.* A mythical and somewhat magical sex act whereby a lesbian puts a *strap-on dildo* on her forehead and goes at her partner like a bull at a gate.

**scrote** *n. Knacker, bollock brain.* A versatile testicular term of abuse.

**scrotum pole** *n.* Old Red Indian erection at the foot of which lie *John Wayne's hairy saddlebags,* and around which *Madam Palm and her five sisters* do ritual dances to precipitate *spunkfall.*

**scrubber** *n. Slapper,* vulgar woman, *dollymop.*

**scrubbing the cook** *v. milit.US. Bashing the bishop.*

**scruff** *n.* Pornography, *muck, grumble. "Look what I've got', said William breathlessly , as he emptied the contents of his jumper at the Outlaws' feet. 'It's a load of scruff. Jumble found it under a hedge."* (from *'William's Milk Race'* by Richmal Crompton).

**scrumping** *1. v. US.* Having sex. *2. v. UK.* Stealing apples.

**scrunchies** *1. n.* Of *slappettes,* the colourful elasticated hairbands captured by rival teenage *slappers* in battle. *2. n.* Excess batter in a chip shop. Scraps.

**scrunger** *n.* Another name for one of those bicycle seat sniffers found lurking around the bicycle racks of convents and women's drop-in centres.

**scrunt** *n. coll. Blart, flange, gusset.* A group of attractive women. *'Suddenly, at the age of 25, the Prince was cast as the world's most eligible bachelor. On a Royal tour of New Zealand in 1973, he found himself having to batter off top-end scrunt with a shitty stick.'* (from *'HRH The Prince of Wales'* by Jim Bob Dimbleby).

**scuffer** *n.* A *cozzer*, a *rozzer*, a *tit-head*, a *filth.*

**scum shovel** *n.* Any form of public transport used extensively by the underprivileged, eg. the no.11 Torry to Northfield bus in Aberdeen.

**scumbag** *n.* The ultimate term of abuse known to tabloid journalists.

**scumper** *n.* Someone who lays sheets of bog roll on the seat of a public toilet so as his *arse* does not touch the same place as someone else's *arse* has touched. The late Carry-on star Kenneth Williams was known to *scump.*

**scumwad** *n. US.* The ultimate term of abuse known to American tabloid journalists.

**scuns** *n. Scads.*

**scutter** *n. Slut, shag bag.*

**scuttle** *v.* To *sink the pink*, or

*brown*, in a hurried fashion from behind.

**sea monster** *n. Swamp donkey, hipocrocapig.*

**seagulling** *v.* The mischievous act of *bespangling* a passer by from a height, eg, a tree, a roof or a Status Quo hotel room balcony. Could lead to *Graham Norton's hair.*

**secaturds** *n. medic.* The muscles surrounding the *nipsy.*

**second sitting** *n.* An immediate unavoidable return visit to the *shitter* after wiping and washing.

**secret smile** *n.* A *cunt.*

**see a friend to the coast** *euph. Drop the kids off at the pool.*

**see you next Tuesday** *acronym.* Parting nicety alluding to the initials 'CU'NT.

**seed** *n.* That which is scattered in a *ladygarden.*

**seeing to** *n.* Sexual servicing, a 'jolly good' one of which is often said to have been given to a woman by a man.

**semen** *n. Aphrodite's Araldite, joy Gloy, gunk, spunk, goo.*

**semen-olina** *n. Spunk* of an especially lumpy nature.

**semi** *1. n. Lazy lob on, a dobber,* a half erect penis. *2. n.* A house joined to one other house.

**semi-demi-on** *n.* A *quarter-on, half a lob on.* The first stirrings of *dobberdom.*

**semi-on** *n.* A partially tumescent generative organ. *Half a teacake.*

**send a sausage to the seaside** *euph. Sink a few U boats.*

**separate-us apparatus** *n. Condom, stiffy stocking. 'Did you remember to bring the separate-us apparatus?' 'Oh, Rat's cocks! I didn't. Perhaps we'd better just play the bagpipes tonight.'*

**serpent socket** *n.* That hole with which the *one eyed trouser snake* connects.

**setting the video** *v.* Sexual position, in which the lady is on her knees and elbows, with her *arse* in the air, tutting exasperatedly.

**sex** *1. n. It, the other, dirties. 2. v.* To pump someone full of semen. *'Babe, I'm gonna sex you up' ('Sex You Up'* song lyric, George Michael). *3. n.* A lady's *mingepiece.*

**sex act** *n.* Versatile, vague tabloid term used to describe and denigrate specifically non-specific acts of *shenani-*

*gans.* Usually prefixed 'vile', 'lewd' or 'sordid.'

**Shabba** *n.* See *J. Arthur.*

**shaft** *1. v.* To *shag, screw. 2. n.* Penis. *3. n. pro.* The black private dick that's a sex machine to all the chicks in town.

**shag** *1. v.* To copulate, to *fuck.* A once shocking term, now lame enough to be used by 'right on' vicars. *2. n.* Sexual encounter, *a screw. 3. n. US.* Fifties dance craze. *4. n.* Type of sea bird. *5. n.* Tobacco. *6. n.* Something to do with *arse grapes* or carpets.

**shag bag** *n.* Loose woman, *a bike.*

**shag dust** *n. Fuck powder.* Make-up.

**shag factory** *n.* Joint which is heaving with *blit, knickerville, blart city.*

**shag monster** *n.* A (not necessarily ugly) woman who has a voracious appetite for sex. A *nymphomentalist.*

**shag slab** *n.* The *altar of lurve,* bed, *passion pit, cock block, fart sack, scratcher.*

**shag tags** *n.* Love bites, *hickies, suckers.* Bruises from a physical game of *tonsil hockey.*

**shaggability** *n.* Measurement of how *shaggable* a person is on an arbitrary, non-scientific scale.

**shaggable** *adj.* Having a high degree of *shaggability*.

**shagged out** *adj.* Exhausted, *jiggered*, *buggered*, *zonked*, *fucked*.

**shaggin' wagon** *n.* A *passion wagon*, a *fuck truck*.

**shagging a bike** *sim.* To describe sex with an extremely thin woman. *'These supermodels, nice faces, some of 'em, but get 'em in the fart sack and it'd be like shagging a bike.'*

**shagging a waterbed** *sim.*To describe sex with an extremely fat woman. *Riding the waves.*

**shagnasty** *n.* A *shag monster* who is extremely ugly.

**shake hands with the wife's best friend** *v.* To perform an act of *self-pollution*.

**shake hands with the Wookie** *v.* Another in the 'Wanking with Star Wars' series. See *Hand Solo, duel with the pink Darth Vader, masturbate the purple-headed light sabre.*

**shake the bishop's hand** *v.* Have a *piss,* as opposed to *bashing the bishop.*

**shake the lettuce** *v.* Of females, to *pee.* Specifically, to give the *beef curtains* a quick tumble dry afterwards.

**shake the snake** *v.* Male equivalent of *shaking the lettuce* the object being to dislodge any *forget-me-nots* before returning the *schlong* to the *shreddies.*

**shaking hands with the unemployed** *v. Wanking.*

**shaking like a shitting dog** *sim.* A bad attack of the DTs after a night on the *sauce.*

**shaking like an flatpack wardrobe** *sim.* Descriptive of the female equivalent of *vinegar strokes.*

**shampoo the rug** *v.* To lose one's *population paste* on a *mapatasi.* Perhaps when *getting off at Edge Hill.*

**shamu** *n.* An overly-acrobatic *dreadnought* that splashes the spectating testicles. From the performing whale of the same name.

**shandy andy** *n.* A *jizzmop.*

**shark . sharking** *v.* Go on the *pull,* using aggressive, sly or cunning tactics.

**shark's fin** *n.* The profile of a neighbour's *beetle bonnet* viewed through a tight bikini bottom whilst sunbathing on the beach.

**sharks sniffing, have the** *euph.* Of a lady, to be afflicted with monthly uncleanliness. *"My darling, at last we are alone' murmured Heathcliffe, as he took Cathy in his arms. 'I cannot wait a moment longer. I must have you now.' 'Sorry, love, I've got the sharks sniffing', she replied."* (from *'Wuthering Heights'* by Tracey Bronte).

**shart** *v.* To pass wind with an unexpected non-gaseous component. To *follow through*.

**shat on from a height** *v.* To have been badly exploited, humiliated, let down.

**shat trick** *n.* The professional goal of the salaried worker, ie. three *Mr. Browns* in one working day.

**shave a horse** *v.* To have a *piss, take a leak*.

**shaven haven** *n.* Bald *monkey's forehead*.

**shed** *n.* Large, promiscuous woman. Somewhere to stick one's *tools*.

**shedded** *adj. Trousered, cattled*.

**sheep sitting** *adj.* To be *on the blob, dropping clots*.

**Sheffield hammer** *n.* A rolled-up newspaper, used to hammer nails into bits of wood, and which can be unrolled before the *scuffers* arrive.

**Sherman** *rhym. slang.* Have a *tug*. From Sherman tank *~wank*.

**shift** *v.* To *shag, screw*.

**shims** *n. Ladyboys*.

**Shipman, to do a** *v.* From Harold Shipman. To inject a lady much older than oneself. *Granny banging*.

**shirt fly** *n.* A 'yes man'. One who is always up the gaffer's *arse*. A *fart-sucker*, a *brown noser*, a *Penfold*.

**shirt lifter** *n.* One who gently lifts the tails of another man's shirt before sticking his *cock* up his *brown eye*. An *uphill gardener*, a *brown hatter*.

**shirt potatoes** *n. Tits, melons, top bollocks*.

**shirtful** *n.* A well stocked *rack. 'My, what a shirtful. You've got the job.'*

**shit . shite** *1. v.* To *shit*, defecate, *sink the Bismarck, build a log cabin, crimp one off, light a bum cigar. 2. n. Crap*, excrement, stools, faecal matter. *3. n. Git, sod, get*, a *shitty* person, usually 'little'. *4. adj. Crap*, useless. *'Shit weather for this time of year, eh, vicar?'*

**shit a brick** 1. *interj.* Exclamation of surprise. 2. *v.* To be scared, to *papper* one's *trollies.*

**shit eating grin** *n.* Exaggerated, smug, self-satisifed smile as worn by the likes of Noel Edmonds.

**shit faced** *n. Arseholed,* intoxicated, *para-fuckin-lytic.*

**shit kiss** *n.* A small, star-shaped brown mark left on the chin of a none too fussy *cumulonimbulist.*

**shit locker** *n. Arse, bomb bay, chamber of horrors.*

**shit on your own doorstep** *euph.* Foul the nest. eg. *shag* one's mother-in-law whilst totally *pissed. Piss on your chips.*

**shit stabber** *n.* A homosexual *pork swordsman.*

**shit tickets** *n. Bumwad, arsewipes, turd tokens, brown shield stamps.* Bathroom tissue.

**shit your pants** *v.* To *drop a brick, cake your kecks, papper your trolleys.*

**shitcloud** *n.* A common meteorological phenomenon involving a silent movement of wind and a strong smell of bad eggs.

**shite house . shit house** *n.* Outside lavatory, *dunny, netty.*

**shiter** *n. Arse, kak cannon.* That which *shites.*

**shits, the** *n.* Of *smallroom dancing,* those up-tempo *trots* which include the *Tijuana cha-cha,* the *sour apple quickstep* and the *Aztec two-step.*

**shitsophrenia** *n. medic.* The condition where the sufferer alternates between having wild *squirts* and normal bowel movements.

**shitter** 1. *n.* Anus, *kakpipe, council gritter.* 2. *n.* A sit down lavatory, the pan.

**shitter chatter** *n.* Long-winded anal babble emitted when a *shit* is expected.

**shitter's ridge** *n. scranus* etc.

**shitty shitty gang bang** *n.* A particularly messy *arsefest.*

**shitty stick** *n.* A stick, covered in *shit,* used by men with powerful cars to stave off advancing *scrunt.*

**shitwreck** *n.* The broken-up remnants of a scuttled *dreadnought,* lying in deep water by the S-bend.

**shniffle-piffler** *n.* One who sniffs lady's bicycle seats.

**shoot in your boot** *euph.* To be so sexually excited as to ejaculate into the top of one's footwear.

**shoot your load / bolt / wad** *v.* To ejaculate, *lose your mess, discharge the mutton musket.*

**shooting bunnies** v. Polite euphemism for *farting.* Pass wind, *blow off.* Also *kill the Easter bunny.*

**shopping** *n.* The underpant aftermath of *follow through. 'Did I detect a twin tone there, your Honour?' 'I'm afraid so. Court adjourned for fifteen minutes whilst I check my trolleys for shopping.'*

**shotgun fart** *n.* A sudden ballistic *fart* which peppers pellets of *crapnel* into the toilet bowl or underpants.

**shoulder boulders** *n.* Big breasts, *gazungas.*

**shreddies** *n. Undercrackers, kecks, trolleys.*

**shrimp** *v.* To suck someone's toes for sexual gratification.

**shtup** *v. Yiddish.* To have sex, *bonk, bang.*

**shunt** *v.* To *shag* a lady.

**side winders** *n. Spaniel's ears* which appear to be gravitating towards the oxters. *Pit fillers.*

**sideburns** *n.* The marks left on multi-storey car park walls by women who could really do with power steering.

**sign the guest book** *v.* To leave large, unmoveable *tread-marks* in someone else's toilet.

**Sigourney Weaver** *rhym. slang. Beaver.*

**silencer** *n.* A *pap-baffle.*

**silicone valley** *n.* The cleavage 'twixt adjoining *bazongers.* The *Bristol Channel.*

**silly string** *1. n.* A light-hearted novelty *shit* that squirts out of one's *aeros-hole* in a rapid and erratic manner. Breaks the ice at parties. Occasionally incorporating small solid lumps, when it is known as a *bicycle chain. 2. n.* Sticky substance light-heartedly sprayed in the face of an actress in a slapstick *art film.* Kept in a cannister that requires vigorous shaking.

**sing a rainbow** *v.* To *shout soup.*

**sing sweet violets** *v.* Airy alternative to *building a log cabin,* to *take a dump.*

**Singer** *n.* Sexual athlete, he or she who goes *at it* like a sewing machine.

**singing into the mic** *sim. Horatio* performed in the style of a hen-night karaoke star.

**sink a few U boats** *v.* To drop a few *depth charges.*

**sink plunger** *n.* A *tug* administered by an inexperienced woman where she appears to be attempting to snap your *banjo* and pull your *fiveskin* over your *clock weights*- the action she would use when unblocking a sink. Opposite of a *squid wank*.

**sink the Bismarck** *v.* To pass one fucking enormous stool, deposit a *U blocker*.

**sink the sausage** *v.* To get one's *leg over*.

**siphon the python** *v.* To take a *Chinese singing lesson, see a man about a dog*. To go for a *piss*.

**Sir Anthony** *rhym. slang.* A proper Charlie. From Sir Anthony Blunt ~*cunt*.

**Sir Cliff's neck** *n.* The bit of taut, elongated *scrotum* just above the bit that's got your *knackers* in.

**Sir Douglas** *rhym. slang.* Shit. From Sir Douglas Hurd ~*turd*.

**sitting on an elephant** *adj.* To be highly *burbulent*, to have *brewed a massive one up.* "Would you kindly evacuate to the drawing room, my dear, and take the girls with you' Mr. Bennet whispered. 'I indulged myself in partaking of rather a surfeit of cook's magnificent sprouts this lunchtime, and I fear I am now sitting on an elephant." (from 'Pride And Prejudice' by Jane Austen).

**six nowt** *n.* Descriptive of something performed with gusto and enthusiasm.

**six-pack grip** *n.* See *tenpin*.

**sixteen valve** *n.* A stunner, a corking *bird*.

**sixth gear** *n. Wanking*, especially in a parked car. See *stick shifter*.

**sixty-eight** *n.* Oral sex undertaken on the understanding that the favour will be returned. *"Ere, give us a sixty-eight and I'll owe you one.'*

**sixty-nine** *n. Soixante neuf, loop the loop.*

**skeet** *1. v. US.* To shoot clay pigeons. *2. v.* To *shoot your load.* To come off at the *Billy Mill roundabout.*

**skeeze** *v. US.* To *shag, schtup.*

**skelpit erse** *sim. Scot.* Descriptive of a face that looks like a *smacked arse.*

**skid marks** *n.* Severe *russet gusset, pebble dashing* of the *undercrackers*, the *turtle's bryllcreem.*

**skidmata** *n.* The miraculous wounds which manifest themselves on the fingertips of one who is a martyr to thin *bumwad.* Also *taxi driver's tan.*

**skiing position** *n.* *Wanking* two men off at the same time while wearing only a helmet, goggles and snow skis.

**skin boat** n. Penis. *'I think I'll sail the old skin boat to tuna town.'*

**skin chimney** *n.* A flue that requires regular sweeping with a *womb broom.*

**skin flick** *n.* A tame *fuck feature,* blue movie, *mamba matinee.*

**skin flute** n. A *fleshy flugel-horn, bed flute, pink oboe.*

**skin grafts** *n.* Somewhat unimpressive *tits.*

**skin-clad tube** *n.* A *live sausage,* a *girlometer.*

**skipper** *n.* A lady's *clematis,* a *love button,* a *wail switch.* From *a man in a boat.*

**Skippy** *n.* A promiscuous male who jumps about from *bush* to *bush.* A *fanny ferret.*

**skirt lifter** *n.* The female equivalent of a *shirt lifter.* A *carpet muncher,* a *lezza.*

**skirt** *n. coll.* Fanny, blart, *toosh, talent. 'I'm on a pink ticket the neet. Let's get down the bar and pick up a bit of skirt.'*

**skit . skitter** *v.* To *shit* diarrhoea.

**skittered** *adj.* To be afflicted with the *skitters.*

**skitters, the** *n.* Diarrhoea, the *shits,* the *squirts,* the *Earthas.*

**skittuin** *n.* The product of the *skitters,* especially in dogs, *canine paint stripper,* puddles of brown acidic gunge on the carpet.

**skull buggery** *n.* *Pugwashing, salami sucking.* Also *skull fucking.*

**slack mabbut** *n.* A *hippo's mouth,* a *beef wellington.*

**slag** *1. n.* A woman of little virtue, slapper. *2. n.* Waste material from a mine, slag heap. *3. n* Term of abuse (pronounced *slaaaaaag*) applied liberally to male criminals in 'The Sweeney.'

**slag heap** *n.* A run-down pub or nightclub in any northern town.

**slag wellies** *n.* Knee-high boots.

**slam hound** *n. US. Slapper, slut.*

**slam in the lamb** *v.* Bayonet manoeuvre involving the *mutton musket.*

**slam on the brakes** *v.* To stop wiping one's *arse* for some reason, eg. the house burning down, with the full knowledge that the process is incomplete, resulting in *skid marks* or *russet gusset.*

**slam spunk** *v.* To have sex.

**slap and tickle** *n.* A sex act, a bit like *rumpy pumpy*, whereby a man wearing a dress shirt and sock suspenders chases an excited lady round a bed before catching her, playfully slapping her *buttocks*, tickling her ribs and *fucking* her. A *romp.*

**slap the monkey** *v. Bash the bishop.* Also *spank the monkey.* To do a *Mary Chipperfield.*

**slaphead** *n.* A *chrome dome*, a *baaldie.*

**slaphood** *n.* A *slapper's* prime of life.

**slapper** n. *Slag,* dirty woman. She who has been around a bit. From the Yiddish schlepper meaning 'I don't fancy yours much.'

**slapper trapper** *n.* A man who, lacking the wherewithal to trap a *fox*, settles for hunting *swamp hogs.*

**slappertite** *n.* A hunger for loose women. *'Do you fancy a fuck, Bill?' 'No thanks, Hillary. I don't want to ruin my slappertite.'*

**slappette** *n.* Betracksuited, *hickied*, bubblegum-chewing, *scrunchie*-wearing fledgling *slapper.*

**slapster** *n.* A *slaphead.*

**slapstick** *n.* A light-hearted, comical *wank.*

**slash and burn** *1. n.* Third world deforestation technique. *2. n.* A painful symptom of the *pox* and the *clap.*

**slash** *n.* A *piss, wee wee.*

**slash palace** *n.* Public lavatory.

**slate layer's nailbag** *sim.* Descriptive of very saggy or battered *labia.*

**slats** *1. n.* Ribs. *'I'm gonna rattle her slats with me womb broom.' 2. Aus.* Beef curtains. *'I'm gonna part her slats with me womb broom.'*

**sledge** *n.* A bloke who is constantly *pulled* by *dogs.*

**sleep in a tent** *v.* To have a large penis. *'Fancy coming back to my place? You'll not be disappointed. I sleep in a tent.'*

**sleeping beast** *n.* Flaccid *cock, marshmallowed main pipe.* A *dead budgie.*

**slice** *n.* A portion of *hairy pie.* A vagina.

**slime** *v. Aus.* To ejaculate, *chuck one's muck. 'Hev yer slimed yet Rolf?'* To reach *Lake Wendouree.*

**slip a length** *v.* To *fuck*, from the male viewpoint. *'I'd slip her a length any day of the week.'*

**slip her a crippler** *v.* A few notches up from *slip her a length*, to *shag* someone so hard they can't walk.

**slippery as a butcher's cock** *sim.* Untrustworthy, sly. From the well known fact that all butchers take carnal advantage of the meat in the back room before selling it.

**slit** *n. Blit, fanny, vertical bacon sandwich.*

**sloppy seconds** *n.* To *stir the porridge.* To stick one's *naughty paintbrush* into a *bill poster's bucket.*

**slot** *n. Slit.*

**slut** *n. Slapper, slag, bike.*

**smear test** *1. n. medic.* Medical procedure aiming to detect precancerous cells in the cervix. *2. n.* Toilet procedure to determine if one has got all the *shit* off one's *nick.*

**smeg** *1. n. Knob cheese. 2. n.*

*prop.* Amusingly named Swedish manufacturer of white goods. *3. n.* A substitute for *fuck* overused in 'Red Dwarf.'

**smegma dome** *n.* A baby *bell end*, with a waxy, red skin. The *lid.*

**smegma** *n.* See *smeg.*

**smoke the bald man** *v.* To light up a *salami cigarette.*

**smoke the white owl** *v. Horatio.*

**smoking bangers** *sim.* Descriptive of a woman with a lovely personality, ie. who looks as though she's been lighting up fireworks.

**smoo** *n. Aus.* A *minge*, a *sportsman's gap.*

**smuggling a brownie** *v.* To have the *turtle's head. 'He seemed quite anxious to get away. I suspect he was smuggling a brownie.'*

**smut** *n.* Mild porn. *Porn lite*, as seen on Channel 5.

**snag your jeans on a nail** *v.* To emit a high pitched, rasping *ringtone.*

**snail trail** *n. Smoo juice* in a lassie's well-worn *scuns.*

**snail's doorstep** *n.* A *clapping fish* that is as *wet as an otter's pocket.*

**snake charmer** *n*. A girl who has an uplifting effect on your *pant python*. *'Phoar! She's a bit of a snake charmer. I'm pitching a trouser tent right here and now.'*

**snake** *v*. To *fuck, poke, bang, futter*.

**snapdragon** *n*. A normally agreeable female who under certain circumstances, ie. when *up on blocks* or full of *tart fuel*, becomes a vicious, fire-breathing monster.

**snatch 22** *n*. A woman whom one requires so much beer to *poke*, that one can't *get it up*.

**snatch mouse** *n*. Tampon. A *cotton mouse*, a *Prince Charlie*, a *chuftie plug*.

**snatch** *n*. *Quim*, vagina, *liver sock*.

**snatch patch** *n*. A feminine hygiene product. A *fanny nanny*.

**snatch quack** *n*. *medic*. One who has the sexy, enviable job of examining malfunctioning *minges*. A *box doc*. A gynaecologist.

**snatchlings** *n*. Young talent.

**snatchment area** *n*. The geographical radius from which a drinking establishment draws its female clientele.

**snatchphrase** *n*. A particularly successful chat up line.

**snedge** *1. n*. Snow. *2. n. Jism*.

**sniping** *v*. Accidentally shooting a jet of *slash* through the gap between the rim of the *chod bin* and the underside of the seat and onto your *kex* whilst sat down having a *tom tit*. A *Wee-Harvey Oswald*.

**snitches** *n*. *Two aspirins on an ironing board, stits, fried eggs*.

**snob sick** *n*. Vomit with plenty of canapes and Chardonnay in it outside a wine bar.

**snobtoss** *n*. An act of *self pollution* committed whilst watching a sophisticated, subtitled movie on FilmFour.

**snog** *v*. To *swap spit, tongue wrestle, play tonsil hockey*.

**snogging water** *n*. A male grooming lotion that smells like *Joan Collins' knickers*. After shave.

**snookered behind the red** *v*. Unable to *sink the pink* due to the time of month. The only pot on is a *difficult brown*.

**Snoopies** *n*. *Spaniel's ears, Ghandi's flip-flops*.

**snoregasm** *n*. A wet dream.

**snorkeller's lunch** *n*. A fish dish which is a particular favourite amongst *muff divers*.

**snorker** *n.* Sausage, both eating and hiding varieties.

**snowball** *v.* To blow *salami cigarette* smoke back into the tobacconist's mouth... sort of thing.

**snowdropper** *n.* Underwear fetishist who steals to sniff, usually from washing lines. A *knicker bandit*.

**snudge** *v.* To sniff a lady's bicycle seat after she leaves it chained to park railings. *Quumfing*.

**snufty** *n.* One who *snudges*.

**snurglar** *n.* *Quumfer, snudger,* bicycle *snufty*.

**snurgle** *v.* To *snuft*, to *quumf*.

**soap-on-a-roper** *n.* One who prefers not to bend down in communal showers.

**soapy tit wank** *n.* Sausage *sandwich* served in the bath or shower.

**sock method** *n.* To *roll the dice* into a sock in the absence of anything else to *roll the dice* into. See *crunchie*.

**sod** *n.* A loose piece of turf in an uphill garden.

**soixante neuf** *n.* Top to tail *horatiocumulonimbus*. French for *sixty-nine*. *Loop the loop*.

**solicitor's tie** *n. Fr.* A *pearl necklace*. Costing £160 an hour.

**soup but no croutons** *adj. medic.* To have a low *springle count, spoogeless spaff*. To be *firing blanks*.

**soup cooler** *n.* A lipless *fart* that has the characteristics of a gourmet gently and silently blowing across a bowl of lobster bisque in a posh restaurant.

**sour apple quickstep** *n.* Another diarrhoea dance. *'Your wife is taking rather a long time in the powder room'. 'Yes, I'm afraid she's dancing the sour apple quickstep tonight.'* See also *Tijuana cha-cha*.

**sow** *n.* One notch up from cow on the female insult scale.

**SPAD** *acronym.* Signal passed at danger. To drive your *Interclitty 125* at full pelt into the tunnel, despite seeing the red warning signs at the entrance. To stick your *cock* into *Billy Connolly's beard*.

**spaddel** *n. Spooge, spoff, spaff, spangle, gunk, jittler.*

**spadger** *n. Aus.* Vagina.

**spaff** *v.* To *spoff* or *spod*. *'No, no, no, Gunter! Be professional, spaff on the chest, not in the pussy.'* (from an unidentified grumbleflick, circa 1980).

**spam alley** *n.* The target zone for *spam javelin* throwers.

**spam butterfly** *n.* A finger-assisted *close-up pink* shot in a *bongo mag.* A *peel.*

**spam castanets** *n.* Percussive *scallops.*

**spam fritters** *n.* Labia. *Vertical bacon sandwich*, especially when served in *batter.*

**spam javelin** *n.* An eight foot long *cock* with a sharpened end.

**spam monkey** *n.* A monkey that is partial to indulging itself with *spam.*

**spam sceptre** *n.* The ceremonial rod that sits atop the *crown jewels.*

**spambidextrous** *adj.* The ability to *beat one's truncheon meat* with either *wanking spanner.*

**spandrels** *n. Men overboard, croutons, tiger nuts.* General vaginal detritus.

**spangle** *1. n.* A sticky, unpleasant mouthful that is most often spat out. *2. n. Spunk.*

**spaniel's ears** *n.* Sagging, flat *thruppenny bits. Snoopies, Fred Bassets.*

**Spanish archer** *n.* The push, the 'El Bow.' '*She caught me in bed with her sister and her mum, and she gave me the old Spanish archer. Tchoh! Women, eh?'*

**Spanish cravat** *n.* A *pearl necklace.* Also *Dutch cravat, Chinese bow tie.*

**spank banks** *n.* A mental reference library of erotic imagery, which can be consulted when *spanking the monkey.* Also *mammary banks.*

**spank the monkey** *v.* To *bash the bishop, burp the worm.*

**spank the plank** *1. v.* To play the electrical guitar in a 'pop' beat combo. *2. v.* To *toss* oneself off.

**spankerchief** *n.* A tissue, or square of fabric for mopping up post *monkey-spanking cock* produce.

**spanking** *n.* A form of corporal punishment still practised in *rub-a-tug* shops. See *Mr Whippy. Fladge and padge.*

**spanky hanky** *n. Jit gel rag, wank sock.* Anything used for clearing up *gunk* after a *tug.*

**spanner** *1. n.* Not the sharpest tool in the shed, a right *fuckwit. 2. n.* Top *stoat*, one who tightens one's nuts.

**spare elbow skin** *n. John Wayne's hairy saddlebags,*

*chicken skin handbag.* The scrotal sac.

**spare** *n.* In a *meat market*, that *flap* which is not yet sold.

**spasm chasm** *n.* See *spam alley.*

**spawning** *v.* The saucy act of masturbating in a public swimming pool.

**speak Welsh** *v. Shout soup, blow chunks, yoff.*

**spear the bearded clam** *v.* A trick involving a *spam javelin* and a hairy bivalve.

**spend tuppence in ha'pennies and farthings** *v.* To pass loose stools, have diarrhoea. To release a *flock of pigeons.*

**sperm** *n. medic.* Doc speak for *spunk, gism.*

**sperm wail** *n.* A low grunting noise emitted at the moment of spouting. An ejaculatory ejaculation. See *spuphemism.*

**sperm worm** *n.* Penis.

**spew** *1. v.* To vomit, *park a tiger*, be sick. *2. n.* The sick itself. *'Mum. This fucking soup tastes like tramp's spew'.*

**spice island** *n. Stinkhole Bay, Dilberry Creek.* A foul smelling archipelago favoured by sailors on their *trips around the world.* The *arsehole.*

**spider's legs** *n.* Of *muffs*, rogue pubic hairs which protrude beyond the knicker line, a *pant moustache.*

**spinning plates** *v.* An old-fashioned novelty act in which the performer attempts to keep both of a lady volunteer's nipples erect at the same time.

**spit roast** *n.* Someone simultaneously skewered at both ends by *pork swords*, a *sausage jockey* who plays a *pink oboe* whilst still in the saddle. A *corn on the cob.*

**spit** *v.* What fussy women do instead of *swallowing.*

**spla water** *n.* Semen, *gunk.*

**splash me boots** *v.* To have a *piss*, take a *leak.* Not to be confused with *fuck me shoes.*

**splashback** *1. n.* An area of tiles behind a sink. *2. n.* Unfortunate tidal effect of a *depth charge* or *belly flopper* within the pan, resulting in splashing of the *arse* and *barse.*

**splat** *n. medic. Bollock batter, fetch.*

**splay** *v. US.* To *schtup, snake, skeeze.* Specifically, to draw back the *beef curtains* and enter.

**splice** v. British version of *splay*.

**splinge** n. A particularly lubricious *kipper mitten*. A *bag of slugs*.

**split a kipper** v. To *part the whiskers*, to have sex.

**split the beard** v. To *part the whiskers*, again.

**split the winnings** euph. To halt the *laying of a cable* halfway through. *'And after four days without movement Job took up his toilet and great was his relief. But even as he released his burden there came a voice and it was the Lord. And the Lord spake in a loud voice saying Come unto Me Job. And Job replied saying Oh God, what is it this time, for I have only just sat down. And great was the wrath of the Lord. And He commanded Job to split the winnings and come now unto Him. And great was Job's discomfort.'* (from *'The Book of Job'* Ch.6).

**splosh** 1. n. Sex, *crumpet, fanny. 'Gor bloimey, squire, I fink I'll go dahn the old rub-a-dub and get moiself a bit o'splosh, innit.'* 2. n. Money. 3. n. Britain's leading periodical for those interested in genito-spaghetti pursuits.

**splurry** n. *Fizzy gravy.* Diarrhoea.

**spock** v. To make a 'V' with one's fingers and boldy go where no man has gone before, ie. two up the *fanny* and two up the *arse*.

**spod** n. See *spooge*.

**spof** n. *Spod*.

**spoilers** 1. n. Aerodynamic wing modifications that allow Citroen Saxos to grip the road when driving up and down in Burger King car parks. 2. n Buttocks, *mudflaps*.

**sponge** 1. n. Of homosexual relationships, the submissive partner, the *noshee* as opposed to the *nosher*. Usually the thin one. See also *stone*. 2. n. prop. A silent character played by Colin Bean in 'Dad's Army'.

**spooge** n. US. *Spof*.

**spooge scrooge** n. *Blob*, condom, *rubber policeman*.

**spooge stick** n. *Gut stick, fuck rod*. The penis.

**sports bag** n. A handy *cottaging* accessory in which one partner stands to conceal his feet and avoid detection by lavatory attendants looking under the door.

**spouse** *1. n.* Marital partner. *2. n.* Her *fanny*.

**spreader** *n.* A variation on a *moonie*, whereby the buttocks are manually pulled apart to reveal the *freckle*.

**spreadsheet** *n.* Shiney, crinkly toilet paper found in public lavatories which only succeeds in smearing the *shit* around one's *arse* like a plasterer's float.

**sprew** *n. Spongle, jitler, spragg. Spunk.*

**sprogdrop** *n. medic.* Pregnancy. A state of *up-the-duffness*, to be expecting a *lawn monkey*.

**spuds deep** *n. Up to the maker's nameplate.*

**spunk** *1. n.* Semen, *seed. 2. n.* Spirit, pluck. *3. n. Aus.* Good looking man, dish, hunk. *4. n.* Tinder made from fungus. *5. v.* To ejizzulate, to *spooge*, esp. *~up*.

**spunk dustbin** *n.* A *spooge bucket, box of assorted creams*. An exceptionally accommodating young lady.

**spunk gurning** *n.* The delightful faces a *grumble-flick* actress pulls as she excitedly anticipates the *tipping* of the romantic lead's *cement* onto her face.

**spunk juggler** *n.* An *onanist*.

**spunk rat** *n.* Good looking bloke, as described by females. Not to be confused with *fanny rat*.

**spunk shuffle** *n.* The walk adopted by one's girlfriend to stop the *congregation* leaving the *cathedral* before reaching the *bog*.

**spunk-drunk** *adj.* Delirious nature brought on by over-consumption of *root beer*.

**spunkled** *adj.* Besprinkled with *spunk*.

**spunkling** *adj.* Sparkling or glistening as a result of being *spunkled*. eg. Gillian Taylforth's chin.

**spuphemism** *n.* A humorous *sperm wail*. A jolly shout upon *spoffage,* eg. *'There she blows!' 'Tim-berrrrr!'* and *'Yabba Dabba Dooooo!'*

**Spurt Reynolds** *n.* Pet name for the tearful *bald man* sitting on the *hairy beanbags*.

**spurt your curd** *v.* Spread your *spunk*, to *spunkle* others with your pluck and spirit.

**squatter** *n.* An annoying little *turd* that takes up residence in one's *arse* and refuses to leave, unless threatened by Bermondsey Dave.

**squeak the breeze** v. US. To *fart, talk German, pass wind.*

**squeeze the cheese** v. Dairy equivalent of *sausage stretching,* to *wank.*

**squid legs** n. The thin, rubbery tentacles found floating on the water after a bath time *dolphin waxing* session.

**squid marks** n. Fishy *skids* in a lady's *fairy hammock.*

**squid wank** n. The kind of *wank* received from a lady inexperienced in the provision of *wanks.* Derived from the distinctive cuttlefish-like movement of the hand.

**squirrel covers** n. A lady's *dung hampers.*

**squirts** n. medic. In proctology, a series of fiery eruptions from the *chamber of horrors* resulting in a pyroclastic flow from the *farting fissure.* A condition also known as the *skitters,* the *Earthas.*

**squishpot** n. US. The area right below the *devil's doorbell.*

**squits** n. medic. Dangerous wet *farts,* constantly bordering on the *follow through.* Junior *squirts.*

**St. George** v. To lance one's old dragon from behind. A *dog's marriage.*

**St. Ivel** n. An imperial measurement of beer, equal to 2½ quarts or ⅝ of a gallon. Five pints. *'Mr. Barratt appeared unsteady on his feet as he got out of the car. I asked him if he had been drinking and he replied 'Not really. I've only had a St. Ivel."* (from the traffic officer's charge sheet after the arrest of Michael 'Shakin' Stevens' Barratt, Dec 31st, 2001).

**stabbin' cabin** n. A secondary residence kept for the sole purpose of quick extra-marital encounters, eg a discreet flat in Belgravia, a small cottage in the Cotswolds, or a 12-foot caravan on the cliffs at Scarborough.

**stabbing the cat** v. Wanking. From the motion of stabbing an invisible cat on one's lap. Same as *feeding the ducks,* but with emphasis on the downward stroke.

**stack blow** n. A gentleman's *organism.*

**stacked** adj. Overstocked *rack* in the *snork* department. *'I fell in love with my wife at first sight. She is particularly well stacked.'*

**stagecoach** n. A cramped, filthy ride which leaves you in need of a wash. Also *riding shotgun.*

**stalagshites** *n.* Naturally-occurring, upward-pointing turdiferous deposits which form in porcelain basins.

**stalk fever** *n.* Condition affecting men on *big cock day.*

**stalk** *n.* Erection, *stiffy.* *'Excuse me, if I look like a tripod. I just can't seem to get rid of this stalk. Anyway, let's carry on. Ashes to ashes, dust to dust...'. A third leg, middle stump.*

**stand . stand on** *n.* See *stalk.*

**standing on the fireman's hose** *sim.* At the conclusion of the evening's fourth or fifth bout of *Jesuit boxing,* a complete failure to release *jaff.* An *air horn.*

**stanky** *n.* The glaze that is left on the *shaft* of the *choad* after a bout of *kipper splitting.* May be *zuffled* on curtains or wiped on a *stankychief.*

**starfish trooper** *n.* An *arsetronaut.*

**start the horn mower** *adj.* The particularly vicious upstroke best demonstrated by the inexperienced female *masturbatrix.*

**starting line at Brands Hatch** *sim.* Descriptive of severely *be-skidmarked*

*undercrackers.* Guaranteed to cause embarrassment the first time they are handed to newly-wedded bride for washing.

**steak drapes** *n. Gammon goalposts, beef curtains.*

**steakwich** *n.* The external genitalia of a lady of a certain age which resembles the traditional British pub snack.

**stealth bomber** *n.* Subtle *leg lifter,* undetectable *benefactor,* phantom raspberry blower. An anonymous *donor.*

**stealth moose** *n.* An *LRF.*

**steg** *n.* Woman resembling a ferocious, spiny, squat, prehistoric dinosaur. Abbrev. ~stegosaurus.

**Stellavision** *n. Beer goggles,* but specifically with the help of Stella Artois.

**stench trench** *n. Fanny.*

**step on a duck** *v.* To create a quack, *fart. 'Pardon me, Ladies and Gentlemen. Do not adjust your wireless set, Mrs. Simpson just stepped on a duck.'* (from The Abdication Broadcast of Edward VIII, 1937).

**step on a frog** *v. Step on a duck.*

**Steptoe's face** *n.* A saggy non-too-fussy set of *flackets*. ie, will take in any old *rag* or *bone*.

**stick shifter** *n. Wanker.*

**stickman** *n.* A *fanny hopper*, a *skippy*.

**sticky belly flap cock** *n.* Post *curd*-spurting condition enjoyed by *monkey spankers*.

**sticky toffee pudding** *n.* A thick, dense *Thora* that sticks to everything it touches, particularly one's *arse cress*.

**stiff lock** *n.* A *piss-proud spooge stick*.

**stiffy . stiffie** *n.* A *stalk*.

**stiffy stocking** *n. Rascal wrapper, cheesepipe clingfilm, Spurt Reynolds' sickbag.*

**stilton muffle** *n.* Pungent and unwashed *fish mitten*. A particularly stenchsome *trench*.

**stilton** *n.* A long, thin, cheesey erection.

**stink** *1. n.* The distinctive odour of well-matured *knob cheese*, eggy *air biscuits*, a *stilton muffle* etc. *2. v.* To emit such a smell, to *ming*. *3. n.* A fuss. *4. n. Aus.* A scrap, fight, *pagga*.

**stinky finger** *n.* Having ate the *captain's pie* without a knife and fork. *Stinky pinky*.

**stinky Mervin** *n.* The Fins-

bury bridge. *Biffin bridge, barse, carse, taint, notcher,* etc.

**Stirling** *rhym. slang.* A *wank.* From Stirling Moss ~*toss.*

**stirring the porridge** *v.* To have *sloppy seconds*, to dip into a *billposter's bucket*.

**stits** *n.* Small *tits*.

**stoat** *n.* In the world of pant nature, the natural prey of the *one-eyed trouser snake*.

**stone** *n.* Of gay men and women, the opposite to a *sponge,* the dominant partner. And usually no oil painting neither.

**stones** *n. arch.* Olde Worlde *balls. Bollocks, knackers*.

**stonker** *n.* Erection, *hard on, stiffy*.

**straightening your hat** *v.* Raking one's kex out the crack of one's *arse*.

**strain your greens** *v.* To have a *piss*.

**strangle Kojak** *v.* Male masturbation, to *peel the carrot*.

**strapadictomy** *n.* Routine operation to strap on a *dildo*.

**Stretch Armstrong** *n.* One gifted with the ability to eat *gorilla salad* whilst simultaneously *finding radio Luxembourg*. Also *superman*.

**stretched quimosine** *n.* An extremely elongated *fanny* that has taken plenty of people for a ride.

**strike up the colliery band** *euph.* To produce a protracted *trouser cough* of a particularly musical timbre.

**string** *n.* *Wood,* tumescence. *'Quick, everybody, Gunter's got string. Fluffer off set, please and roll camera.'*

**string of pearls** *n.* A series of tiny *botty burps* released in quick succession whilst walking. *Air croutons.*

**stringbean** *n.* A long, thin, probably green, penis.

**stripper's clit, face like a** *adj.* Of a woman, to have a charming personality.

**stripy laugh** *n.* A *parked tiger*, a *Welsh monologue.*

**stroke mag** *n.* An item of top shelf literature, *art pamphlet, gentleman's interest magazine.*

**stroke of midnight** *n.* A free *one off the wrist,* courtesy of the Adult Channel. A *discount wank.*

**stroke the dog through the letterbox** *euph.* To slide one's hand down the front of a lady's knickers.

**strum** *v.* A relaxed *tug.*

**strumpet** *n.* *arch.* Olde Worlde Prostitute.

**strumping** *v.* Predatory behaviour by a *bird,* female equivalent of *sharking.*

**stuffing a marshmallow in a piggy bank** *v.* Of those unfortunate situations involving *brewer's droop,* attempting to force one's *loose sausage meat* into the *slot.*

**stunt cock** *n.* In a *bongo vid,* when the leading thespian is unable to sustain *wood* or provide a *money shot;* cue the stunt cock, a fat ugly cameraman with a *concrete donkey* on a *hair trigger.*

**succubus** *n.* A phantom nighttime *cock* sucker once thought to be responsible for nocturnal emissions.

**suck face** *v.* *US.* To kiss. *'Git a goddamn move on an' finish your mother fuckin' popcorn, you sonofabitch. I wanna suck some face.'*

**suck off** *v.* To perform *horatio,* to do a *chewie,* give some *head.*

**suckers** *n.* *Shag tags.*

**suckhole** *n.* In radio studios, one who laughs at everything Chris Moyles says. *Brown noser, toady, arselick, sycophant.*

**sugar walls** *n.* Sheena East-on's *slice* sides.

**sugared almond** *n. Clematis.*

**summoning Moira** *v.* The desperate act of frantically conjuring up a mental picture of cadaverous newsreader Moira Stewart in order to suppress a potentially embarrassing *diamond cutter* just before getting off the bus.

**sunnies** *n. Aus Tits, baps.*

**supermarket smack** *n.* Special Brew.

**surfboard** *1. n.* Flat chested female, *Miss Lincolnshire. 2. n. Aus.* A piece of equipment used by women to catch the waves when the *red flag is flying.* A *fanny nanny* for a heavy *aunt Flo.*

**surfing the crimson wave** *v. Riding the menstrual cycle.*

**surprise, sur-fucking-prise!** *exclam.* Remark made at a depressingly predictable event, eg. England losing on penalties.

**swagman's hat** *n. medic.* Condition of the anus when infested with numerous *tagnuts. 'Holmes surveyed the lavatory cubical before announcing, 'The game is afoot, Watson, and our quarry has a bandy legged gait'.*

*'How the devil do you know that, man?' exclaimed Watson. 'Elementary. The Izal toilet paper means he will almost certainly have a ring-piece like a swagman's hat."* (from *'The Red-Ringed League'* by Sir Arthur Conan Doyle).

**swallow the oysters** *exclam.* A phrase of friendly encouragement to a lady who is being a little too fussy about eating all her porridge up.

**swallow** *v.* What proper women do.

**swamp donkey** *n.* Female not overly endowed with physical beauty. A *tug boat, boiler, sea monster, steg.*

**swamp** *v. milit.* To *piss,* urinate.

**swap spit** *v. Suck face.*

**sweatermeat** *n.* Phrase used to alert friends to the presence of a nice pair of *tits.* Usually accompanied by clockface directional information. *'Sweatermeat at three o'clock.'*

**sweaty Morph** *n.* A *mudchild,* a *turd.*

**Swedish** *n. Greek.*

**sweep the yard** *v.* To loudly scratch one's pubic area making a sound like sweeping

paving slabs with a hard bris-
tled broom.

**sweet FA** *acronym*. Sweet
Fanny Adams, *fuck all*,
absolutely nothing. Nowt.

**sweet tits** *n*. Affectionate
male term of endearment for
females. *'Goodnight, goodnight! Parting is such sweet
sorrow/ That I shall say
goodnight until it be morrow,
sweet tits.'* (from *'Romeo and
Juliet'* by William Shakespeare).

**sweetcorn itch** *n*. An itchy
ringpiece due to insufficient
wiping. *IRS*.

**swill out the trough** *v*.
Female equivalent of cleaning *inside the farmer's hat*.

**swim against the tide** *v*. To
take a dip whilst the *red flag*
is flying.

**swing both ways** *v*. To be a
*switch hitter*.

**swiss** *adj*. Completely useless.
*'Did you see Henman play at
Wimbledon? He was com-
pletely fucking swiss.'*

**Swiss kiss** *n*. A *post-horatio
spangle*-flavoured snog.

**switch hitter** *n*. *US*. Person
who *bats with both hands*,
bisexual, *AC/DC*. One who
approaches the oyster and
snail buffet with a broad
plate.

**swive** *v*. *17thC*. Fuck. *'A horse,
a horse. My kingdom for a
swiving horse.'*

**swope** *n*. The hairstyle affect-
ed by balding men whereby
strands of hair on one side of
the head are grown long and
swept over the dome, giving
the impression of a full head
of hair, eg. Robert Robinson,
Bobby Charlton, Desmond
Morris.

**sword swallower** *n*. A circus
*fellatrix*.

**syrup** *n*. Hairpiece. From
syrup of fig ~*Irish jig*.

# Tt

**tackle** *n.* The *family jewels* and the *spam sceptre*. The *fruitbowl*.

**tackleshack** *n. Trolleys, underpants, kecks, nut chockers.*

**taco tickler** *n. Gusset typist.*

**tadger** *n. Todger.*

**tadpole net** *n. Blob, rubber Johnny, cheesepipe clingfilm.*

**tadpole yoghurt** *n. Gentleman's relish,* dressing for a *sausage sandwich.*

**tagnuts** *n. Toffee strings, winnets, clinkers, dangleberries, bead curtains.*

**tail** *1. n. arch.* Penis. *2. n. Fluff, totty, skirt, talent. 3. n. Bum.*

**tail ender** *n.* Small dollop of *do* that one must wait for after the main stool has been expelled, the finial on a *log cabin* roof.

**tail gunner** *n.* A *rear admiral. Arse bandit at 6 o'clock.*

**tail shot** *n.* The release of *tail wind.*

**tail wind** *n. Botty gas. Air biscuits* tending to push one forwards.

**tailpipe** *n. US. Ass-hole.*

**taint** *n. Nifkin's bridge.* Because *"tain't your arse and 'tain't your fanny.'*

**take an air dump** *v.* To *fart, blow off.*

**take Captain Picard to warp speed** *v.* TV baldy/cock euph. Masturbate. To *strangle Kojak, pull Paul Daniels' head off.*

**talent** *n. coll. Crumpet, bush,* attractive females.

**talent scout** *n.* A designated member of a group who looks round the pub door to check that the *blart* inside is worth pushing one's way to the bar for.

**talk German** *v.* To *fart, blow off,* puff on an imaginary *bum cigar.*

**talk on the great white telephone** *v.* To be sick in the lavatory. *Drive the porcelain bus.*

**talk to the judge** *n.* To *suck a copper's truncheon* by way of avoiding a speeding ticket. eg. *'I know I was doing 50 in a 30 zone, officer, but is there any way we can work this out? Perhaps if I spoke to the judge behind that skip...'*

**tallywhacker** *n. 18thC.* Penis, *old man.*

**tam rag** *n.* Variation of *jam rag.*

**tammy huff** *n.* A monthly feminine mood swing. A *blob strop.*

**tampon** *n.* A small, highly sophisticated implant which enables women to play tennis.

**tamtrum** *n.* A monthly exhibition of petulance. From Latin *tampus* ~fanny rags & *trum* ~hissy fit. A *blobstrop, a tammy huff.*

**tango butter** *n. Fanny slobber.*

**tank driver's hat** *n.* A particularly hairy *fanny* with flaps that come under your chin. A *biffer.*

**tank slapper** *n.* An ugly biker's moll.

**tank** *v.* To *scuttle, roger.*

**tanked up** 1. *adj.* Usefully drunk, sufficient to fight or drive a car very fast. 2. *adj. milit.* To be sufficiently equipped with tanks.

**tantric shit** *n.* An extremely prolonged visit to the porcelain *chod bin*, where one sits for four hours, humming.

**tap** *n.* See *oot on the tap.*

**tap off** *v.* To successfully *tap up.*

**tap up** *v.* To chat up, attempt to instigate a sexual liaison.

**tapioca toothpaste** *n.* Dental gel for a *trouser leg trombonist.*

**TAPS** *acronym. medic.* Technical term used by doctors on medical notes, Thick As Pig Shit.

**tardis fanny** *n.* Deceptively spacious *snatch*. A disappointing *cathedral* when one was expecting a *priest's hole.*

**tarmac round the garage** *sim.* Descriptive of a slightly grubby *path to the back door*, making rear entry an unpleasant prospect.

**tart farmer** *n.* A *pimp.*

**tart fuel** *n.* Any alcoholic drink consumed by young women which gets them going. *'She's very light on tart fuel. She'll go all the way to Cockfosters on 3 bottles of Hooch.'*

**tart** *n. Slapper, dolly bird.*

**tart's window box, a** *n.* What one smells like when one has too much after shave on.

**Tarzan cord** *n.* The narrow cord which attaches *Kojak's roll-neck* to the *bobby's helmet*. The *guy rope*, the *banjo.*

**tash** *n.* See *Hitler tash.*

**taste the rainbow** *v.* To have a little taste of everything from the 'All You Can Eat' *pant buffet.*

**tatties** *n.* Testicles, *spuds.*

**tatty watta**. *n. Nat. Am.* Red Indian word for *spud juice*, semen. Literally *'potato water.'*

**taxi driver's tan** *1. n.* An area of sunburn on the right index finger caused by hooking it on the top of the cab whilst driving along. *2. n.* A similar tan caused by *breaching the hull.* A *filter tip.*

**taxi tiger** *n.* A desperate last-chance lunger on the way home.

**Taylforth** *1. n.* A disastrous *blowjob* in a car. *2. n. medic.* A severe attack of pancreatitis which can only be relieved by being *sucked off* in a layby.

**TBS** *abbrev.* Toxic Bott Syndrome. To suffer from severe noxious emissions or *brewer's farts. Burn bad powder.*

**TCM** *abbrev. medic.* Turd cutting muscle, *crimper,* anal sphincter. The *nipsy, secaturds.*

**tea pot** *n.* Gay male from the Larry Grayson school of posturing.

**tea towel holder** *n.* Anus, *ringpiece, freckle.* From the 1950s plastic 'finger poke' style kitchen accessory.

**teabagging** *v.* To make a strong brew with *Fussels milk* and two lumps. A last resort sexual practice whereby the man lowers his *pods* into the lady's mouth.

**teaching William a lesson** *n. Punishing Percy, pulling the Pope's cap off. "What's all this banging and groaning?' bellowed Mr. Wilkins as he burst into the dorm. 'Please, Sir,' piped-up Venables. 'It was Darbishire teaching William a lesson."* (from *'Jennings and the Mysterious Body Hairs'* by Anthony Buckeridge).

**teapot sucker** *n.* A *bottom shelf drinker,* a teetotaller.

**tear in a coalman's jacket** *sim.* A large, raggy *blart.*

**tear off a piece** *v. US.* To have sex. *Tear one off.*

**technicolour yawn** *n.* A *yoff.*

**teddy's leg** *n.* State of stool expulsion somewhere beyond the *turtle's head,* but prior to *touching sock.* Midway through *smoking a bum cigar. Bungle's finger.*

**tee off** *v.* To *wank* and/or *fart.* Not necessarily at the same time.

**teeter meter** *n.* Calibration scale assessing the attractiveness of women based on how far from sober one would have to be to *slip them a length.* eg, Kylie Minogue would be 0 on the teeter meter, whereas Gail Tilsley off Coronation Street would be 15 pints of Stella with whisky chasers.

**teggat** *n.* A short-necked *turtle's head* which is unable to *touch cloth*, and retreats back into the *bomb bay*.

**temazepalm** *n. medic.* Hand induced insomnia relief.

**ten pint princess** *n.* A *donner.*

**tennis fan** *n.* A woman who takes the *other bus* to Wimbledon. A *lady golfer.*

**tenpin** *v.* To place digits simultaneously in the *tea towel holder* and the *fish mitten.* From the grip used in ten pin bowling. To *spock.*

**tent pole** *n. Stiffy*, erect penis, especially in bed. A *trouser tent, morning glory, wake up with Jake up.*

**Terry Waite's allotment** *sim.* Descriptive of a badly overgrown *ladygarden.* *'Marriette was powerless to resist. His eyes burned into hers like emeralds. His muscular arms enfolded her body as she felt herself being swept away in a monsoon of passion. 'Bloody hell! You've got a twat like Terry Waite's allotment!' he cried, as he pulled out the waistband of her bloomers and peered inside.'* (from *'The Peasant Girl and the First World War Soldier'* by Barbara Cartland).

**test card wank** *n.* A *tug* one has, not because one is feeling particularly *fruity,* but simply because there is nothing else to do. A *loose end away.*

**textbook dog** *n.* The recognition of an absolutely perfect *doggy-style* position seen in everyday situations, eg. a secretary crawling on the floor to find a contact lens.

**thatch hatch** *n.* Vagina, *hairy pie.*

**the other** *n. It*, the old *how's your father.*

**the third place** *n. Splaystation 2.* The *arse.*

**Thelonius** *rhym. slang.* Semen. Named after the jazz pianist Thelonius Spunk.

**thesbian** *n.* A *grumbleflick* actress who does *girl on girl* professionally, but is not a *tennis fan* in real life.

**thick as a ghurka's foreskin** *sim.* Descriptive of someone who is as *thick as a Welshman's cock.*

**thick repeater** *n.* A large bore semi-automatic, single barrel *mutton musket.*

**thighbrows** n. A profusion of bikini overspill. *Loose baccy.*

**third leg** 1. n. Cricketing position between mid-off and gully. 2. n. The *middle stump.*

**thirty four and a halfer** n. A gentleman blessed with the miraculous ability to perform *horatio* upon himself.

**Thora Hird** 1. n. prop. Pelican-throated actress of stairlift testimonial fame, alive at time of going to press. 2. rhym. slang. A *turd.*

**thousand island dressing** n. The sauce which coats one's *naughty spoon* after mixing the *gorilla salad* when *cranberry dip* is on the menu.

**thrap . thrape** v. To masturbate furiously, to give it six nowt on the *Right Honourable Member for Pantchester.*

**three card trick** rhym slang. Prick. 'She got her jazz bands round me three card trick and started giving it six nowt.'

**three coiler** n. Dog *turd*, the curled and crimped result of not having walked the dog, usually found on a carpet.

**three dick gob** n. A capacious mouth. 'The next record is 'You're So Vain' by Carly Simon, the lady with the three dick gob. And it's for Terry, who is seven today. Lots of love from mummy, daddy, nana and granpa Johnson and nana Robins.' (Ed 'Stewpot' Stewart, *Radio 1 Junior Choice*, 1974).

**three legged race** n. When *fuckstruck*, to stumble up the stairs with a *bone-on.*

**three mile island** n. An extremely noxious rectal meltdown with a half life of about ten minutes. A *Smellafield.*

**three piece suite** n. *Meat and two veg, wedding tackle,* the male *undercarriage.*

**three wheeler** rhym. slang. Dyke, lesbian. From three wheeled trike.

**throb on** n. A *wide on.*

**throne** n. The Queen's *crapper.*

**throne room** n. The Queen's *shit house.*

**throttle pit** n. Aus. The *dunny.* Toilet.

**throttle the turkey** v. To masturbate in Norfolk.

**through a hedge backwards** exclam. Phrase to indicate the sexual attractiveness of a lady. 'Phoar! I could fuck her through a hedge backwards.'

**througher** *n.* A 24-hour drinking session. A *Leo Sayer.*

**throw out the garbage** *v.* To flush out one's *spooge pipe.*

**throw** *v.* To *barf, hoy, chuck.*

**throwabout** *n.* A petite woman who can be easily and casually 'thrown about' from one position to another during sex. A *laptop.*

**throwing a Woodbine down Northumberland Street** *sim.* In Newcastle, unsatisfying sex with a *bucket-fannied* individual. *'Why man, it was like hoyin' a Woodbine doon Northumberland Street'.* Leeds ~*throwing a sausage up Briggate,* HM Navy ~*throwing your kit bag in the Ark Royal's dry dock,* etc. The *last hot dog in the tin, wall of death.*

**thrupenny bits** *1. rhym. slang. Tits. 2. rhym. slang.* The *shits.*

**thumb a ride on the rocket** *adj.* To *take Captain Picard to warp speed.*

**thumbing in a slacky** *v.* The first act of an optimistic bout of lovemaking for which the gentleman's spirit is willing, but his flesh is weak. *Pushing a marshmallow into a moneybox.*

**thumper** *n.* A big, pounding erection, a *stalk,* a *stiffy.*

**thunder bags** *n.* Underpants, *trolleys.*

**thunder box** *n. arch.* Lavatory, *shitter.* Also *thunder bowl.*

**thunder mug** *n.* Chamber pot, *piss pot.*

**thunderbirds** *n.* Women of ample proportions. *Barge arses.*

**thundercrack** *n.* The kind of *fart* that requires one to check one's *kex* for *bullets.*

**ticket to tottieville** *euph.* See *token for the cockwash.*

**tickle tackle** *n. Anteater's nose, cock collar.* The *fiveskin.*

**tickle the pickle** *v.* See *jerkin' the gherkin.*

**tickle your pip** *v.* To be aroused sexually by Leslie Philips or Terry-Thomas.

**ticklers** *n.* Corrugated condoms, amusing *French letters.*

**tickling the scampi** *v.* A means of getting *fish fingers.* Feminine *monkey spanking.*

**tiffin** *n.* An afternoon *fuck* off Sid James in a pith helmet.

**tiffter** *n.* Unwanted erection, *Jake.*

**Tijuana bible** *n.* A *jazz mag.*

**Tijuana cha-cha** *n.* The *trots.* See *sour apple quickstep*, *Mexican screamers*.

**tile hanger's nailbags** *sim.* Sagging, lumpy *Charlies.* 'She had tits like a tile hanger's nailbags'.

**tin of Vim with an apple on top** *sim.* A fictitious penis measurement.

**tinter** *1. n.* High class *totty*, top class *talent*. 'That Mick Hucknall's a jammy get. A face like his and he still gets all the top tinter'. *2. n.* A lady's *barse*, because *'tin't 'er arse and 'tin't 'er fanny.'* The *taint.*

**tip your concrete** *v.* A sophisticated term for ejaculation when *cough your filthy yoghurt* seems inappropriate.

**tisnae** *n. Scot.* The *taint, tintis, barse, biffin bridge.*

**tit fairies** *n.* Mythical visitors who magically transform the wife's *fried eggs* into *TNTs* during and after *sprogdrop.*

**tit man** *n.* He who prefers *tits* to *arses* or *gams.*

**tit pants** *n.* A bra.

**tit pizzas** *n.* Big, round, mottled, crusty aereolae.

**tit splitter** *n.* A lady's fashion bag worn diagonally across the torso such that it bisects the *headlamps.*

**tit wank** *n.* A *soapy tit wank*, without the soap.

**Titanic** *n.* A lass who goes down first time out.

**titnotised** *adj.* To be involuntarily mesmerised by a smashing pair of *tits.*

**tits** *1. n.* Breasts, *knockers.* 'What a pair of tits.' *2. n.* Foolish or derisory people. 'What a bunch of tits.' *3. n.* Nerves. 'Christ, he gets on my tits.'

**tits on a fish** *n.* Descriptive of a supremely useless thing. 'Did you see (insert name of striker currently having a run of bad form) play on Saturday? He was as much use as tits on a fish.'

**titty fuck** *n.* A *sausage sandwich*, a *diddy ride.*

**TNTs** *abbrev.* Two Nifty Tits.

**toaster** *n.* A crumb-filled vagina with two slots and a spring mechanism that ejects the *cock* once it has finished.

**Toblerone tunnel** *n.* The gap, triangular in cross section, between the tops of a slender woman's thighs and her *skin gusset*, into which a Toblerone would slide neatly.

**tockley** *n. Aus.* A *gut stick*, a *choad.*

**todger dodger** *n.* One who leaps out of the way of an oncoming *cock*. A lesbian.

**todger** *n.* Penis. Also *tadger, tockley, tool.*

**toffee strings** *n.* See *bead curtains.*

**toilet snails** *n.* Cryptozoological molluscs that slither around the *bog pan* in student houses, leaving *skid-marks* that no-one claims responsibility for.

**toilet suicide** *n.* A loud explosion followed by a low groan from a lavatory cubicle.

**token for the cockwash** *n.* A romantic gift bestowed upon a lady by a man, (eg. flowers, chocolates, bottle of wine) in the hope that it will get him *a bit. 'I'm just nipping down the off licence to get a token for the cockwash.'* See *cock wash.*

**Tom** *1. n.* Prostitute. *2. v.* To carry out prostitution. *'Are you tomming it?' 3. rhym. slang.* Tomfoolery ~jewellery.

**toms . tom tits** *rhym. slang.* The *squits.*

**tongue job** *n.* A lick, as opposed to a *blow job.*

**tongue punchbag** *n.* A *bald man in a boat,* a *clematis.*

**tongue shui** *n.* See *tongue wrestling.*

**tongue wrestling** *n.* Tonsil hockey.

**tonk** *v.* To *fuck, poke.*

**tonsil hockey** *n.* Kissing, *spit swapping.*

**tookus** *n.* Totty, scrunt.

**tool** *n.* Penis, *manhood.* All the *DIY* enthusiast needs, along with his *wanking spanners,* to get the job done.

**toosh** *n.* Totty, blart.

**toot meat** *n.* Penis. From the fictional musical sweet of a similar name. *Bed flute, meat flute, pink oboe.*

**toot toot** *1. n.* Risque BBC parlance for vagina. *2. onomat.* The noise made by a *chewie.*

**toot** *v.* A child and vicar-friendly term for a *fart.*

**toothless gibbon** *n.* A *clapping fish.*

**toothless sea lion** *sim.* Smelly and unkempt *minge.* *'I don't think I'll see her again, Cilla. She had a fanny like a toothless sea lion.'*

**top banana** *exclam.* Give that man a coconut, whacko-the-diddle-oh. Jolly good.

**top bollocks** *n.* Breasts, *jubblies.*

**top deck** *v.* Of a house guest, to defecate in one's host's cistern, rather than, more conventionally, in the toilet, for comic effect. *"I say, Jeeves, he was a bit of a rum cove, what? Did you see him pass the port from left to right?' 'Indeed I did, Sir,' replied the sage retainer. 'I took the liberty of top decking the servants' bathroom before leaving."* (from *'Heil Hitler, Jeeves!'* by Sir PG Wodehouse).

**top hat** *n.* The implausible achievement of a lady with three blokes up her *wizard's sleeve.* After a dish of the same name in the Restaurant on the Stenna Ferry, consisting of three pork sausages in mashed potato sitting in a Yorkshire pudding.

**top stealth** *n.* The art of entering a shop, grabbing your desired *bongo mag,* paying and leaving with such cunning that no-one bats an eyelid.

**topless hand shandy** *1. n.* A lemonade and beer drink, pulled from a pump by a barmaid naked from the waist up. *2. n.* A milky drink pulled from a *love pump* by a masseuse naked from the waist up. *Topless relief.*

**topless relief** *n.* Bordello-speak for a *tart* with her *tits* out giving you a *wank.*

**tops and fingers** *adj.* Scale on which sexual achievement is measured by teenage males. *'Get far last night?' 'Not bad. I got my tops and two fingers.'*

**toss** *1. v.* To *wank,* usually *'oneself off.' 2. v.* To flip pancakes through 180° during cooking.

**toss parlour** *n.* A *rub-a-tug shop.*

**toss pot** *1. n.* a jar for keeping *toss* in. *2. n.* A person held in low esteem, a *fuckwit.*

**tossed salad** *n. US.* Anal sex between male prisoners. *'More tossed salad, Lord Archer?' 'No thanks, Mr. Big, I'm completely stuffed.'*

**tosser's twitch** *n.* Nervous affliction suffered by *wankers* during periods of abstinence.

**tossing the caber** *v.* Having *one off the wrist* with a 16 foot long, splintery *cock.*

**tottle** *n.* A bath-time *air biscuit.* From the joke with the punchline *'But, sir. I distinctly heard you say, 'What about a water bottle, Tottle?"*

**totty** *n. coll.* Girls, *fanny.* *'Hey, this car's a fanny magnet .*

*Since I bought it I've been beating off the totty with a shitty stick.'* Singular if prefixed 'a nice bit of~.'

**touch** *v.* To *fondle*, usually 'up'.

**touching cloth** *adj.* That stooling stage immediately after *turtle's head* when the movement establishes contact with the *trollies*. *'Is there a bog round here mate? I'm touching cloth.'*

**touching socks** *adj.* The stage by which time it is too late to look for a toilet, but time to look for a trouser shop.

**towbar** *n.* A bulbous *turtle's head*. With a 12 volt output.

**towel hook** *n.* A *hard-on* that's strong enough to support the weight of a damp bath towel.

**trade spit** *v.* To *swap spit*.

**tradesmen's entrance** *n.* *Back passage*.

**traff** *v.* To *fart, let off*.

**train** *n.* See *pull a train*.

**tramp's breakfast** *n.* A *docker's omelette*. A pavement greb.

**tramp's day out** *n.* An alfresco act of frenzied masturbation conducted in a bush. Also *tramp's picnic*.

**tramp's delight** *n.* Low cost cider.

**tramp's jackpot** *n.* A perfectly intact discarded cigarette.

**tramp's mate** *n.* Someone who looks like they probably stink, eg. Danny Baker, Jocky Wilson.

**tramps' truffles** *n.* Discarded chips.

**tranny** *1. n.* An old fashioned radio. *2. n.* Transvestite, transparency or transit van. eg. A fetish photographer might say *'Shit. I left that tranny of the tranny in the back of the tranny.'*

**trap** *n.* A toilet cubicle in a line of toilet cubicles.

**travel fat** *n.* Unwanted *stalk* which sprouts during bus journeys.

**traveller's marrow** *n.* A large root vegetable unconsciously cultivated on buses that usually ripens just before your stop. *Diesel dick, root master, travel fat.*

**tread on a frog** *v.* A wetter sounding version of *step on a duck*.

**treading water** *v.* Light *strumming* on the banjo in order to keep one's interest up during the dull plot bits in a *grumbleflick*. To maintain a *satiscraptory* level of *wood.* 'You're under arrest, Mr Sinstadt.' 'But officer, I wasn't wanking, I was just treading water.'

**tree log** *n.* A *chocolate shark* whose snout is in the water before its tail leaves one's *arse*, a *Cuban bum cigar*, a *bridger.*

**tree monkey** *n.* A *fart.*

**trick** *n.* Customer in a *rub-a-tug shop*, a *Hilman Hunter*, a *gonk.*

**trilogy** *n.* Also known as *brown Star Wars.* A *turd* of such epic proportions it has to be released in three instalments. The first can stand on its own as a complete adventure. The second links to the first, but has a dark, inconclusive feel generating an air of foreboding and leaving itself wide open for an unknown ending. The final chapter has drama, excitement and moments where you think all is lost. A grand battle is waged where good overcomes evil and peace is restored in your gut.

**trim** *n.* Tidy *bush, talent, totty.*

**tripe hound** *n.* A *fugly dog.*

**triple crown** *1. n.* The Holy Grail of Rugby Union players; to win matches against the other three home nations. *2. n.* The Holy Grail of Rugby Union players; to throw up, *piss* and *shit* oneself in the back of a taxi.

**Trisha trash** *n.* The kind human vermin that appear on mid-morning riff-raff debates. British *trailer trash.*

**trogg** *n.* Simpleton, *fuckwit.* See also *pranny.*

**Trojan arse** *n.* A toilet bowl invasion that takes one by surprise in the middle of the night and sends one back to bed in a state of sleepy bemusement. A somnambulodefecation.

**Trojan** *n. US.* A war-like, Greek contraceptive.

**trolley dash** *n.* Of a punter, to chase a prostitute who has stolen his trousers down a back alley, wearing his underpants, shoes and socks.

**trolleys** *1. n. Kecks 2. n. Underkecks.*

**trollop** *n.* See *trull.*

**tromboning** *v.* A thoroughly impractical sex act in which the woman (or *Colwyn* man) *rims* a man's *brass eye* whilst simultaneously reaching round the front to give it some elbow on his *horn*, the action being akin to playing a trombone. A *George Jism*.

**trots, the** *n.* Frequent rapid foot movement required to convey a diarrhoea sufferer to the lavatory. See also *Tijuana cha-cha, sour apple quickstep, Turkish two-step*.

**trouser arouser** *n.* Fit lass, good looking *bird*.

**trouser bandit** *n.* Slightly more polite version of *bum bandit*.

**trouser chuff** *n.* *Trouser cough*.

**trouser cough** *n.* Fart, botty burp.

**trouser department** *1. n.* Section of a department store dealing with men's legwear. *2. n.* Area of the body where middle aged men experience problems.

**trouser leg trombonist** *n.* Popular female musician who plays in the same ensemble as the *skin flautist* and *pink oboe* virtuoso.

**trouser Mauser** *n.* A small rapid firing *porridge gun*. A *pump action mottgun, mutton musket*.

**trouser rake** *n.* Stiffer version of the *trouser snake*. Often pops up and hits women in the face when stood on.

**trouser rouser** *n.* Fart, Bronx cheer.

**trouser snake** *n.* See *one eyed trouser snake*.

**trouser tent** *n.* Embarrassing portable erection made from canvas or other trouser material, with a zip up one side, supported by a rigid shaft. If occurring whilst seated this can easily be concealed with a bowler hat.

**trouser trout** *n.* Something one tickles in one's *trolleys* before taking it out and banging its head against a rock.

**trouser trumpet** *1. n.* Fart. *2. n.* The *anus*.

**trouser truncheon** *n.* The stiff pole a copper takes out in the back of his van on a Saturday night.

**trousered** *1. adj.* To be wearing trousers. *2. adj.* Wasted, arseholed, wankered, shit faced.

**trout** *v.* To pull. '*I was out trouting last night. Ended up with a right old five-to-twoer. Had to chew me own arm off this morning.*'

**trucker's mate** *n.* Someone who looks like he could be a sex case, eg. Roy off Coronation Street.

**truffle hunting** *v.* To take a

*trip around the world.* To *rim.*

**trull** *n. 19thC.* Prostitute, a *hoo-er.* With fat *tits* but not many teeth, as killed by Jack the Ripper.

**trump** *v.* To *fart* or *pass wind* in a chair-shaking way.

**trumpeter's lips** *n.* The involuntary pursing of the *tea towel* holder at moments of extreme fear. *'Any man who tells you he is not afraid to go into battle is either a fool or a liar. It is the fear that makes him fight. I personally had the trumpeter's lips throughout the North African campaign.'* (from *'The Memoirs of Field Marshal Montgomery').*

**truncheon voucher** *n.* A *ticket to the policeman's ball.* A constabulary bribe.

**try on the comedy beard** *v.* To perform *cumulonimbus.*

**trying to get the last pickled onion from the jar** *euph.* Deep *gusset typing.*

**tubby chaser** *n.* A man who thinks *thunderbirds* are go, eg. Geoffrey 'The Great Soprendo' Durham. Also a woman who prefers her *beefcake* to be a *salad dodger*, eg. Victoria Wood.

**tubesteak** *n. Beef bayonet on the bone.*

**TUBFUF** *acronym.* Thumb Up Bum, Finger Up Fanny. All business.

**tug boat** *n.* A woman of plain appearance and compact, muscular build. A *swamp donkey.*

**tug** *v.* To *pull*, as in a *pud*. A light hearted *wank. 'Dinner's ready, Sidney!' 'Down in a minute, dear. I'm just having a little tug.'*

**tugwax** *n. Spongle, spadge, jitler.*

**tumblepube** *n.* A fur ball of *clock springs* and other discarded pubic hairs which wafts around when the bog door opens.

**tummy banana** *n.* A *gutstick.*

**tummy truncheon** *n. Sixth gear stick, porridge gun,* penis.

**tuna taco** *n.* A hot dish, not requiring cutlery, served when *dining at the Y.* If eaten with a side order of *cranberry dip*, could lead to *Mexican lipstick.*

**tuna town** *n.* Female genitalia, *Billingsgate box.*

**tup** *1. v.* To have sex, *fuck. 2. v.* Of sheep-to-sheep shagging, red hot horny ram on ewe action.

**tuppence licker** *n. Lesbo, bean flicker.*

**turbo shit** *n.* The high speed *dump* required to fool a lady into thinking you had only gone for a *gypsy's kiss*. A *greyhound's egg.*

**turbot for tea** *exclam.* Announcement that the *fish supper* is served. *'Never mind that tug, Sidney. It's turbot for tea.'*

**turd burglar** *n.* Stealthy thief who forces entry into the rear of a person's premises via the inside of the *chocolate drainpipe.*

**turd clippers** *n. US.* Buttocks.

**turd** *n.* A cylindrical unit of *shit,* longer than a *tod.* A link of *feeshus.*

**turdis** *n.* One of those detached, modern, portable, space age looking public conveniences. A *turd tardis.*

**turistas** *n.* See *Turkish twostep.*

**turk** *v.* To take someone or something up the *council.* *'Sit down please, Lord Archer'. 'If it's all the same with you, Governor, I'd rather stand. I've just been turked in the showers by Jonathan King.'*

**turkey** *n.* The *cracker* you think you've pulled whilst drunk at the office Christmas party who turns out to be a rough old *bird* who only gets *stuffed* once a year.

**turkey's wattle** *n.* A *ragman's coat,* a *club sandwich.*

**turkey-neck** *n.* That which is throttled in Norfolk. See *throttle the turkey.*

**Turkish bath** *n.* A *Glasgow shower.*

**Turkish** *n. Irish.*

**Turkish two-step** *n.* Small-room *dance* not disimilar to the *sour apple quick step, Tijuana cha-cha, Aztec twostep.*

**turn Japanese** *v.* Of *wanking,* to *apploach the Birry Mill Loundabrout.*

**turn your bike round** *v.* Go to the lavatory. *'Excuse me, I'm just going to turn my bike round. Have you got any arse paper?'*

**turps nudger** *n.* A *top shelf drinker.* *'Have you seen that bloke who reads the news on Tyne Tees? Jesus, what a fucking turps nudger.'*

**turpsichord** *n.* A public house pianoforte, as played by rubber-fingered drunks.

**turquoise** *n.* A lady who allows the *dog in the bathtub.*

223

One who doesn't object to being *turked* up the *bonus tunnel*.

**turtle** *1. n.* Passive sexual partner. *'Get her on her back and she's fucked.'* 2. *n. Blit, fanny, fluff, talent.* Birds, collectively.

**turtle bungee** *n.* The dangerous sport of releasing and retracting *turds* by clever use of the sphincter muscles just before they *touch cloth*. *Prairie dogging, gophering.*

**turtle recall** *v.* The brief retraction of the *turtle's head* whilst on route to the *thunderbox*.

**turtle's breath** *n.* The very final warning *fart* before the turtle pokes its head out to *autograph the gusset*.

**turtle's head** *n.* The initial protrusion of a stool though the *tea towel holder*, the point at which contracts are exchanged for the building of a *log cabin. Touching cloth.*

**tush. tushie** *n. US. Bum, ass.*

**tussage** *n. Talent,* female *buffage.*

**TV** *1. abbrev.* A television. *2. abbrev.* A *tranny.*

**twang the wire** *v.* To pluck out a *jazz rhythm* on the *one stringed banjo.*

**twanger** *n.* See *whanger.*

**twankunt** *n.* Descriptive of someone who is not just a *twat,* but also a *wanker* and a *cunt* to boot. *'Lord Archer – author, politician and twankunt, 62 today.'* (*The Times* birthday column, April 15th 2002).

**twat** *1. n.* A *minge.* 2. *n.* Stupid person. *3. v.* To hit, beat up.

**twat burglar** *n.* A man, presumably wearing a mask and stripy jersey, who steals another bloke's missus.

**twat mag** *n. Bongo literature.*

**twat nappy** *n.* See *clot mop.*

**twat rattler** *n.* A *plastic cock,* a vibrator.

**twatriot** *n.* Someone who waves a Union Jack and shouts 'Come on Tim', between every point whilst Tim 'Spoilt Bastard' Henman gets thrashed at Wimbledon again. Also found wearing a plastic Union Jack hat singing 'Land of Hope and Glory' at the Last Night of the Proms.

**twin peaks** *1. n. prop.* An experimental television series of the early 1990s created by David Lynch. *2. n.* Smashing *tits* like Audrey's in the series.

**twin tone** *n*. A *fart* which suddenly and ominously drops in pitch, indicating something other than marsh gas may have been expelled. A *follow through*.

**twinkie** 1. *n*. US. *Turd, chocolate log.* 2. *n*. An apprentice *mudhole plumber.*

**twist** 1. *rhym. slang. US.* Girl. From twist and twirl. 2. *n*. Of *carpet munching* relationships, the carpet, as opposed to the muncher. A passive *lesbo*.

**twister** *n*. *US*. Pervert, a *nonce*.

**twitter** *n*. A lady's perineum, that area of the anatomy between the *twat* and the *shitter*. The *chin rest, duffy's bridge, biffin bridge, tinter*.

**Twix lips** *n*. A *front bottom* version of *hungry arse*. See also *camel's foot*.

**two aspirins on an ironing board** *sim*. Descriptive of the slimmer-figured lady. Flat *stits, fried eggs, lung warts.*

**two bagger** *n*. Someone so ugly that two bags are required in order to go *quim wedging* with them – one over their head and one over yours, just in case theirs falls off.

**two pot screamer** *n*. *Aus*. Someone who cannot hold their beer. A more reserved British equivalent would be the *halfpint Harry*.

**two puppies fighting in a bag** *n*. Large, mobile and unrestrained breasts.

**two ring circus** *n*. *Over the shoulder boulder holder,* bra.

**two up** *n*. A *twos up*, a *threesome* with two gentlemen and a lady.

**twoc** *v*. Take Without Owner's Consent. To borrow someone's car, not in order to steal it, but to merely drive it through Dixon's window and set it on fire. Also *twock*.

**twocker** *n*. A cheeky rapscallion who *twocks*. A loveable rogue, a lively urchin.

**twunt** *n*. Useful, satisfying yet inoffensive combination of two very rude words which can safely be spoken in the primmest and properest company.

**Tyne bridge** *adj*. Descriptive of the position adopted by a dog trying to lay a particularly tenacious *egg*.

# Uu

**U blocker** *n.* A titanic *dreadnought* so big it causes a *jobbie* jam in the foul drainage system. The Moby Dick of *brown trouts*.

**udder scudder** *n.* See *sausage sandwich*.

**UDI** *abbrev.* Unidentified Drinking Injury. Mysterious bodily damage sustained during a *bender* and of which the victim has no recollection.

**ugly bus** *n.* A vehicle that mysteriously turns up after one has had 8 pints on a Friday night and takes all the ugly women home, leaving the pub full of beautiful ladies.

**ugly taxi** *n.* A vehicle which mysteriously delivers an ugly *bird* into one's bed on a Saturday morning.

**unblock the sink** *sim.* To have a vigorous and impatient *wank*, presumably with both hands.

**Uncle Albert's beard** *n.* Jelly jewellery.

**Uncle Doug** *rhym. slng.* Self abuse. From Uncle Doug ~ tug.

**Uncle Fester** *n.* A *goolie*-ish bald headed man from the *old Adam* family, who occasionally rises up and puts the willies up your missus.

**undefuckable** *adj.* Bust, damaged beyond repair. *'Oh, and there goes Barricello's engine on the warm up lap. He'll head straight for the pit lane, but that looks pretty undefuckable. It's certainly the end to his Portuguese Grand Prix, Martin.'* (Murray Walker as Frentzen's front left wheel came off on the final lap, Belgian Grand Prix 1999).

**under thunder** *n.* Violent rectal belching of the *arse's* natural *kak gases* which erupt from the *fart fissure*.

**undercarriage** *n.* Genitals, usually male. *Wedding tackle, pudendas*.

**underchunders** *n.* Trolleys.

**undercrackers** *n.* Trolleys, bills.

**underdaks** *n.* Trolleys, bills, farting crackers.

**underkecks** *n.* Trolleys, bills, farting crackers, dunghampers.

**unit** *1. n.* Genitals, usually male. *2. n. Bird*, an individual piece of talent.

**unload** *v.* To drop a *depth charge* or launch an *air biscuit*.

**unmentionables** *n.* Roman Catholic word to allow mother-in-laws to mention genitals or underwear.

**untidy sock drawer** *n.* A *ripped sofa, badly packed kebab, ragman's coat.*

**unwrap the meat** *v.* To *let the twins out. Tits oot for the lads.*

**up on blocks** *adj.* Of a woman. A monthly *MOTT* failure due to a recurring leak under the *beetle bonnet.*

**up periscope** *n.* Bathtime game for up to one person. *Polish the lighthouse.*

**up the duff** *adj. medic.* See *up the pasture.*

**up the pasture** *adj. medic.* See *up the poke.*

**up the poke** *adj.medic.* See *up the stick.*

**up the stick** *adj. medic.* See *in the club.*

**up to the apricots** *adj. Up to the plums.*

**up to the buffers** *adj.* Variation of *up to the bumper* used by train spotters to describe the sex that they never have. *Up to the maker's nameplate.*

**up to the bumper** *adj.* Of *pork sword* fencing, to be inserted *up to the hilt*, to the full extent. To *fuck* Grace Jones *up to the apricots.*

**up to the eggs** *adj.* Engaged in full penetrative sex. *Up to the maker's nameplate.*

**up to the maker's nameplate** *adv.* An engineering term for being *conkers deep.* Also, *up to the boilermaker's nameplate.*

**up to your nuts in guts** *adj. Aus.* Engaged in sexual intercourse.

**up to your pots** *adj.* Amazingly enough, not to be *up to the eggs*, but to be *ripped to the tits* on drink. *Pissed.*

**up, in, out and off** *phr.* Plot synopsis essential to all *grumbleflicks.*

**upchuck** *v.* To *chuck up.*

**uphill gardener** *n.* He who sows his seed on the *brown allotment*, pusher of a *pork wheelbarrow* up the *lavender* path. A male homosexual.

**upstairs** *n.* The *rack, top bollocks. 'What's she got upstairs?' 'Stacked mate! Looks like a dead heat in a zeppelin race.'*

**Urals, the** *n.* Vague and tenuous British film comedy euphemism for the testicles. See also the *Balkans.*

**Uranus** *1. n.* A large planet with brown rings around it. And a big smelly *shit* coming out a hairy hole in the middle of it. *2. n. Urarse.*

**urine shroud** *n.* A cotton or nylon artefact, clearly showing the miraculous crusty image of a *bearded clam*. ie, a pair of discarded *scads* found sunny side up on a lady's bedroom floor.

**UTBNB** *abbrev.* Up The Bum, No Babies. A reliable, yet malodorous contraceptive device. Opposite of an IUD.

# Vv

**vadge** n. See fadge.

**vag** n. US. American *pie*, the *hairy* variety.

**vaggie** n. An uncomfortable front-tuck for a lady. A vaginal *wedgie*.

**vagina decliner** n. The male equivalent of a *todger dodger*. A *beaver leaver*, a *pie shy guy*.

**vagitarian** n. He who only eats *hairy pie, fur burgers*, and *vertical bacon sandwiches*. Plus the occasional *fish supper*. An inveterate *diner at the Y.*

**vagitation** n. Agitation of the vagina. *Bean flicking*, female masturbation.

**Valentine's day porridge** n. *Semen-o-lina, spaff, spangle, snedge, gunk, liquid pearls.*

**varnish the cane** v. To give the old *walking stick* a one-handed waxing.

**Vatican roulette** n. *Pull out and pray.* A method of contraception practised by *left footers* with very large families.

**v-bone steak** n. A sumptuous, meaty meal, eaten off a *hairy plate.*

**veiny bang stick** n. Penis, the *choad*, the *giggle stick.*

**velcro arse** n. medic. Descriptive of the condition of the *bum cheeks* after a long hot day.

**velcro triangle** n. *Minge, mott, mapatasi.*

**Velma, to give her a** v. The act of deliberately or accidentally shooting *jitler* into one's *bird's* eyes, reproducing the disorientating effects suffered by Velma from 'Scooby Doo,' each time she lost her glasses. *Spunkblind. St. Valentine's Day mascara.*

**venetian bind** n. An awkward situation in which a gentleman finds himself when there isn't a curtain available to wipe his *cock* on.

**verminillionaire** n. A lottery winner who doesn't deserve it, has a criminal record as long as your arm and spends all the money on helicopters and Ferraris.

**versnatche** n. A designer *cunt.*

**vertical bacon sandwich** n. That which is clearly visible in *hamburger shots*. Also *vertical smile, vertical taco.*

**vertical eyebrow** n. A *fanny* that has been trimmed to within a quarter of an inch of its life. A *Pires's chin.*

**vesser** n. A silent *fart.*

**vicar's calling card** n. Sticking the organ up the reredos. A *sting in the tail*. *Bumming*.

**vicar's piss** *n*. Any particularly weak beer.

**Victorian photographer** *n*. A gentleman *cunning linguist* who performs under the skirts of a lady.

**video cripple** *n*. One who can normally walk perfectly well, but loses this ability when returning a video to the shop and has to park right outside, even if it's a double yellow line or is restricting traffic. Similar to *cashpoint cripple*.

**Viennetta** *n*. A rich and satisfying multi-layered toilet pudding, consisting of several alternating layers of *turd* and *bumwad*.

**vinegar Joe** *n*. The *stick vid* actor responsible for causing the *porn trauma*.

**vinegar string** *n*. The *banjo*.

**vinegar strokes** n. Of males *on the job*, the final climactic stages of intercourse or masturbation. *'Would you believe it? The phone rang just as I was getting onto the vinegar strokes. I nearly ran into the car in front.'* From the similar

facial expression associated with sipping vinegar.

**visit from aunt Flo** *euph*. To *have the painters in*. To be *sheep sitting*.

**vitamin S** *n*. A naturally-occurring substance which men insist is very good for women when taken orally in 5ml doses. Often added to fast food burgers by disgruntled staff.

**vixen** *n*. Wily *bird*, a young temptress, a foxy *chick*. eg. Stevie Nicks in about 1978.

**vommunition** *n*. Anything eaten to line the stomach before a drinking session.

**voodoo butter** *n*. The raw material of *squid marks*.

**vote for Tony Blair** *v*. To rush enthusiastically into the cubicle expecting big things, only to get a pathetic little *fart*. To be constipated.

**VPL** abbrev. Visible Panty Line.

**vurp** *n*. A burp which brings up a small but foul tasting quantity of stomach contents small enough to be gulped straight back down again. A *broat*.

# Ww

**wab** *n.* Penis.

**wad** *1. n.* The large sum of money which Harry 'Loadsamoney' Enfield waved around. *2. n.* That featured in a *money shot.* A small package of *hot fish yoghurt* flying out the end of a *mutton musket.* A *jizzbolt.*

**wade in** *1. v.* To move in for the kill immediately prior to pulling a *bird.* *2. v.* To walk towards the centre of a *pagga,* with one's arms above one's head in order to join the fun.

**wail switch** *n.* An excitable lady's *clematis.*

**waist height delight** *n.* A fun-size lady, ideal for vertical *horatio* or enthusiastic *cowboy.* A *lap-top,* a *throwabout.*

**wake up with Jake up** *v.* To have a *dawn horn, morning glory.*

**walk the plank** *rhym. slang.* To masturbate. Whilst a jeering monocular unidexter jabs a cutlass in your *arse.*

**walking condom** *n.* Descriptive of a breed of Scouse male, up to no good in a baggy tracksuit with hood.

**walking tripod** *sim.* Well-endowed male, *donkey rigged* individual. When admiring *buffage* a sexist lady might offensively remark *'Look at the third leg on that. He's a walking fucking tripod.'*

**wall of death** *1. n. Attack of the helicopters. 2. n. Last hot dog in the tin.*

**wallace** *rhym. slang.* To vomit. From Wallace and Gromit. *'He's wallaced all over my new carpet.'*

**wallop** *n. Cookin'.* Any beer bought by a hearty twat with a beard who calls the barman Landlord or Squire.

**walnut manoeuvre** *n.* The legendary method by which good looking nurses are trained to poke one's prostate in order to obtain an instant *Thelonius* sample.

**walnut** *n.* Gland up the male *arse* which causes immediate ejaculation when poked by a good looking nurse.

**walnut whip** *rhym. slang.* A minor operation which removes the *cream,* but leaves the *nuts* intact. The *snip.*

**wand waver** *n. Flasher,* sexual exhibitionist.

**wang** *n.* See *whanger.*

**wangst** *n.* Post masturbatory anguish. A *wank hangover.*

**wanic** *n.* The state of perturbation that occurs when a wife or girlfriend returns home unexpectedly as one is reaching the *vinegar strokes* in front of one's favourite *scud mags*. A *wank panic*. A *jazz funk*.

**wank** *1. n.* Masturbation. *'If you have a wank every day you'll go blind.'* *2. n.* Rubbish. esp. a pile of~. *'Don't talk wank.'* *3. v.* To masturbate. *'My brother wanks all the time and he's got perfect eyesight.'*

**wank crank** *n. medic.* Elbow.

**wank hangover** *n.* Post self-abuse self-loathing.

**wank pie** *n.* Something third rate, eg. any programme with Anthea Turner in it.

**wank séance** *n.* Whilst masturbating, the eerie feeling that one is being watched disapprovingly by dead relatives. Also *Doris Strokes*.

**wank sock** *n.* Sock tied to a bedpost designed to indicate when wind conditions are suitable for masturbation.

**wank stain** *n. Bum scrape, piss flap, dip shit, toss pot.* General purpose insult.

**wank tanks** *n. Balls, nads, knackers.*

**wank xerox** *1.n.* One who *knocks one out* repeatedly throughout the day, only to find the quality diminishes as his *toner* runs out. *2. n.* To masturbate over and over again to the same *jazz mag*. A *groundhog wank*.

**wanker** *1. n.* One who *wanks*. *2. n.* A fellow road user, a motorist at whom one waves.

**wanker's block** *n.* A complete absence of imagination or inspiration when trying to stimulate feelings in the *trouser department*. Often occurs when one has the *horn* but is too *pissed* to think of anything rude.

**wanker's hankie** *sim.* Descriptive of something very brittle. *'Come along to the Rupali Restaurant, Bigg Market, Newcastle on Tyne, where the curry is hot, the beer is cold and the popadoms are as brittle as a wanker's hankie.'* (Press release from Abdul Latif, Lord of Harpole).

**wanker's tache** *n. medic.* The vertical line of hair between the navel and the top of the *pubes*. Develops as a consequence of masturbation, along with spots, hairy palms, shortsightedness, insanity and growth-stunting.

**Wankerchief** *n.* A *spanky hanky*, a *jizz sock*, a *toss rag*.

**Wankered** *adj.* Very drunk, *arseholed, shit-faced*.

**Wanking chariot** *n.* A single bed.

**Wanking Jap, grin like a sim.** To smile broadly in the style of a Nissan executive *turning Japanese*.

**Wanking parlour** *n.* Brothel, house of ill repute, any club popular with *gonks*. A *toss parlour*.

**wanking spanners** *n.* Hands, *cunt scratchers*.

**wank-me-downs** *n.* Heirloom *bongo mags* inherited from an elder brother or friend. Also *one-hand-me-downs*.

**wankrupt** *adj.* To have no *money shots* left. To have *spent your wad*.

**wanksmith** *n.* An enthusiastic or workmanlike *onanist*.

**wankstop** *n.* medic. The flange that prevents the *wanking spanner* disengaging from the end of the *shaft* when revving your *single cylinder engine*. The *brim* of the *herman gelmet*. The sulcus.

**wankton** *n.* A unicellular lifeform that inhabits the shallow waters of the bath after a session of *dolphin waxing*. *Dutch jellyfish*.

**wanky** *adj.* Self-indulgent, pretentious.

**wannocks** *n.* The area of noman's land between the *nuts* or the *fadge*, and the *ringpiece*. The *biffin bridge, notcher, barse, taint, tintis*.

**wap-waps** *n. medic.* A lady's mammary glands.

**war paint** *n.* Of *birds* getting ready to go out at night, their make-up.

**warm Norman** *n.* A *hotplate, Cleveland steamer*.

**warren** *n.* Generic term for one not blessed with attractive features ~*'Warren ugly bastard.'*

**warthog whammies** *n.* Fantastic *tits* on an ugly woman. *Heffalumps*.

**wash the cosh** *v.* To polish the *love truncheon*.

**water sports** *n. Recreational Chinese singing*. To express romantic feelings for another by *pissing* onto their face, etc.

**watering can wazz** *n.* The uncontrollable multi-directional *gypsy's kiss* taken after a bout of *horizontal jogging* or a *five knuckle shuffle*.

**waving a sausage in the Albert Hall** *v.* To stick one's *cock* in a *fanny* that can seat 5000 people and the London Symphony Orchestra.

**wax the bonnet** *v.* To *spoff* over a woman's bodywork, then lean over and polish it in until the desired shine is achieved.

**wax the dolphin** *v.* To drop fish down the end of one's *bed muscle.*

**wazoo** *n. Jacksie,* anus.

**wazz** *v.* Variously to *piss,* to *puke,* to *wank.*

**wazzed** *adj. Pissed* on, *puked* on and *wanked* off.

**wazzock** *n.* One who is *pissing, puking* and *wanking* all at the same time.

**wear a Twyfords collar** *v.* To *drive the porcelain bus,* to *shout soup,* to *yoff.*

**wear the beard** *1. v.* To perform *cunning linguistics* on a woman. *Impersonate Stalin. 2. v.* Of *bean flickologists,* to be the *stone. 'You can tell which one of them two wears the beard.'*

**webbed tits** *n.* Breasts of elderly Hollywood actresses with a highly stressed membrane between, caused by the sheer weight of implants.

**wedding tackle** *n.* The male genitalia. Also *wedding furniture.*

**wedge** *v.* To pull another's *bills* up the crack of their *arse.*

**wedgie** *n.* Wedged *bills.*

**weenie** *n. US.* Penis. Also *wienie, wiener.*

**weenie waggler** *n.* A *wand waver.*

**weft** *n.* Of a lady's *pubes,* to all lie in one direction after wearing particularly tight briefs. *Twat nap.*

**weigh anchor** *v.* To drop an immensely large *turd,* being careful not to break the porcelain.

**welder's bench** *sim.* Ugly woman, *a face like a~.* Also *blind cobbler's thumb, burglar's dog, box of frogs, sack of chisels, bag of spanners.*

**welly top** *sim.* A term used to describe the larger *Mary. 'She had a fanny like a welly top.'* A *yawning donkey.*

**Welsh mist** *n.* A particularly dense and clammy *fart* which hovers around ankle level and chills the bones.

**Welsh** *n.* Masturbation by *frottering* with a leek while listening to a male voice choir.

**Welshman's cock** *sim.* Descriptive of someone who is short and thick, eg. Dennis Wise.

**wendy** *n.* An uncomfortable front tuck for a lady. A vaginal *wedgie*, a *vaggie*.

**wet as an otter's pocket** *sim.* Descriptive of the moistness of an object, eg. a face flannel, a raincoat, a *frothing gash*.

**wet one** *1. n.* A pre-moistened cleaning tissue. *2. n.* An untrustworthy *fart*, possibly a *twin tone* that would require the use of *1.* A pre-moistened *fart*.

**wet penny in your pocket** *n.* A circular *piss*-stain on the trouser frontage, caused by insufficient shaking of the *wang*.

**wet season** *n.* That time of the month when the *crimson tide* comes in.

**wet the baby's head** *v.* To have intercourse with a woman who has a *bun in the oven.* *'And so it was that Mary and Joseph came to an inn in Bethlehem. And Mary was heavy with child and the innkeeper spake unto them saying, Behold, there is no room at the inn. And Joseph replied unto him saying, Yea, we have travelled from Nazareth, and my wife is heavy with child, and I have great need to wet the baby's head. And he gave unto the innkeeper a wink. And lo the wink was cheeky.'* (from *St. Matthew,* Ch.2, vv 14-16).

**whammers** *n. Bazoomas, Gert Stonkers, big tits.*

**whanger** *n.* An extremely large *wang.*

**wheek** *v. Scot.* To remove *jobbies* from an aeroplane toilet.

**wheelie bint** *n.* A woman so ugly that she's only taken out once a week. In the dark. By dustmen.

**whidgey** *n. Front bottom.*

**whiff of lavender** *n.* Of a marriage, the suspicion of a bearded bride. *'I don't know about Edward. There's a whiff of lavender about that marriage.'* See *lavender, beard.*

**whirling pits** *n.* See *helicopters.*

**whisker biscuit** *n.* A *fur burger.*

**whisker pot** *n. Fanny, minge, whidgey.*

**whistle down the Y fronts** *v. Fart,* pass wind.

**whistling gorilla** *n.* An inviting and voluptuous *toothless gibbon.*

**whistling in the dark** *v.* *Muff diving,* eating *hairy pie.*

**white knuckle ride** *n.* A solo thrill which makes your eyes bulge and lasts about three minutes. *One off the wrist.*

**white mouse** *n.* Tampon. A *cotton mouse, fanny mouse, chuftie plug.*

**white pointers** *n.* Extremely impressive *tits* found inhabiting a wet t-shirt.

**white wee-wee** *n.* Planet Skaro Dalek term for semen.

**white-out!** *exclam.* When two large, pale breasts are exposed. *Unwrap the meat.*

**whitewash the hall** *v.* To *spoff* up a lady's *cunt.* A far more fulfilling job than *painting the ceiling.*

**whitewater wristing** *v.* Rapid paddling of the *skinboat.* To *pull your pud,* masturbate.

**whoof** *v.* To *fart.*

**whoof whoof!** *1. exclam.* Term of approval directed at passing *talent.* 'Whoof whoof! Give that dog a bone.' *2. exclam.* Term of disapproval aimed at passing women who haven't made the effort to look attractive.

**whoopsy** *n.* A *piss,* usually in Frank Spencer's beret.

**wick** *1. n.* Penis. See *dip your wick. 2. n.* Nerves, *tit ends.* 'I wish that Mark Kermode would fuck off. He really gets on my fucking wick.'

**wicked pisser** *n. US.* Good egg or a good show, top notch person or experience. As in 'Thank you very much for your kindness and generosity. You really have been the most wicked pissers.'

**wide-on** *n.* Female equivalent of a *hard-on.*

**widow's memories** *n.* Penis-shaped sausages, cucumbers etc. Indeed, anything vaguely cylindrical in supermarkets fingered nostalgically by old ladies.

**wife beater** *n.* An unnecessarily strong lager. *Wreck the hoose juice.*

**Wigan rosette** *n.* The state of the *freckle* after a particularly fierce *Ruby Murray.* A *Johnny Cash.*

**willets** *n.* A type of *jugs.*

**willie and the hand jive** *n.* Rhythmic, throbbing cork-popping combo who perform the *Bologna bop* among other dances.

**willie** *n.* A ten-foot penis that has to be cut with a rake. *John Thomas, Percy the pork swordsman,* he who gives *Gert Stonkers* a *pearl necklace.* The *tassel,* the *Peter,* the *Charlie.*

**willie welly** *n. French letter, French safe, English overcoat.*

**willie woofter** *rhym. slang. Poofter.*

**willipedes** *n.* genital arthropods. *Mechanical dandruff.*

**willnots** *n. Tagnuts, dangleberries.* Toffee entwined in the *kak canyon* undergrowth which simply 'will not' come off.

**wind jammer** *n.* A *botternist.*

**window cleaner's pocket** *n.* A large, sad, damp, dishevelled *fadge.*

**windy pops** *n. Bunny shooting bullets, chuffs, anal announcements.*

**winking walnut** *n. Brown eye, chocolate starfish.*

**winkle picking** *v. medic.* Anal sex with one afflicted with piles.

**winky** *1. n.* Tiny *cock. 2. adj.* Having a tendency to wink a lot.

**winkybag** *1. n.* Tiny scrotum. *2. n.* Ugly old woman with a tendency to wink a lot.

**winnet . winnit** *n. Klingon, dag, dangleberry, willnot, brown room hanger on.*

**winnie** *n.* Lesbian, she who licks the *honey pot.*

**wire spider** *n.* The hairs around the *chocolate starfish* that come to life when you are in a meeting or in the checkout queue at Asda.

**witch doctor's rattle** *n.* descriptive of a woman with a nice personality. A *monk's pin-up.*

**witten** *n.* See *winnet.*

**wizard's sleeve** *n.* A *clown's pocket.* A particularly capacious *sausage wallet.* 'I can't feel a bloody thing, Mother Theresa. You must have a fanny like a wizard's sleeve.'

**wizards' hats** *n. Dunces' hats.*

**WOAT** *acc.* A woman at a football, rugby or cricket match. Waste Of A Ticket.

**wobbly boots** *adj.* Uncontrollable alcoholic footwear. *Seven pint boots.*

**wobbly landing** *n.* Trying, when drunk, to moor your under-inflated *zipper zeppelin* into your wife's *hairy hangar.*

**wolf bait** *n.* An unusually meaty, pungent *fart,* similar to the smell of opening a tin of Butcher's Tripe Mix.

**wolfbagging** v. To have sex with a wolf inside a large bag.

**woman in comfortable shoes** n. A *tennis fan*, a *lady golfer*.

**wombies** n. *Tits,* breasts, *baps.*

**womfer** n. The female equivalent of a *barse*. *Chinrest* used to avoid cramp at a *hairy pie* tasting.

**wongle** v. To rive one's *passion cosh* up and down one's wife's *arse* in an attempt to wake her up for a *poke*.

**wood** n. Erectivity of the penicular appendation.

**woodpecker** n. A woman who performs rapid, hands-free *horatio*. From the movement of the *bird's* head as she hammers your *trunk*.

**woody** n. An erectivation.

**wookie hole** n. A *Mary Hinge*, a *biffer*.

**wool** n. *coll. US. Fluff, blart, fanny, totty.*

**woolly wardrobe** n. A bulky, cavernous receptacle in the bedroom where gentlemen stuff their *roll neck sweaters*.

**working from home** v. *Wanking.*

**world of leather** n. The parts of an aged lady. *Granny's oysters.*

**worth a squirt** adj. Sexually desirable.

**wring the rattlesnake** v. *Siphon the python.* To *piss, strain the greens.*

**wrist flick** n. A *grumblevid*, a *stick film*.

**write the letter 'M'** v. To inscribe the letter 'm' in *arse* sweat on the toilet seat whilst having a *Queensway*.

**wuffle nuts** n. The fruits of the *dangleberry* tree.

**wu-wu** *1.* n. Childish name for a *fufu*. *2.* n. Noise a train makes.

# Xx

**X-piles** *n.* Mysterious unidentified throbbing objects from your *anus*.

**X-ray specs** *n.* Spectacles available only by mail order from the back of pubescent boys' comics which enable the wearer to see through a woman's clothing. 50¢.

**XXX** *adj.* Special video certificate awarded to pornographic films of exceptionally poor sound and picture quality.

**xylophone** *1. n.* Like a piano, but you twat it with little sticks. *2. v.* To move along a line of naked women who are all bending down, and spank their bottoms – which are of varying sizes – with one's penis, to play a tune on women's buttocks. From the Greek *xylo* ~wood & *phonnicus* ~to hit tunefully.

# Yy

**Y bone steak** *n.* Female opposite of a *tube steak*. The *beef curtains*.

**yabba dabbas** *n.* The climactic stages of intercourse which immediately precede the dooooooos! The *vinegar strokes*.

**yachting** *n.* The stirring sight of a dog in full sail, tacking its way across the living room carpet attempting to remove the barnacles from its keel.

**yaffle the yoghurt cannon** *v.* Suck the *cock,* voraciously.

**yak** *1. n.* Big hairy animal of untidy appearance. *2. n.* A big hairy *fanny* of untidy appearance. A feminist's *beaver*, a *minge* with a *pant moustache.*

**yambag** *n.* The *nut sack.*

**yang** *n.* *US.* A *wang.*

**yank** *1. n.* An inhabitant of the Northern states of America. *2. n.* A 'one-man-band' type device with which an American attaches his penis to his ankle in order to *pull himself off* whilst walking about. $4.99.

**yank off** *v.* Wank off, *tug the T-bone.*

**yank the plank** *v.* To *tug* one's *wood.*

**yarbles** *n.* Testicles.

**yard** *1. n. arch.* Olde Worlde Penis. *2. n.* The *ladygarden.*

**Yarmouth clam** *n.* Similar to a *Viennese oyster,* only performed by a malodorous woman from Yarmouth.

**Yasser** *abbrev. US.* Erection. From 'Yasser Crack-a-fat'. Pun on the name of the teatowel-titfered Palestinian.

**Y-box** *n.* Much more fun than an X-box, and only costs the price of a bunch of flowers from the 24-hour garage.

**yeti's welly** *n.* A voluminous *fadge*, a *donkey's yawn.*

**yinyang** *1. n. US.* Arse, bum. *2. n.* Fuckwit, dupe.

**yitney** *n.* One who is *yitten.*

**yitten** *adj.* To be scared of something very tame.

**yobble** *v.* To *shit* somewhere other than a toilet, usually for the amusement of others. eg, onto a cow from a tree.

**yodel in the canyon / valley** *v.* To *growl* at a very *capacious badger.*

**yodel** *v.* To vomit, to *sing a rainbow.*

**yoinkahs** *n.* A pair of *twin peaks* that cause a volcanic eruption in your *underkrakatoas.*

**yongles** *n. US. Clockweights,* testicles.

**yoni** *n.* Ancient Hindu Female genitals, *fanny.*

**yonks!** *exclam.* Popular vocal reaction to finding a tenner on a cartoon pavement.

**york** *onomat.* To vomit, *call Huey.*

**yo-yo knickers** *n. Bike,* loose woman, woman whose knickers go up and down faster than Richard Branson's hot air balloons.

**yummy mummy** *1. n.* A middle aged woman worthy of a good *seeing to,* eg. Helen Mirren. *2. n.* A young mother with a fantastic *arse* pushing a buggy.

# Zz

**Zebedee** *n.* A tea-time erection that pops up unexpectedly, signalling that it is time for bed.

**zeps** *abbrev. Zeppelins.* Large, hydrogen-filled, flammable breasts, *Hindenburgs.*

**zig-a-zig ahhhh!** *onomat.* To have a bloody good *wank* watching a Spice Girls video.

**Zinzanbrook** *rhym. slang. NZ.* To *fuck.*

**zipper sniffer** *n.* Hunter of the *pant python*, male or female.

**zipperfish** *n.* Penis, *trouser trout, eel in the pants.*

**zit** *n.* A *pluke.*

**Zoes** *n. Balls,* testicles. From the Radio 1 presenter Zoe Bollocks.

**zonked** *adj. Pissed, wankered, wazzed.*

**zoob . zubrick** *n.* Penis.

**zook** *n.* A prostitute, a *ho'.*

**zorba** *1. rhym. slang.* To have a *piss.* From Zorba the Greek ~leak. *2. v.* To have sex in the *Greek* style. *'Sorry I can't sit down. I've been zorba-ed.'*

**zounds** *n. arch.* God's wounds. 17th C swear word banned by Act of Parliament in 1651, but okay now if used in moderation. Also *gadzooks.*

**zucchini** *n. US. Cock.*

**zuffle coat** *n.* The topmost coat of the pile on the bed at a party. Used by the male party guest to get the slime off his *choad* after a furtive *poke.*

**zuffle** *v.* To wipe one's *cock* on the curtain after having sex, usually in a posh *bird's* house.

**ZZ bottom** *n.* An exceptionally long haired *muff,* from the resemblance to the beards sported by the rock band ZZ Top. But not the drummer.

**ZZ tops and fingers** *n.* The act of fondling one's missus while she's asleep.